13.25

THE PSYCHOLOGY
OF LEARNING
AND TEACHING

Edited by
Patricia C. Stetson
University of Delaware
Wm. Ray Heitzmann
Villanova University

MSS INFORMATION CORPORATION

Distributed by **ARNO PRESS**
3 Park Avenue, New York, N.Y. 10016

This is a custom-made book of readings prepared for the courses taught by the editors, as well as for related courses and for college and university libraries. For information about our program, please write to:

MSS INFORMATION CORPORATION

MSS wishes to express its appreciation to the authors of the articles in this collection for their cooperation in making their work available in this format.

Library of Congress Cataloging in Publication Data

Stetson, Patricia C   comp.
  The psychology of learning and teaching.

    1. Education, Psychology of--Addresses, essays, lectures.   I.   Heitzmann, William Ray, joint comp. II.   Title.   [DNLM: 1.   Learning--Collected works. 2.   Psychology, Educational--Collected works. 3.   Teaching--Collected works.   LB1051 S841p 1973] LB1051.S7245   1973   370.15'2'08   73-10258 ISBN 0-8422-5113-8 ISBN 0-8422-0336-2 (pbk.)

CONTENTS

To the Student   5

SECTION ONE: THE LEARNING PROCESS

What Psychology Can We Feel Sure About?
    GOODWIN WATSON   7

Theories of Learning
    MORRIS L. BIGGE.   12

The Learning of Concepts
    ROBERT M. GAGNÉ   15

Learning and Thinking
    JEROME S. BRUNER.   25

The Motivating Effect of Learning by Directed Discovery
    BERT Y. KERSH   34

Jean Piaget: Notes on Learning
    FRANK G. JENNINGS.   41

Acquisition of Conservation through Social Interaction
    FRANK B. MURRAY.   44

The Validity of Social Science Simulations: A Review of
Research Findings
    WILLIAM RAY HEITZMANN   50

The Language and Values of Programmed Instruction
    DONALD G. ARNSTINE   58

Some Changing Concepts about Learning and Memory
    JAMES L. McGAUGH.   66

The Chemistry of Learning
    DAVID KRECH   73

SECTION TWO: THE LEARNER

The Commonness of Creativity
    RALPH J. HALLMAN.   79

IQ: God-Given or Man-Made?
    GILBERT VOYAT   84

Arthur Jensen and His Critics: The Great IQ Controversy
    THOMAS SOWELL.   90

Goodbye IQ, Hello EI (Ertl Index)
    Phi Delta Kappan Interview with JOHN ERTL   101

Classroom Aggression: Determinants, Controlling Mechanisms,
  and Guidelines for the Implementation of a Behavior
  Modification Program
    GERALD R. ADAMS 112
Intent, Action and Feedback: A Preparation for Teaching
    NED A. FLANDERS 126

SECTION THREE: THE TEACHER

Systematizing Teacher Behavior Research
    ALLAN C. ORNSTEIN............................. 136
People Poll
    PHILADELPHIA DAILY NEWS...................... 145
'Best' Teachers 'Demand,' 'Care'
    ELLEN ELLICK 147
Teachers' Expectancies: Determinants of Pupils' IQ Gains
    ROBERT ROSENTHAL and LENORE JACOBSON.......... 150
The Self-Fulfilling Prophecy
    THOMAS L. GOOD and JERE E. BROPHY 154
For a Disciplinarian's Manual
    DON L. EMBLEN 158
The Reinforcement Hierarchy
    STEVEN R. FORNESS............................. 161
The Use of Behavior Modification by Student Teachers —
  A Case Study in Contingency Management
    WILLIAM RAY HEITZMANN 171
Behavior Modification: Some Doubts and Dangers
    BRYAN L. LINDSEY and JAMES W. CUNNINGHAM........ 172
Quality Research — A Goal for Every Teacher
    BYRON G. MASSIALAS and FREDERICK R. SMITH........ 175
Humanizing Teacher Education
    ROBERT BLUME................................. 183
Notes on Teacher Education
    RICHARD H. BROWN 191
Classroom Incident
    TODAY'S EDUCATION............................. 198

TO THE STUDENT

Ideally, teachers are expected to perceive and respond to the psychological needs of the students they teach. Needless to say, those involved in the teaching profession know this is not an easy task. One reason for the difficulty results from the fact that specialists in the fields of education and psychology have often failed to provide adequate answers to questions concerning the nature of human behavior. In other words, we do not have all the knowledge necessary to solve our present educational problems. Despite such a shortcoming, prospective teachers need an opportunity to learn what *is* currently known about human behavior. The present course is designed to afford you such an opportunity. Hopefully, this book will provide an introduction to some of the important issues confronting educators involved everyday in the teaching-learning process. Our objective in having you read and reflect upon these articles is not solely to increase your cognitive knowledge of the principles of educational psychology. Ultimately, we hope this experience will provide personal insight into the phenomenon known as schooling and the acquisition of a positive attitude towards the children whose lives you will influence.

Prior to a course in education it is sometimes necessary to review how the course will contribute to one's total education. Courses and programs in education fulfill a dual function in that they serve to educate as well as train. Specifically students in a course in educational psychology will not only obtain compentencies that will enable them to function successfully in the classroom, but obtain knowledge that will be of a cultural or liberal arts value (See chart).

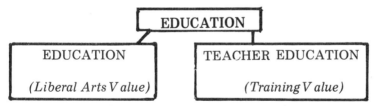

Some courses contribute more to one's cultural knowledge than others. For example, courses in Historical Foundations of Education and Comparative Education contribute more in the liberal arts dimension whereas *Methods* courses are most likely to have their greatest value in the training of teachers.

The authors of this book of readings have chosen the selections for their practical value to the pre-service teacher. It is hoped they will be of utility when he or she enters the classroom and suggest that class discussion related to the articles take that direction also. Obviously not all of the readings have training value (this will differ with the individual) for the authors feel that teachers should not only be trained but also be educated.

Patricia C. Stetson
Wm. Ray Heitzmann

What Psychology Can We Feel Sure About?

GOODWIN WATSON

EDUCATORS and others who wish to apply psychology in their professional work have long been troubled by controversies among psychologists themselves. Behaviorism arose to challenge the introspective method; Thorndike's connectionism was controverted by Gestalt concepts; psychoanalysts talked an almost completely different language. It was natural for teachers to say, "Let's wait until the psychologists themselves straighten out their various systems!" It looked for a while as if one could support almost any educational practice by choosing which psychologist to cite.

Gradually, however, a body of pretty firm facts has accumulated. While it remains true that research findings will be somewhat differently expressed and explained within different theoretical frameworks, the findings themselves are fairly solid.

A workshop of educators* recently asked me to formulate for them some statements of what we really know today about children and learning. To my own surprise, the list of propositions with which few knowledgeable psychologists of any "school" would disagree, grew to fifty.

* The New Jersey State Curriculum Workshop, Atlantic City, November 12, 1959.

In no science are truths established beyond the possibility of revision. Einstein modified thinking about gravity, even though Newton's observations were essentially correct. Psychology is much younger and more malleable than physics. New facts are constantly accumulating in psychological research, and these will doubtless introduce some qualifications and modifications—conceivably even a basic contradiction. The educator who bases his program on these propositions, however, is entitled to feel that he is on solid psychological ground and not on shifting sands.

What follows is a listing of fifty propositions, important for education, upon which psychologists of all "schools" would consistently agree. These are presented in twelve classifications.

NATURE-NURTURE

1. Every trait in human behavior is a product of the interaction of heredity (as determined at conception by genes) and environmental influences. Some traits (preferences in food or clothing, for example) are easily influenced by nurture; others (height, rate of skeletal ossification) seem to be affected only by extreme differences in environment.

2. There are specific stages in indi-

THE RECORD-TEACHERS COLLEGE, 1960, pp. 253-257.

vidual development during which certain capacities for behavior appear. The manner in which these capacities are then utilized sets a pattern for later behavior which is highly resistant to change. If unutilized then, they are likely not to develop later (for example, visual perception, mother attachment, language pronunciation, sports skills, peer relations, independence from parents, heterosexuality).

3. The significance of the important biological transformations of pubescence (growth of primary sex organs, development of secondary sex characteristics, skeletal and muscular growth, glandular interaction) lies mainly in the *meaning* which cultural norms and personal history have given to these changes.

LEARNING PROCESS

4. Behaviors which are rewarded (reinforced) are more likely to recur.

5. Sheer repetition without indications of improvement or any kind of reinforcement is a poor way to attempt to learn.

6. Threat and punishment have variable and uncertain effects upon learning; they may make the punished response more likely or less likely to recur; they may set up avoidance tendencies which prevent further learning.

7. Reward (reinforcement), to be most effective in learning, must follow almost immediately after the desired behavior and be clearly connected with that behavior in the mind of the learner.

8. The type of reward (reinforcement) which has the greatest transfer value to other life-situations is the kind one gives oneself—the sense of satisfaction in achieving purposes.

9. Opportunity for fresh, novel, stimulating experience is a kind of reward which is quite effective in conditioning and learning.

10. The experience of learning by sudden insight into a previously confused or puzzling situation arises when: (*a*) there has been a sufficient background and preparation; (*b*) attention is given to the relationships operative in the whole situation; (*c*) the perceptual structure "frees" the key elements to be shifted into new patterns; (*d*) the task is meaningful and within the range of ability of the subject.

11. Learners progress in any area of learning only as far as they need to in order to achieve their purposes. Often they do only well enough to "get by"; with increased motivation they improve.

12. Forgetting proceeds rapidly at first—then more and more slowly; recall shortly after learning reduces the amount forgotten.

MATURATION: LIFE TASKS

13. The most rapid mental growth occurs during infancy and early childhood; the average child achieves about half of his total mental growth by the age of five.

14. Ability to learn increases with age up to adult years.

15. During the elementary school years (ages 6 to 12) most children enjoy energetic activity — running, chasing, jumping, shouting, and roughhouse. For most staid adults this is uncomfortable. Boys are generally more vigorous, active, rough, and noisy than girls.

16. Not until after eleven years of age do most children develop the sense of time which is required for historical perspective.

17. Readiness for any new learning is a complex product of interaction among physiological maturation, prerequisite learning, the pupil's sense of the

importance of this lesson in his world, and his feeling about the teacher and the school situation.

INDIVIDUAL DIFFERENCES

18. No two children make the same response to any school situation. Differences of heredity, physical maturity, intelligence, motor skills, health, experiences with parents, siblings, playmates; consequent attitudes, motives, drives, tastes, fears—all these and more enter into production of each child's unique reaction. Children vary in their minds and personalities as much as in their appearance.

19. Pupils vary not only in their present performance but in their rate of growth and the "ceiling" which represents their potential level of achievement. Some "late bloomers" may eventually surpass pupils who seem far ahead of them in grade school.

20. Gains in intelligence test scores by children are positively related to aggressiveness, competitiveness, initiative, and strength of felt need to achieve.

21. Pupils grouped by ability on any one kind of test (age, size, IQ, reading, arithmetic, science, art, music, physical fitness, and so forth) will vary over a range of several grades in other abilities and traits.

LEVEL OF CHALLENGE

22. The most effective effort is put forth by children when they attempt tasks which fall in the "range of challenge"—not too easy and not too hard—where success seems quite possible but not certain.

23. According to some studies, many pupils experience so much criticism, failure, and discouragement in school that their self-confidence, level of aspiration, and sense of worth are damaged.

TEACHING METHOD

24. Children are more apt to throw themselves wholeheartedly into any project if they themselves have participated in the selection and planning of the enterprise.

25. Reaction to excessive direction by the teacher may be: (a) apathetic conformity, (b) defiance, (c) scape-goating, (d) escape from the whole affair.

26. Learning from reading is facilitated more by time spent recalling what has been read than by rereading.

27. Pupils *think* when they encounter an obstacle, difficulty, puzzle or challenge in a course of action which interests them. The process of thinking involves designing and testing plausible solutions for the problem as understood by the thinker.

28. The best way to help pupils form a general concept is to present the concept in numerous and varied specific situations, contrasting experiences with and without the desired concept, then to encourage precise formulations of the general idea and its application in situations different from those in which the concept was learned.

"DISCIPLINE" AND LEARNING

29. Over-strict discipline is associated with more conformity, anxiety, shyness and acquiescence in children; greater permissiveness is associated with more initiative and creativity in children.

30. When children (or adults) experience too much frustration, their behavior ceases to be integrated, purposeful and rational. Blindly they act out their rage or discouragement or withdrawal. The threshold of what is "too much" varies; it is lowered by previous failures.

GROUP RELATIONS

31. Pupils learn much from one another; those who have been together for years learn new material more easily from one of their own group than they do from strangers.

32. When groups act for a common goal there is better cooperation and more friendliness than when individuals in the group are engaged in competitive rivalry with one another.

33. At age six, spontaneous groups seldom exceed three or four children; play groups all through childhood are smaller than school classes.

34. Children learn that peer consensus is an important criterion; they are uncomfortable when they disagree with their peers, and especially when they find themselves in a minority of one against all the others.

35. Groups which feel some need (internal coherence or external pressure) to work together try to influence deviates toward the group norm. If there is no felt need to stay together, the deviate may be ignored and thus excluded.

36. Leadership qualities vary with the demands of the particular situation. A good leader for a football team may or may not be a good leader for a discussion group, a research project, or an overnight hike; leadership is not a general trait.

37. In most school classes, one to three pupils remain unchosen by their classmates for friendship, for parties, or for working committees. These "isolates" are usually also unpopular with teachers.

SUBJECT MATTER

38. No school subjects are markedly superior to others for "strengthening mental powers." General improvement as a result of study of any subject depends on instruction designed to build up generalizations about principles, concept formation, and improvements of techniques of study, thinking, and communication.

39. What is learned is most likely to be available for use if it is learned in a situation much like that in which it is to be used and immediately preceding the time when it is needed. Learning in childhood-forgetting-and relearning when needed is not an efficient procedure.

40. Television is the most frequently reported activity of elementary school pupils, occupying about the same number of hours per week as are given to school—far more than would voluntarily be given to school attendance.

ATTITUDES AND LEARNING

41. Children (and adults even more) tend to select groups, reading matter, TV shows, and other influences which agree with their own opinions; they break off contact with contradictory views.

42. Children remember new information which confirms their previous attitudes better than they remember new information which runs counter to their previous attitudes.

SOCIAL STRATIFICATION

43. Attitudes toward members of "out-groups" are usually acquired from members of one's "in-group."

44. Children who differ in race, nationality, religion, or social class background, but who play together on a footing of equal status and acceptance, usually come to like one another.

45. Children who are looked down upon (or looked up to) because of their

family, school marks, social class, race, nationality, religion, or sex tend to adopt and to internalize this evaluation of themselves.

46. Two thirds of the elementary school children of America come from lower-class homes; the one third who come from the lower-lower class usually find school very uncongenial.

47. Children choose most of their "best friends" from homes of the same socioeconomic class as their own.

48. More girls than boys wish, from time to time, that they could change their sex.

EVALUATION

49. If there is a discrepancy between the real *objectives* and the *tests* used to measure achievement, the latter become the main influence upon choice of subject matter and method.

50. The superiority of man over calculating machines is more evident in the formulation of questions than in the working out of answers.

Theories of Learning

MORRIS L. BIGGE

SINCE ancient times, most civilized societies have developed and, to some degree, tested theories about how man learns. As each new theory has gained support, it has seldom displaced its predecessors but merely competed with them. For this reason, the educational philosophies and practices of many teachers may include ideas from a variety of learning theories, some of which are basically contradictory in nature.

Each theory of learning is linked to a conception of the basic nature of man: In basic moral inclination, is he innately good, is he evil, or is he neutral? Then, in relation to his environment, is he active, passive, or interactive? Each of the different conceptions has its adherents, and each has its own approach to learning.

The accompanying chart outlines the concepts involved in ten major learning theories (Column I) either prevalent in today's schools or advocated by leading psychologists. Reinforcement and conditioning (No. 7), especially as represented by B. F. Skinner's "operant conditioning" and the cognitive-field theory (No. 10), first advanced by Kurt Lewin but refined by contemporary psychologists, are two leading contenders in the present scene.

Teachers may find this chart useful in thinking through and noting possible inconsistencies in their own educational outlook and how their outlook agrees or disagrees with that of their school administration. Although some of the theories have roots that go back to antiquity, they all still exert influence in presentday schools.

Each theory has its unique approach to education. However, some of them have enough in common to justify grouping them in families. Thus, in a more general sense, there are only five basic outlooks in regard to learning—the three families plus theories 3 and 4.

NEA JOURNAL, March 1966, pp. 18-19.

	I THEORY of LEARNING	II PSYCHOLOGICAL SYSTEM or OUTLOOK	III ASSUMPTION CONCERN- ING the BASIC MORAL and PSYCHOLOGICAL NATURE of MAN
MIND SUBSTANCE FAMILY	1.Theistic ment- al discipline	faculty psycho- logy	bad-active mind sub- stance continues act- ive until curbed
	2.Humanistic mental disci- pline	classicism	Neutral-active mind substance to be dev- eloped through ex- ercise
	3.Natural un- foldment	romantic natural- ism	good-active natural personality to un- fold
	4.Apperception or Herbartion- ism	structuralism	neutral-passive mind composed of active mental states or ideas
	5.S-R bond	connectionism	neutral-passive or reactive organism with many potential S-R connectionism
CONDITIONING THEORIES OF STIMULUS- RESPONSE(S-R) ASSOCIATIONISTIC FAMILY	6.Conditioning (with no rein- forcement	behaviorism	neutral-passive or reactive organism with innate reflex- ive drives and emo- tions
	7.Reinforcement and condition- ing	reinforcement	neutral-passive or- ganism with innate reflexes and needs with their drive stimuli
	8.Insight	Gestalt psychology	naturally-active be- ing whose activity follows psychological laws of organization
COGNITIVE THEORIES OF GESTALT-FIELD FAMILY	9.Goal insight	configurational- ism	Neutral-interactive purposive individual in sequential relation- ships with environment
	10.Cognitive- field	field psychology relativism	neutral-interactive purposive person in simultaneous mutual interaction with en- vironment, including other persons.

IV BASIS FOR TRANSFER LEARNING	V MAIN EMPHASIS IN TEACHING	VI KEY PERSONS	VII CONTEMPORARY EXPONENTS
exercised facul- ties, automatic transfer	exercise of facul- ties-the "muscles" of the mind	St.Augustine, John Calvin, J.Edwards	many Hebraic- Christian funda- mentalists
cultivated mind or intellect	training of in- trinsic mental power	Plato,Aristole	M.J.Adler,St. John's College
recapitulation of racial his- tory, no trans fer needed	negative or per- missive education	J.J.Rousseau, F.Froebel	extreme progres- sivists
growing apper- ceptive mass	addition of new mental states or ideas to a store of old ones in subconscious mind	J.F.Herbart, E.B.Tichener	many teachers and administrators
identical ele- ments	promotion of ac- quisition of desired S-R connections	E.L. Thorndike	J.M. Stephens, A.I. Gates
conditioned re- sponses or re- flexes	promotion of ad- hesion of desired responses to ap- propriate stimuli	J.B.Watson	E.R. Guthrie
reinforced or conditioned re- sponses	successive system- atic changes in organisms'environ- ment to increase the probability of desired responses	C.L. Hull	B.F.Skinner, K.W.Spence
transposition of insignts	promotion of in- sightful learning	M.Wertheimer K.Koffka	W.Kohler
tested insights	aid students in trial-and-error, goal-directed learning	B.H.Bode,R.H. Wheeler	E.E.Bayles
continuity of life spaces,ex- perience or in- sights	help students re- structure their life spaces-gain new insignts into their contemporan- eous situations	Kurt Lewin,E. C.Tolman,J.S. Bruner	R.G.Barker,A.W. Combs,H.F.Wright M.L.Bigge

14

ROBERT M. GAGNÉ

The Learning of Concepts

For those interested in the design of effective instructional conditions in the school situation, the learning of concepts is a matter of central concern. School learning is preponderantly conceptual in nature. Nevertheless, there is great variation in the ways in which the term "concept" is used by educational writers and, accordingly, a variety of descriptions of the essential conditions for learning concepts by students. What *is* a concept, anyhow, in a generic sense? How is it related to a "fact" or a "principle" or a "generalization"? How is it related to methods of learning, such as repetition, or to discovery?

Being a psychologist, I naturally think that one should attempt to seek an answer to such basic definitional questions in that body of partially organized knowledge that has originated from controlled experimental research on behavior. For surely it is true that human learning of concepts can be studied in the framework of controlled laboratory experimentation. Whatever may be the variation in concepts of science, mathematics, language, art, or other content sub-

THE SCHOOL REVIEW, Autumn, 1965, vol. 75, pp. 187-196.

15

jects, when people speak of concept-learning they must be referring to a kind of change in human performance that is independent of such content. And if it is independent, then it would seem possible to arrange a set of conditions under which the learning of a concept can be studied systematically.

When one examines the experimental literature on concept formation," "concept-learning," and related matters, it appears that here too the word "concept" is not being used with great consistency. Under the heading of concepts, one can find experimental studies dealing with such things as the learning of nonsense words, the acquiring of a new category word by children, the inferring of common functions of a set of objects, the combining of object qualities to achieve new categories, and even the solving of mathematical puzzles. All of these kinds of experiments undoubtedly represent studies of learning. What is not entirely evident, however, is whether they reflect the learning of the same kinds of capabilities. It is truly difficult to describe what it is that these experimental studies have in common, or whether they are in fact devoted to the study of a common problem.

What does "learning a concept" mean? The approach I should like to take here is one that depends largely on observations of what happens in school learning. I do this, not to suggest that one can study the problem systematically in this way, but rather that perhaps one can begin to *define* the problem in such a manner. Perhaps if there can be agreement on what a concept is, and on how it is typically acquired in practice, then it will be possible to design experimental studies to find out the effects on its learning of various conditions of the learning situation.

AN INITIAL DISTINCTION

Some anticipation of my conclusions needs to be stated at the outset in order to spare you the details of a historical account. As a result of examining the kinds of situations that are said to represent concept-learning, I have arrived at the following propositions:

16

1. There are at least two different, important kinds of phenomena commonly referred to as concept-learning. One refers to the acquiring of a common response, often a name, to a class of objects varying in appearance. This may best be called *concept-learning*. The second refers to the combining of concepts into entities variously referred to as "ideas," "facts," "principles," or "rules." I prefer to call this *principle-learning*.

An example of these two different kinds of capabilities can perhaps be illustrated by *number*. First of all, there are such things as number concepts. When a young child is able to correctly assign the name "three" to collections of any three objects, and at the same time not assign it to collections of two or four objects, it may be said that the child has learned the concept "three." But as mathematics educators will be quick to point out, this is only the most elementary meaning of what they have in mind when they speak of the child "knowing the concept three." Obviously, they want the child to know that three is a set that may be formed by joining the sets two and one, by taking one member away from the set four, by subtracting zero from the set three, by dividing six into two equal parts, by taking the square root of nine, and so on. Perhaps all of these together could form what might be called the "meaning of three." But each of these is a separate *idea* or *principle*. Each of them is achieved by *combining* the concept three (in the simple sense previously described) with some other concept, perhaps equally simple. There is, then, the concept three, the correct choosing of objects to which the name three can be legitimately assigned. And in addition there is a set of principles of three, which are actually combinations of simpler concepts.

2. The basic reason for the distinction between *concept* and *principle* is that they represent two different kinds of learned capabilities. In the first case, the criterion performance is simply being able to answer such a question as "Which of these collections of objects is three?" In the second case, the criterion performance is being able to *use* the concept three in combination, as in the ques-

tion "What number added to two will give three?" These are quite different performances. Obviously, a child who is able to do the first may not have learned to do the second. If the second question is asked in a way which excludes the possibility of verbal parroting (as it needs to be), then it seems very likely that a child who does it correctly *will* be able to answer the simpler question correctly.

3. If it is true that knowing a concept and knowing a principle are two different capabilities, then it is also quite possible that the conditions for learning them are also different. I shall have more to say about this presently.

LEARNING CONCEPTS

How is a concept learned? What are the conditions that need to obtain in the instructional situation in order for a new concept to be acquired? It should not be too difficult to identify these conditions. For one thing, we know that animals can acquire concepts. The Harlows' monkeys acquired the concept "odd" when they had learned to choose the odd one of any three objects presented, two of which were nearly identical. If two identical cubes and a sphere were presented, they would choose the sphere; if two boxes and a stick were presented, they would choose the stick.[2] It is instructive to note that what the monkeys learned was the capability of choosing an "odd" one, regardless of the physical appearances of the objects presented. They learned to respond to a *class* of situations which the experimenter could classify as "odd."

How did the animals learn the concept "odd"? Actually, it required a lot of practice with a variety of specific situations each containing "an odd one" which was correct and each differing from the preceding one in the actual objects it contained. Human beings, too, can learn concepts this same way. In fact, sometimes psychologists force them to learn concepts this way in order to analyze the phenomenon. But one should not be led to suppose that humans *have* to learn concepts this way. In one way or another, it is almost bound to be true that the process of concept-learning gets shortened by human beings. Language is one thing that operates to bring this about. For example, studies by the Kendlers indicate that four-year-olds learn a reversal problem by extended trial-and-error, whereas seven-year-olds learn to reverse a discrimination in virtually a single trial.[3] The strong suggestion is that seven-year-olds can say something like "opposite" to themselves, whereas four-year-olds do not yet have the language to do this.

Suppose the concepts "liquid" and "solid" are to be taught to a young child. It seems likely that the learning situation would be something like the following:[4]

1. Show the child a glass containing water and a glass containing a rock. Say "This is a solid" and "This is a liquid."

2. Using a different container, show the child some powdered substance in a pile in a container and some milk in another container. Say "This is a solid; this is a liquid."

3. Provide still a third example of solid and liquid, using different materials and containers.

4. Show the child a number of examples of liquids and solids which he has not seen before. Ask him to distinguish the liquids and the solids. (In this example, I assume the child has previously learned to repeat the words "liquid" and "solid" readily when he hears them; they are familiar in sound.)

The characteristics of this learning situation are, first, that several varieties of the class, themselves of varying physical appearance, were used to exemplify the class to be responded to. Second, words already familiar as responses were used to guide the learning. Under such circumstances, one might expect a child to learn a fairly adequate set of concepts of "liquid" and "solid." This is tested by asking the child to identify liquids and solids from a set that he has not seen before and that has not been used in the learning.

It is also important to note two things that were *not* present in this situation. First, this is not repeated trial-and-error learning. Only three examples are used, all different. The situation is not repeated identically over and over again. Second, although there is language here, it is by no means extensive. One has not tried to teach the concepts, for example, by making such verbal statements as "A liquid is a substance whose particles move freely over each other so that its mass assumes the shape of the container in which it is placed." This characteristic of a liquid is directly exhibited, rather than being verbally described.

Presumably, much the same sort of conditions may obtain when an older student learns a new technical term. Something like this must have to be done when a student learns a concept like "point of inflection" in mathematics, or when he learns concepts such as "cell," "nucleus," or "mitochondrion" in biology, or when he learns what a "simile" is in English. Sometimes, it is true, even more extensive verbalization is used, and I shall return to this point in a moment.

LEARNING PRINCIPLES

What is meant by learning a principle (or rule)? And how does this differ from learning a concept? It needs to be recalled here that a principle is a combination of concepts.

Principles, being combinations, can become very complex. But let us start with an extremely simple one, such as "liquids pour." What kind of learning situation would be set up to bring about the learning of such a principle? Actually, there are two possibilities, and this does not make my task easier.[5]

Possibility one is this: After determining that the concepts "liquid" and "pour" can be identified, make the statement that "liquids pour." To test the learning, give the student a liquid in a container, and say, in effect, "Show me." This technique is what is often called *reception learning*, and there is little doubt that a very large proportion of school learning is basically of this sort, as D. P. Ausubel says.[6]

Possibility two is this: First determine that the concepts "liquid" and "pour" can be identified. Then, give the student a number of different liquids in a number of different containers. Ask him to

20

demonstrate ways in which the liquids are alike and different from solids. One thing he will do is pour them; he may also make the verbal statement, "Liquids pour." This learning technique is called *discovery learning*, and there is some evidence, though not much, that the principle learned this way is better retained and transferred than is the case with reception learning.

Regardless of the learning technique, however, the important thing to note is that what is learned is a combination of concepts, called a principle. There is no particular reason to think that there are any important formal differences between a simple principle of this sort and the great variety of more complex principles that are learned at later ages, such as principles of using adjectives, or of dividing quantities into fractional parts, or of specifying the functions of a legislature, or of relating force and mass and acceleration.

The characteristics of the learning situation for principles are, first, that the concepts of which it is composed must be previously learned. Second, the principle is either stated verbally or discovered by the learner. The acquisition of the principle is tested by asking the student to demonstrate its application to a particular case which he has not encountered during the learning.

Note particularly that the conditions of learning for a principle are *not* the same as those for a concept. Perhaps the outstanding difference is that the concepts which make up the principle must already be learned; they are prerequisite to the learning. Second, there is no requirement to illustrate the principle by two or three examples (although of course this may be done *after* the learning, for other purposes). Third, it is possible to discover a principle, since the two or more concepts which make it up may be theoretically "combined" in a number of different ways. But pure discovery, without verbal guidance, does not usually occur as a process in the learning of concepts by human beings. One could more aptly describe what monkeys do in attaining concepts as "discovery." Since they cannot be guided by language, they must go through a rather lengthy trial-and-error procedure to get to the point where they can choose the odd one or go to the middle door. If human beings had to "discover" new concepts in this way, it would take them a very long time to learn all the things they have to learn. Using a familiar word accomplishes the instruction much more rapidly. But it also short-circuits the process of discovery.

CONCEPT-LEARNING BY DEFINITION

While the distinction between concepts and principles in terms of conditions required for learning seems fairly clear, there is another source of confusion between them: When people are verbally sophisticated, they often learn concepts verbally, as pointed out by J. B. Carroll in a recent article.[7] That is to say, individuals learn concepts "by definition." If a person does not know the concept "caliche," he may learn what it is by reading or hearing the verbal statement, "a crust of calcium carbonate formed on stony soil in arid regions."

It is important to note that in this kind of learning situation, a *principle* is being used to provide instruction for the learning of a *concept*. The verbal statement itself is obviously a principle, because it contains several concepts: crust, calcium carbonate, stony soil, arid, region. And just as obviously, the learner will not be able to acquire "caliche" as a concept unless he does indeed know what each of these other concepts means, that is, unless he has previously learned each of them.

There can be little doubt that many new concepts are learned in this verbal manner by literate students and adults. Lest one think, however, that this method of learning concepts is a flawless one, a caution should be noted. A concept that is learned by way of verbally stated principles may have some inadequacies. For example, if an individual visits Texas for the first time in his life after hearing a verbal definition of caliche, will he make a certain identification of this material? Or will he be somewhat hesitant about it, and tend to confuse it with something else? Perhaps everyone would agree that for learning what caliche is, nothing can quite take the place of actually observing it.

This principle of "seeing is believing" is of more than passing importance to the problem of concept-learning. It is, for example, a fundamental reason why science educators are so firmly convinced of the value of the laboratory. If the student is to learn concepts like "power," "energy," "osmotic pressure," and many others, he can, to be sure, learn them in some sense by means of definitions. But there is a danger that the concepts he learns this way are inadequate in one way or another. Accordingly, most science educators would maintain that the performing of operations, including observation in the laboratory, is an essential part of the learning situation required for the learning of fully adequate, generalizable concepts. The role of the laboratory in school learning serves to remind us of the concrete basis for learning concepts and of the potential insufficiencies of concept-learning which is based solely upon verbally conveyed definitions. This is equally true in subjects other than science. The requirement for direct observation exists in all school subjects.

SUMMARY

In summary, it appears to be of some importance for the design of curriculum content and instructional method to recognize a distinction between concepts and principles. Different conditions are applicable to the learning of concepts and the learning of principles. Two differences that I have mentioned are perhaps of greatest importance. The first is that concepts are prior to principles and, in this sense, are simpler than principles. To learn a principle, one must have previously learned the concepts of which it is composed. A second difference pertains to verbal guidance versus pure discovery as a learning method. Learning concepts by pure discovery would appear to be an inhumanly inefficient thing to do, given the existence of language. But principles can be learned by discovery. There is some slight evidence to suggest that such a method of learning principles may be advantageous for retention and transfer, although it is likely to be more time-consuming for initial learning. Additional soundly designed research could well be devoted to this latter question.

NOTES

1. Paper given as part of a symposium on "Concept-Learning and the Curriculum" at the annual meeting of the American Educational Research Association, Chicago, Illinois, February 12, 1965.

2. H. F. Harlow and M. K. Harlow, "Learning To Think," *Scientific American*, CLXXXI (1949), 36–39.

3. H. H. Kendler and T. S. Kendler, "Effect of Verbalization on Reversal Shifts in Children," *Science*, CXLI (1961), 1619–20.

4. See my *The Conditions of Learning* (New York: Holt, Rinehart & Winston, 1965).

5. See *ibid.*

6. *The Psychology of Meaningful Verbal Learning* (New York: Grune & Stratton, 1963).

7. "Words, Meanings and Concepts," *Harvard Educational Review*, XXXIV (1964), 178–202.

Learning and Thinking[1]

JEROME S. BRUNER

I

I HAVE BEEN ENGAGED, these last few years, in research on what makes it possible for organisms—human and subhuman alike—to take advantage of past learning in attempting to deal with and master new problems before them now. It is a problem with a deceptively simple ring to it. In pursuit of it, my colleagues and I have found ourselves observing children in schoolrooms, watching them learning. It has been a revealing experience.

We have come to recognize in this work that one of the principal objectives of learning is to save us from subsequent learning. This seems a paradox, but it is not. Another way of putting the matter is to say that when we learn something, the objective is to learn it in such a way that we get a maximum of travel out of what we have learned. A homely example is provided by the relationship in arithmetic between addition and multiplication. If the principle of addition has been grasped in its deeper sense, in its generic sense, then it is unnecessary to learn multiplication. For, in principle, multiplication is only repeated addition. It is not, as we would say in our curricula, another "unit."

Learning something in a generic way is like leaping over a barrier. On the other side of the barrier is thinking. When the generic has been grasped, it is then that we are able to recognize the new problems we encounter as exemplars of old principles we have mastered. Once over the barrier, we are able to benefit from what William James long ago called "the electric sense of analogy."

There are two interesting features in generic learning—in the kind of learning that permits us to cross the barrier into thinking. One of them is

[1] Paper presented to Massachusetts Council on Teacher Education, February 13, 1958.

HARVARD EDUCATIONAL REVIEW, Summer 1959, vol. 29, 184-192.

25

organization; the other is *manipulation*. If we are to use our past learning, we must organize it in such a way that it is no longer bound to the specific situation in which the learning occurred. Let me give an example from the history of science. It would have been possible for Galileo to have published a handbook of the distances traversed per unit time by falling bodies. School boys for centuries thereafter could easily have been tortured by the task of having to remember the Galilean tables. Such tables, cumbersome though they might have been, would have contained all the necessary information for dealing with free-falling bodies. Instead, Galileo had the inspiration to reorganize this welter of information into a highly simplified form. You recall the compact expression $S = \frac{1}{2} gt^2$: it not only summarizes all possible handbooks but organizes their knowledge in a way that makes manipulation possible. Not only do we know the distances fallen, but we can use the knowledge for bodies that fall anywhere, in any gravitational field—not just our own.

One of the most notable things about the human mind is its limited capacity for dealing at any one moment with diverse arrays of information. It has been known for a long time that we can deal only with about seven independent items of information at once; beyond that point we exceed our "channel capacity," to use our current jargon. We simply cannot manipulate large masses of information. Because of these limits, we must condense and recode. The seven things we deal with must be worth their weight. A simple formula that can regenerate the distance fallen by any free body, past or future, is under these conditions highly nutritious for its weight. Good organization achieves the kind of economical representation of facts that makes it possible to use the facts in the future. Sheer brute learning, noble though it may be, is not enough. Facts simply learned without a generic organization are the naked and useless untruth. The proper reward of learning is not that it pleases the teacher or the parents, nor is it that we become "quiz kids." The proper reward is that we can now use what we have learned, can cross the barrier from learning into thinking. Are we mindful of these matters in our conduct of teaching?

What has been said thus far must seem singularly lacking in relevance to magic, to art, and to poetry. It appears to relate principally to the learning of mathematics, science, and the social studies. But there is an analogous point to be made about the learning of the arts and literature. If one has read literature and beheld works of art in such a way as to be able to think with their aid, then one has also grasped a deeper, simplifying principle. The underlying principle that gives one the power to use literature and the arts in one's thinking is not of the order of a generic condensation of knowledge. Rather it is metaphoric in nature, and perhaps the best way of describing this class of principles is to call them guiding myths.

26

Let me take an example from mythology. Recall when you read for the first time the story of Perseus slaying the hateful Medusa. You recall that to look directly upon the Medusa was to be turned to stone. The secret of Perseus was to direct the killing thrust of his sword by the reflection of Medusa on his polished shield. It is an exciting story, full of the ingenuity that Hercules had taught us to expect. Beneath the story, beneath all great stories, there is a deeper metaphoric meaning. I did not understand this meaning for many years, indeed, not until my son asked me what the myth of Perseus "meant." It occurred to me that the polished shield might symbolize all of the devices by which we are able to take action against evil without becoming contaminated by it. The law suggested itself as one such device, enabling us to act against those who trespassed against morality without ourselves having to trespass in our action. I do not wish to hold a brief for my interpretation of the Perseus myth. But I would like to make one point about it.

Man must cope with a relatively limited number of plights—birth, growth, loneliness, the passions, death, and not very many more. They are plights that are neither solved nor by-passed by being "adjusted." An adjusted man must face his passions just as surely as he faces death. I would urge that a grasp of the basic plights through the basic myths of art and literature provides the organizing principle by which knowledge of the human condition is rendered into a form that makes thinking possible, by which we go beyond learning to the use of knowledge. I am not suggesting that the Greek myths are better than other forms of literature. I urge simply that there be exposure to, and interpretation of, literature that deals deeply with the human condition. I have learned as much from Charley Brown of *Peanuts* as I have learned from Perseus. The pablum school readers, stripped of rich imagery in the interest of "readability," stripped of passion in the erroneous belief that the deeper human condition will not interest the child—these are no more the vehicles for getting over the barrier to thinking than are the methods of teaching mathematics by a rote parrotting at the blackboard.

II

I should like to consider now some conditions in our schools today that promote and inhibit progress across the barrier from learning to thinking. I should point out in advance that I am not very cheerful on this subject.

The passivity of knowledge-getting. I have been struck during the past year or so, sitting in classrooms as an observer, by the passivity of the process we call education. The emphasis is upon gaining and storing information, gaining it and storing it in the form in which it is presented. We carry the remainder in long division so, peaches are grown in Georgia, transportation is vital to cities, New York is our largest port, and so on. Can the facts or the methods presented be mimicked? If so, the unit is at an end. There is little effort indeed which goes into the process of putting the information together, finding out what is generic about it. Long division is a skill, like threading a needle. The excitement of it as a method of partitioning things that relates it to such matters as subtraction is rarely stressed. One of the great inventions of man—elementary number theory—is presented as a cookbook. I have yet to see a teacher present one way of doing division and then put it squarely to the class to suggest six other ways of doing it—for there are at least six other ways of doing it than any one that might be taught in a school. So too with algebra. Algebra is not a set of rules for manipulating numbers and letters except in a trivial sense. It is a way of thinking, a way of coping with the drama of the unknown. Lincoln Steffens, in his *Autobiography,* complains upon his graduation from the University of California that his teachers had taught him only of the known, how to commit it to mind, and had done little to instruct him in the art of approaching the unknown, the art of posing questions. How does one ask questions about the unknown? Well, algebra is one technique, the technique for arranging the known in such a way that one is enabled to discern the value of an unknown quantity. It is an enriching strategy, algebra, but only if it is grasped as an extended instance of common sense.

Once I did see a teacher specifically encourage a class to organize and use minimal information to draw a maximum number of inferences. The teacher modeled his technique, I suppose, on the tried method of the story-teller. He presented the beginnings of the Whiskey Rebellion and said to his pupils, much in the manner of Ellery Queen speaking to his readers, "You now have enough to reconstruct the rest of the story. Let's see if we can do it." He was urging them to cross the barrier from learning into thinking. It is unhappily true that this is a rare exception in our schools.

So knowledge-getting becomes passive. Thinking is the reward for learning, and we may be systematically depriving our students of this reward as far as school learning is concerned.

One experiment which I can report provides encouragement. It was devised and carried out by the research group with which I am associated at Harvard in collaboration with teachers in the fifth grade of a good public school. It is on the unpromising topic of the geography of the North Central States and is currently in progress so that I cannot give all of the results. We hit upon the happy idea of presenting this chunk of geography not as a set of knowns, but as a set of unknowns. One class was presented blank maps, containing only tracings of the rivers and lakes of the area as well as the natural resources. They were asked as a first exercise to indicate where

28

the principal cities would be located, where the railroads, and where the main highways. Books and maps were not permitted and "looking up the facts" was cast in a sinful light. Upon completing this exercise, a class discussion was begun in which the children attempted to justify why the major city would be here, a large city there, a railroad on this line, etc.

The discussion was a hot one. After an hour, and much pleading, permission was given to consult the rolled up wall map. I will never forget one young student, as he pointed his finger at the foot of Lake Michigan, shouting, "Yipee, *Chicago* is at the end of the pointing-down lake." And another replying, "Well, OK: but Chicago's no good for the rivers and it should be here where there is a big city (St. Louis)." These children were thinking, and learning was an instrument for checking and improving the process. To at least a half dozen children in the class it is not a matter of indifference that no big city is to be found at the junction of Lake Huron, Lake Michigan, and Lake Ontario. They were slightly shaken up transportation theorists when the facts were in.

The children in another class taught conventionally, got their facts all right, sitting down, benchbound. And that was that. We will see in six months which group remembers more. But whichever does, one thing I will predict. One group learned geography as a set of rational acts of induction —that cities spring up where there is water, where there are natural resources, where there are things to be processed and shipped. The other group learned passively that there were arbitrary cities at arbitrary places by arbitrary bodies of water and arbitrary sources of supply. One learned geography as a form of activity. The other stored some names and positions as a passive form of registration.

The Episodic Curriculum. In a social studies class of an elementary school in a well-to-do suburb of one of our great eastern cities, I saw groups of twelve-year-old children doing a "project" on the southeastern states. Each team was gathering facts that might eventually end up on a map or a chart or some other graphic device. The fact-gathering was atomized and episodic. Here were the industrial products of North Carolina. There was the list of the five principal cities of Georgia. I asked the children of one team what life would be like and what people would worry about in a place where the principal products were peanuts, cotton, and peaches. The question was greeted as "unfair." They were gathering facts.

It is not just the schools. The informational environment of America seems increasingly to be going through such an atomization. Entertainment is in fifteen minute episodes on TV, to be taken while sitting down. The school curriculum is built of episodic units, each a task to itself: "We have now finished addition. Let us now move to multiplication." Even in our humor the "gag" threatens to replace the shrewd observer of the human comedy. I have seen an elementary school play fashioned entirely on a parody of radio commercials. It was a brave effort to tie the 10-second atoms together.

I do not wish to make it seem as if our present state of education is a decline from some previous Golden Age. For I do not think there has ever been a Golden Age in American public education. The difference now is that we can afford dross less well than ever before. The volume of positive knowledge increases at a rapid rate. Atomizing it into facts-to-be-filed is not likely to produce the kind of broad grasp that will be needed in the world of the next quarter century. And it is certainly no training for the higher education that more and more of our children will be getting.

I have not meant the above as a plea for the "central subject" or the "project" method of teaching. It is, rather, a plea for the recognition of the continuity of knowledge. One hears professional educators speak of "coverage," that certain topics must be covered. There are indeed many things that must be covered, but they are not unconnected things. The object of learning is to gain facts in a context of connectivity that permits the facts to be used generatively. The larger the number of isolated facts, the more staggering the number of connections between them—unless one can reduce them to some deeper order. Not all of them can. Yet it is an ideal worth striving for, be it in the fifth grade or in graduate school. As Robert Oppenheimer put it in a recent address before the American Academy, "Everything cannot be connected with everything in the world we live in. Everything can be connected with anything."

The embarrassment of passion. I should like to consider now the guiding myth. Let me begin with a summary of the young Christopher Columbus as he is presented in a popular social studies textbook. Young Chris is walking along the water front in his home town and gets to wondering where all those ships go. Eventually he comes back to his brother's cobbler shop and exclaims, "Gee, Bart, I wonder where all those ships go, whether maybe if they just kept going they wouldn't come back because the world is round." Bart replies with pleasant brotherly encouragement. Chris is a well-adjusted kid. Bart is a nice big brother. And where is the passion that drove this obsessed man across uncharted oceans? What impelled this Columbus with such force that he finally enlisted the aid of Ferdinand and Isabella over the protest of their advisors? Everything is there in the story except the essential truth—the fanatical urge to explore in an age of exploration, the sense of an expanding world. Columbus did not have a schoolboy's whim, nor was he the well-adjusted grownup of this account. He was a man driven to explore, to control. The justification for the pablum that makes up such textbooks is that such accounts as these touch more directly on the life of the child.

What is this "life of the child" as seen by text writers and publishers? It is an image created out of an ideal of adjustment. The ideal of adjustment has little place for the driven man, the mythic hero, the idiosyncratic style. Its ideal is mediocentrism, reasonableness above all, being nice. Such an ideal does not touch closely the deeper life of the child. It does not appeal to the dark but energizing forces that lie close beneath the surface. The Old Testament, the Greek Myths, the Norse legends—these are the embarrassing chronicles of men of passion. They were devised to catch and preserve the power and tragedy of the human condition—and its ambiguity, too. In their place, we have substituted the noncontroversial and the banal.

Here a special word is needed about the concept of "expressing yourself," which is our conception of how one may engage the deeper impulses of the child. I have seen a book review class in a public school in which the children had the choice of reporting on any book they wished to choose, in or out of the school library, and where the discussion by the other children had to do entirely with the manner in which the reciting child presented his material. Nothing was said about the book in the discussion. The emphasis was on nice presentation, and whether the book sounded interesting. I have no quarrel with rewarding self-expression. I wonder simply whether it is not perhaps desirable, too, to make known the canons of excellence. The children in this class were learning to be seductive in their recounting; they were not concerned with an honest accounting of the human condition. The books they had read were cute, there was no excitement in them, none to be extracted. Increasingly the children in American elementary schools grow out of touch with the guiding myths. Self-expression is not a substitute. Adjustment is a worthy ideal, if not an ennobling one. But when we strive to attain it by shutting our eyes to the turmoils of human life, we will not get adjustment, but a niggling fear of the unusual and the excellent.

The quality of teachers. I do not wish to mince words. The educational and cultural level of the majority of American teachers is not impressive. On the whole they do not have a good grasp of the subject matter that they are teaching; courses on method will not replace the absent subject matter. In time and with teaching experience this deficiency is often remedied. But in so many cases there is no time: the turnover in the teaching profession as we all know is enormous; the median number of years of teaching before departure for marriage or motherhood is around three.

This leaves us with a small core of experienced teachers. Do we use them to teach the new teachers on the job? No. The organization of the school with respect to utilization of talent is something short of imaginative. It consists of a principal on top and a group of discrete teachers beneath her, and that is all. In large metropolitan high schools this is sometimes supplemented by having departments at the head of which is an experienced teacher. The communication that goes on between teachers is usually at a highly informal level and can scarcely be called comprehensive. It is usually about problem-children, not about social studies or mathematics or how to bring literature alive.

I would urge, and I believe that educators have taken steps in this direction, that we use our more experienced teachers for on-the-job training of less experienced, new teachers. I would also urge that there be established some means whereby the substantive topics taught in our elementary and high schools be included in some kind of special extension program provided by our eighteen hundred colleges and universities in the United States for the benefit of teachers. I am not speaking only of teachers colleges, but rather of all institutions of higher learning. Institutions of higher learning have a responsibility to the lower schools, and it can be exercised by arranging for continuous contact between those, for example, who teach history at the college level and those who are teaching history or social studies at the lower levels. And so, too, with literature or mathematics, or languages. To assume that somehow a teacher can be "prepared" simply by going through teacher training and then by taking courses on methods in summer school is, I think, fallacious. Often it is the case that the teacher, like her students, has not learned the material well enough to cross the barrier from learning to thinking.

III

It is quite plain, I think, that the task of improving the American Schools is not simply one of technique—however comforting it would be to some professional educators to think so. What is at issue, rather, is a deeper problem, one that is more philosophical than psychological or technological in scope. Let me put it in all innocence. What do we conceive to be the end product of our educational effort? I cannot help but feel that this rather overly simplified question has become obscured in cant. There is such an official din in support of the view that we are "training well-rounded human beings to be responsible citizens" that one hesitates to raise the question whether such an objective is a meaningful guide to what one does in classroom teaching. Surely the objective is worthy, and it has influenced the techniques of education in America, not always happily. For much of what we have called the embarrassment of passion can, I think, be traced to this objective, and so too the blandness of the social studies curriculum. The ideal, sadly, has also led to the standardization of mediocrity by a failure of the schools to challenge the full capacity of the talented student.

Since the war, there has been a perceptible shift in the problems being faced by schools and parents alike. It is the New Competition. Will Johnny and Sally be able to get into the college of their first choice or, indeed, into any college at all? The origins of the concern are obvious enough—the "baby bulge" has made itself felt. The results are not all bad, I would urge, or need not be. There are, to be sure, severe problems of overcrowding that exacerbate the difficulties already inherent in public education. And it is true that parental pressures for grades and production are increasing the proportion of children with "learning blocks" being referred to child guidance clinics.

But the pressures and the competition are also rekindling our awareness of excellence and how it may be nurtured. The shake-up of our smugness by the evident technical thrust of the Soviet Union has added to this awareness. Let me urge that it is this new awareness that requires shaping of expression in the form of a new set of ideals. Grades, admission to college, followed by admission to graduate school—these are surely not the ideals but, rather, the external signs.

Perhaps the fitting ideal is precisely as we have described it earlier in these pages, the active pragmatic ideal of leaping the barrier from learning into thinking. It matters not *what* we have learned. What we can *do* with what we have learned: this is the issue. The pragmatic argument has long been elaborated on extrinsic grounds, that the higher one has gone in the educational system the greater the economic gain. Indeed, at least one eminent economist has proposed that parents finance college education for their children by long-term loans to be repaid by the children on the almost certain knowledge that higher earning results from such education. All of this is the case, and it is indeed admirable that educational progress and economic success are so intimately linked in our society. I would only suggest that the pragmatic ideal be applied also to the intrinsic aspects of education. Let us not judge our students simply on *what* they know. That is the philosophy of the quiz program. Rather, let them be judged on what they can generate from what they know—how well they can leap the barrier from learning to thinking.

THE MOTIVATING EFFECT OF LEARNING
BY DIRECTED DISCOVERY [1]

BERT Y. KERSH

High school students were taught 2 novel rules of addition by a programed booklet procedure. Subsequently, ⅓ of the 90 Ss were given individual guidance in discovering the explanation for the rules ("guided discovery"), ⅓ were taught the explanation by a programed booklet ("directed learning"), and the remaining ⅓ were given no further instruction ("rote learning"). A questionnaire and a test of recall and transfer given 3 days, 2 weeks, and 6 weeks later favored the Rote Learning and Guided Discovery groups. The questionnaire indicated that the Guided Discovery group practiced the rules during the time interval between the learning and test period more than Ss in other groups (chi square, $p = .05$). The data support the hypothesis that self-discovery motivates the S to practice more and thus to remember and transfer more than he might if taught directly.

Advocates of the process of learning by directed discovery claim a number of advantages, most of which are included in a recent article by Bruner (1961). He has suggested that learning by discovery benefits the learner in four ways: it (a) increases the learner's ability to learn related material. (b) fosters an interest in the activity itself rather than in the rewards which may follow from the learning, (c) develops ability to approach problems in a way that will more likely lead to a solution, and (d) tends to make the material that is learned easier to retrieve or reconstruct.

Research evidence does not entirely support Bruner's arguments. One of the more recent reviewers, Ausubel (1961, p. 47), concludes "that most of the reasonably well-controlled studies report negative findings." However, as is true in other areas of research, the evidence is somewhat equivocal, partly because it is difficult to equate studies in terms of the amount and kind of direction that is provided. The experimental subjects rarely if ever are required to learn completely without help, and the kind of help provided commonly differs. Consequently, there are studies which appear to be somewhat contradictory, such as Craig's (1956), in which the "directed" group learned and retained significantly more principles than the "independent" group, and Kittell's (1957), in which the group which received an intermediate amount of guidance was superior in learning, retention, and transfer to groups receiving either more or less direction. It has been suggested

[1] This study was supported by a research grant from the Graduate School of the University of Oregon, Eugene, Oregon. Grateful acknowledgment is due Jerome C. R. Li, Chairman of the Statistics Department, Oregon State University, for his invaluable assistance in the statistical analysis. Additional research assistance was ably provided by William R. Hogan and Arthur M. Jackson. The research was reported at the APA meeting in Chicago, September 1960, under a different title.

JOURNAL OF EDUCATIONAL PSYCHOLOGY, 1962, vol. 53, pp. 65-71.

34

that the "intermediate" amount of guidance provided by Kittell may have actually exceeded the amount Craig provided to his directed group (Ausubel, 1961, p. 52).

One of the few studies that forced learners to discover almost entirely without help provides data in support of the discovery process (Kersh, 1958). The contrasting directed treatment groups were superior in learning rate and immediate recall, but the "no help" group was superior in terms of retention and transfer after a period of approximately one month following the learning period. No evidence was produced to indicate that the no help group understood the rules better. Instead, an explanation was offered in terms of practice. On the basis of a subjective analysis of the subject's comments written on the retests and reported to the experimenter, it was concluded that the learners were motivated to continue the learning process or to continue practicing the task after the formal learning period.

The present experiment was designed to provide formal data concerning the motivating power in question.

HYPOTHESIS

Each subject had the task of learning the following two rules of addition:

1. Odd Numbers rule. The sum of any series of consecutive odd numbers beginning with 1 is equal to the square of the number of figures in the series. (For example, 1, 3, 5, 7, is such a series; there are four numbers, so 4×4 is 16, the sum.)

2. Constant Difference rule. The sum of any series of numbers in which the difference between the numbers is constant is equal to one-half the product of the number of figures and the sum of the first and last numbers. (For example, 2, 3, 4, 5, is such a series; 2 and 5 are 7; there are four figures, so 4×7 is 28; half of 28 is 14 which is the sum.)

The rules can be learned by simple memorization of the task procedure as above. Further, the learner can become cognizant of certain relations which these rules bear to geometrical and arithmetical concepts, in which case it is assumed that his learning will be more meaningful. The definition of meaning, as well as the geometrical and arithmetical relationships referred to are identified in a previous publication (Kersh, 1958). In the hypothesis statement below, the term "relationships" refers specifically to those in the reference cited above and generally to comparable relationships in related tasks.

As will be explained below, the experimental treatments in the present study differed primarily with respect to the extent of the external direction provided the subjects in learning the relationships referred to above. The present experiment was designed to test the following hypothesis.

To the extent that the external direction provided to the learner is lessened during his attempts to discover the relationships which are considered essential to the understanding of a cognitive task: (a) the learner will tend to use the learned material more frequently after the learning period (i.e., to extend the practice period voluntarily) and, as a result, (b) he will remember it longer and transfer his learning more effectively.

It should be noted that the hypothesis is written in two parts and that the second is dependent upon the first.

PROCEDURE

A total of 90 high school geometry students was utilized, having been selected from a larger group on the basis of a pretest covering the arithmetical and geometrical concepts and procedures that were considered essential prerequisites to the tasks used in the experiment. The entire sample was then taught the two rules of addition given above by being simply told the rules and given practice in their application. They were taught by a programed booklet procedure to the same criterion, six successive applications of each of the two rules. Thereafter, the subjects were divided at random into three main groups of 30 each, and each group was treated differently.

One group, called the Directed Learning group, was taught the rules and their explanation entirely by a programed learning technique. Each subject learned from a booklet in which the learning process was broken down into smaller steps, and answers to questions or solutions to problems were revealed to the subject whether he responded correctly or not.

A second group, called the Guided Discovery group, was required to discover the explanation with guidance from the experimenter. The subjects in the Guided Discovery group were taught tutorially using a form of Socratic questioning which required each subject to perform specific algebraic manipulations and to make inferences without help. The guidance was a practical expedient, since it was necessary to control between groups the quality and quantity of the relationships used in explaining the rules.

The final group was called, appropriately, the Rote Learning group since the explanation for the rules was omitted. This treatment was incorporated in the research design primarily as the control for "meaningful" learning.

After the learning period of the experiment, a test of recall and transfer was given to subgroups of each treatment group after 3 days, 2 weeks, and 6 weeks. For this purpose each of the three main groups was divided into three subgroups of 10 each.

The test consisted of two problems and a short questionnaire. The problems were given first with instructions to show all work including scratchwork. The two test problems were as follows:

1. John's employer agrees to pay him $1.00 for his first day of work and increase his pay by $2.00 each day. How much will he receive for the first month's work if he works all 30 days?

2. A man is left a sum of money by an eccentric relative. The will states that he will receive $10.00 the first month and that each successive monthly payment will be increased by $5.00 (i.e., he will receive $10.00 the first month, $15.00 the second month, $20.00 the third month, etc.). His monthly payment at the end of four years is $245.00. What is the total amount he has been paid by that time?

The questionnaire asked the subject to state each rule, using examples if necessary, and to report whether or not he made use of the rules after the formal learning period.

RESULTS

The number of subjects in each group who used the appropriate rule in an acceptable way on the test was employed as the index of transfer. Acceptable use of a rule for the first test problem meant the use of either rule to obtain the solution; for the second test problem, only the Constant Difference rule was acceptable. Computational accuracy was not required.

The number of subjects in each group who wrote an acceptable statement of each rule was used as a measure of pure retention. To be acceptable, each subject's statement had to be complete and accurate, but not necessarily in the same words as the original statements. Errors in spelling or grammar were overlooked.

Table 1 presents the number who used and stated the rules in the acceptable way on the test problems. A total of 90 subjects served as the basis for the data in Table 1, 10 subjects per cell.

In the statistical analysis, use was made of a chi square technique devised by Li (1957, p. 416-20). The data included under each of the columns of Table 1 were envisioned as a 2×9 contingency table, with 8 df. Four separate analyses were then conducted, each of which broke down the chi square into the following components: (a) differences between teaching treatments (2 df), (b) differences between test periods (2 df), and (c) differences attributed to interaction of treatments and time periods (4 df).

TABLE 1

NUMBER OF SUBJECTS (OF 10 IN EACH CELL) WHO USED AND STATED THE
RULES CORRECTLY ON THE RETEST

Treatment Groups	Used Rules		Stated Rules	
	Odd Numbers[a] 1	Constant Difference 2	Odd Numbers[a] 3	Constant Difference[a] 4
Rote Learning:				
3 days	7	7	7	9
2 weeks	7	6	2	6
6 weeks	4	4	0	3
Guided Discovery:				
3 days	6	6	8	9
2 weeks	3	5	3	4
6 weeks	2	3	3	3
Directed Learning:				
3 days	4	3	3	4
2 weeks	4	3	1	3
6 weeks	0	3	1	1

[a] Differences between treatment groups and between test periods signifacant by chi square at or beyond .05 level.

None of the interaction effects was significant, indicating that the rate of forgetting did not differ significantly across the teaching treatment groups. A trend analysis of the test data indicated also that the rate of forgetting was constant for all groups (Li, 1957, pp. 226-233).

Otherwise, as pointed out by the footnote references in Table 1, the differences between treatment groups and between test periods were found to be significant for all columns except that headed "Constant Difference 2," for which the observed differences were found not to be reliable.

Perhaps the most striking finding in the present study is that the Rote Learning group was found to be consistently superior in every respect to the other treatment groups. Although this completely unanticipated finding has no direct bearing on the hypothesis in question, it does nevertheless bear clearly upon the related question of "meaningful vs. mechanical" learning. This finding will be discussed in a subsequent section.

Strictly speaking, the hypothesis which the present experiment was designed to test involves only the Guided Discovery and Directed Learning treatments. To support the major hypothesis, the data should have shown that the subjects comprising the Guided Discovery group used the rules after the learning period more frequently than the subjects in the Directed Learning group; and, if so, that the former remembered and transferred the rules more effectively than the latter.

With respect to the frequency of using the rules after the learning period, the results do support the hypothesis.

37

Although the number of subjects in each group who reported that they did use the rules was very small, the difference between the frequency patterns of the two groups in question is statistically significant. Eleven subjects of the 30 in the Guided Discovery group reported that they had used the rules as compared with two subjects in the Directed Learning group. In the Rote Learning group, six subjects of 30 reported in the affirmative.

With respect to the relative permanence of the retention and increased transfer effects, the results also support the hypothesis. The Guided Discovery group is clearly superior to the Directed Learning group 3 days after the learning period, and since the rate of forgetting may be presumed to be approximately the same for each treatment group (see statistical analysis above), their initial superiority remains after 6 weeks.

DISCUSSION

The data from this present experiment do not support the generalization that learning by a process which involves discovery is necessarily superior to learning by more highly directed processes. Indeed, these data suggest that under certain conditions of learning, highly formalized "lecture-drill" techniques, ordinarily considered sterile and meaningless, produce better results than techniques which attempt to develop "understanding."

One explanation for the present results is that they reflect a simple and well known phenomenon, retroactive inhibition. The experimental efforts to inject meaning into the rules amounted to following their initial rote learning with a closely related and complex learning task; thus the Rote Learning group may have surpassed other groups simply because retention among the

latter was inhibited by the interpolated learning.

How may the present results be reconciled with those of the previous experiment by Kersh (1958), in which learning by discovery proved markedly superior? The preferred interpretation is that the findings of the two studies are actually complementary. Schematically, the treatments employed in the two experiments may be compared on a line representing the continuum of learning processes: at one extreme, learning without any external direction whatsoever (true self-discovery); at the other, learning by lecture-drill processes (rote learning), as follows:

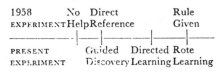

As is indicated above, the Direct Reference treatment in the 1958 experiment is comparable to the Guided Discovery treatment in the present one; similarly, the Rule Given and Rote Learning groups correspond. The present experiment has no counterpart to the No Help treatment of the previous study; and, in the previous one, the Directed Learning treatment was not represented.

When compared as above, the results of the two experiments are remarkably similar. The initial achievement of the comparable groups in both experiments was very high then dropped to where only about half of each group was able to recall and apply the rules after 4 to 6 weeks. In each experiment the difference in the performance of the Rote Learning and Directed Discovery groups was not notable; if anything, the Rote Learning groups tended to perform slightly better.

With respect to the motivating power

of learning by discovery, in the 1958 experiment the superior performance of the No Help subjects on the retest together with their written comments and verbal reports to the experimenter strongly evidenced their increased interest. The present results leave no doubt that there is a tendency for interest to accrue as a result of learning by discovery.

The results of both experiments also are consistent in their failure to support the notion that attempts to provide added meaning will necessarily prolong memory for rules and procedures and will enhance their transfer. On the contrary, both experiments suggest that such attempts may well do more to interfere with learning than enhance it. This does not mean that rote learning is superior to learning with understanding. Rather it means that we need to know much more than we do about meaningful learning and how we come by it.

The relatively poor showing of the Directed Learning group in the present study is partially explained by the subjects' reported failure to practice the rules after the learning period to the extent that the subjects did in other groups. Why the Rote Learning treatment generated more interest than the treatment in question again may reflect nothing more than that the original learning was inhibited by the interpolated programed learning. The subjects' unfamiliarity with the instructional procedure may have contributed to their confusion.

Most certainly the data from the two experiments under discussion suggest that the frequently taught principles of learning that pertain to self-discovery and meaning (see introduction) should be restated or qualified. The following statements are offered for further study.

Learning by self-discovery. Learning by self-discovery is superior to learning with external direction only insofar as it increases student motivation to pursue the learning task. If sufficiently motivated, the student may then continue the learning process autonomously beyond the formal period of learning. As a result of his added experience, the learner may then raise his level of achievement, remember what he learned longer, and transfer it more effectively. The explanation for the elusive drive generated by independent discovery is not evident, but several have been offered, including the Zeigarnik effect of superior memory for unfinished tasks and the Ovsiankina effect of resumption of incomplete tasks.[3] It also could be explained in terms of operant conditioning; specifically, as a kind of "searching behavior" reinforced by the experimenter's comments and by the subject's own successful progress toward a solution. Whatever the explanation, the motivating power evidently does not appear in strength unless the student is required to learn almost completely without help and expends intensive effort over a period of 15 minutes or more.

Meaningful learning. Aside from the advantage the student may come to have academically, he may not benefit from knowing the explanations for rules and procedures he learns, i.e., the pattern of relationships involved. That which is meaningful (understood) may or may not be retained longer and transferred more effectively than that which has been learned by rote. Moreover, superficial efforts to gain understanding after a rule or principle has been memorized may have an inhibitory effect when the student attempts to recall and transfer the original learning. If it is important only that the task be under-

---

[3] The author is particularly indebted to Julius M. Sassenrath and the late Percival M. Symonds for their critical comments and suggestions.

stood (as is most often the case, presumably), the essential relationships may be learned most economically when taught by another person or teaching program, not by process of self-discovery.

REFERENCES

AUSUBEL, D. P. Learning by discovery: Rationale and mystique. *Bull. Nat. Ass. Second. Sch. Principals*, 1961, 45, 18-58.

BRUNER, J. S. The act of discovery. *Harv. educ. Rev.*, 1961, 31, 21-32.

CRAIG, R. C. Directed versus independent discovery of established relations. *J. educ. Psychol.*, 1956, 47, 223-234.

KERSH, B. Y. The adequacy of "meaning" as an explanation for the superiority of learning by independent discovery. *J. educ. Psychol.*, 1958, 49, 282-292.

KITTELL, J. E. An experimental study of the effect of external direction during learning on transfer and retention of principles. *J. educ. Psychol.*, 1957, 48, 391-405.

LI, J. C. R. *Introduction to statistical inference.* Ann Arbor, Mich.: Edwards, 1957.

JEAN PIAGET:
NOTES ON LEARNING

By FRANK G. JENNINGS

T HE MAN behind the ideas of many of the plans and
programs to improve the curricula in the schools is not
an educator. Jean Piaget is the seventy-one-year-old
French-speaking Swiss director of the Jean Jacques Rousseau
Institute in Geneva, the founding director of the International
Center for Genetic Epistemology, director of the International Bureau of Education, and professor of child psychology
and of the history of scientific thought at the University of
Geneva. Some psychologists are convinced that his work
might become as influential as Freud's. Some educators are
fearful that this may be true.

In March, Piaget came to this country to deliver three
lectures on the nature and nurture of intelligence and on
related matters in science, psychology, and education. He
spoke at New York University and addressed the convention
of the American Orthopsychiatric Association in Washington.

It has been said of Piaget that he is by vocation a sociolo-
gist, by avocation an epistemologist, and by method a logi-
cian. He tells his listeners and readers that he is not an
educator, that he is a psychologist with an interdisciplinary
bent, that he is an investigator using the tools of the related
fields of biology, psychology, and logic to explore the genesis
of intelligence in the human young. All his long life he has
drawn upon these three fields to conduct research and to
build his theories of the development of intelligence in
children.

For Piaget, the crucial question in the study of the growing child is how he adjusts himself to the world in which he
lives. And for Piaget there is nothing pejorative in the word
adjustment. It involves backing and filling, winning and los-
ing, understanding and gaining knowledge. As he expresses it:

> Knowledge is not a copy of reality. To know an object,
> to know an event, is not simply to look at it and make a

SATURDAY REVIEW, May, 1967, pp. 81-83.

mental copy, or image, of it. To know an object is to act on it. To know is to modify, to transform the object, and to understand the process of this transformation, and as a consequence to understand the way the object is constructed. An operation is thus the essence of knowledge; it is an interiorized action which modifies the object of knowledge.

This is the voice of the epistemologist, but it speaks from the soul of the teacher. Piaget's techniques for observing, recording, and understanding the way a child thinks is quite literally to get inside of the child's mind and see the world through the child's eyes. One of his notable experiments, for example, was to join in a child's game as an equal. He would "learn how to make a good shot at marbles, how to make bad ones, and even how to cheat.

Rules and standards for three-year-olds, he found, are almost nonexistent. Ask a three-year-old who won and you get the answer, "I won, you won, and we all won." The five-year-old sees and sometimes respects rules. For the seven-year-old they are sacred and immutable. When the Geneva boys were told that the game was played differently in Lucerne, they shouted, "But those kids over there never understood marbles, anyway."

Piaget found that ten-year-olds can get together and modify rules to meet new conditions, and with the onset of puberty, adjustments are freely made to meet unusual cases. In a ball game, the short-sighted child is allowed to stand nearer the pitcher, a cripple will be allowed a runner. Thus there is a logic of operations that is fitted to a logic of social relations. There is continuous observable growth in the way the child learns and adjusts his understanding to the requirements of the world around him.

Piaget sees four major stages of growth through childhood; the first is the *sensory-motor* stage, which lasts from birth to about two years. Here the child learns his muscles and senses and develops certain habits for dealing with external objects and events. Language begins to gain form. He can deal with and know that things exist even when they are beyond his sight or touch. He begins to "symbolize," to represent things by word or gesture.

The second stage is the *preoperational* or *representational* stage. It begins with the beginning of organized language and continues to about the age of six. This is the period of greatest language growth and through the use of words and other symbols the child can represent the outside world and his own inner world of feeling. It is a period when magical explanations make sense, when "God pushes the sun around" and stars must go to bed when he does. The child begins to gain a sense of symmetry, depends on trial and error adjustments, and manages things by a kind of intuitive regulation.

The third stage, between seven and eleven years, is one in which the child acquires the ability to carry out what Piaget calls *concrete operations*. He can move things around, make them fit properly. He acquires fine motor skills and can organize what he has and knows how to solve physical problems.

The fourth stage is one of *formal operations* and prepares the way for adult thinking. It usually begins between twelve and fifteen years and involves the development of "hypothetical reasoning based upon a logic of all possible combinations and to perform controlled experimentation."

In successive studies Piaget and his associates have explored the growth of intelligence, the development of moral awareness, the child's concept of physical reality, and the elaboration of appropriate logic to deal with complex nonrepresentational problems.

Although *The Language and Thought of the Child* was published in English in 1926, it was not until the early 1950s that Piaget's ideas made any significant impact in the United States. Professor Jerome S. Bruner of Harvard is probably responsible for the current public awareness, which can be traced to his important little book *The Process of Education* (1960), and his most recent book, *Toward a Theory of Instruction* (1966). Bruner describes Piaget as "unquestionably, the most impressive figure in the field of cognitive development." Piaget, he says "is often interpreted in the wrong way by those who think that his principal mission is psychological. It is not. . .What he has done is to write the implicit logical theory on which the child proceeds in dealing with intellectual tasks."

Some American psychologists and educators make precisely this "wrong" interpretation. They see Piaget as "cold-blooded," not interested in motivational problems, not responsive to curricular concerns. They criticize him for being intellectually seductive. They object to his children, who seem to have a fair view of the world, who appear to be distressingly happy with their existence.

Put this down, perhaps, to a tough-minded myopia of those who must work in the slums, or to the necessary sentiment of those who give primacy to "feeling" and "socialization." It is not that Piaget overlooks the affective domain, but rather that he appears convinced that the world is manageable only to the degree that orderly intelligence can be brought to bear upon the inescapable transactions each human being must make with it and with his fellows.

One critic recently complained that Piaget's children ". . . react as if they trusted the world, as if the environment were waiting to welcome them." Indeed, they sometimes do, for they are engaged in explorations of the greater world and of the closer environment with patient, resourceful, interested, and perhaps even loving adults who seem to believe that sovereign reason has not yet been dethroned. The great strength of reason, Piaget seems to say, is in its very tentativeness before an uncertain and sometimes disorderly universe. Patience is required, and time to grow, time to take in the outside world, to assimilate it, to understand it, and to use it generously.

Acquisition of Conservation through Social Interaction

FRANK B. MURRAY[1]

In two experiments, groups of three children (generally one nonconserver and two conservers) were required to respond with one group answer to a series of standardized conservation problems. When tested again individually, all subjects made significant gains in conservation judgments and explanations on the same problems, on a parallel form of those problems, and on new problems. Nonconservers made the greatest gains. In all, 108 children with mean age of 6.7 years were studied.

That so many reasonable attempts to train nonconservers in conservation have been surprising failures raises the question of how children normally acquire conserved concepts. In the *Language and Thought of the Child*, Piaget suggested originally that a necessary condition for the movement from the stage of preoperational or egocentric thought to more mature stages of thought was the occurrence of repeated communication conflicts between children. These conflicts would require the young child to attend to another child's point of view and perspective, and the ability to maintain a perspective of another or to take another's role appears to be related to operational modes of thought (Flavell, 1967) and to the opportunities for social interaction (Neale, 1966). Since nonconservation is the salient mode of preoperational thought, one would expect that an effective conservation training procedure would be one in which the child was confronted with opposing points of view. This expectation was investigated in an experiment and a replication experiment in which the child's point of view was brought into conflict with other children's points of view. Specifically it was expected that the young child's ability to give conservation judgments, and to support those judgments with adequate reasons, would improve after he had been subjected to the contrary arguments and viewpoints of other children.

Method

Subjects

In Experiment I, there were 57 white children, 28 boys and 29 girls, whose mean age was 6.70 years ($SD = .72$ years) from kindergarten and first grades of a suburban Minneapolis elementary school. In Experiment II, there were 51 white children, 28 boys and 23 girls, with a mean age of 6.74 ($SD = .31$ years) from the first grade of a suburban parochial elementary school in Wilmington, Delaware. The data were collected by female experimenters in a vacant classroom in the child's school during the months of November and December.

Procedure

In the first of three sessions of both experiments, all subjects were given Form A of the Concept Assessment Kit (Goldschmid & Bentler, 1968), which provided a standardized and individual testing procedure for six conservation problems (two-dimensional space, number, substance, continuous quantity, weight, and discontinuous quantity). Two points were given for each correct problem, one point for a correct judgment and one point for an explanation that noted reversibility, compensation, or invariant quantity. In Experiments I and II, one nonconserver (subjects with scores from 0–4 on Form A) was grouped with two conservers (subjects with scores from 10–12 on Form A).

[1] The assistance of Anne Matthews at the University of Minnesota and Virginia Flynn at the University of Delaware and the cooperation of the children and staff at the Bloomington Elementary School and the St. Mary Magdalan Elementary School is greatly appreciated.

DEVELOPMENTAL PSYCHOLOGY, 1972, vol. 6, pp. 1-6.

In a second session of both experiments, each group of three subjects was given the same problems from Form A of the Concept Assessment Kit. In each group, subjects were told that they could not receive a score until all of them agreed on the answer to each problem. Subjects were given 5 minutes to solve each problem. The experimenter started with the lowest scorers on Form A, and asked each child in a group to answer a problem, and when there was disagreement between children, they were directed to discuss the problem, and explain to each other why they had said what they had. Subjects were allowed to manipulate the conservation stimuli, but the experimenter gave no information or reinforcement for correct or incorrect answers.

One week later in the critical third session each subject was tested alone, as in the first session. Conservation problems from Form B, Form C, and lastly Form A of the Concept Assessment Kit were presented. Form B consisted of parallel problems on the same six concepts as Form A, but different conservation stimuli or different conservation transformations were used. Form C tested the conservation of two new concepts, length and area, with three area and three length conservation problems. As on Form A, each problem on Forms B and C, was scored one point for the correct judgment and a second point for the appropriate explanation of that judgment. Thus the maximum score on any form was 12.

Results

Scores between 0 and 6 were taken to indicate nonconservation on that form, and scores between 7 and 12 were taken to indicate conservation. This somewhat arbitrary division preserved all the data and required that all children labeled as conservers give at least one acceptable reason for their conservation judgments. Since less than 9% of the children earned scores of 5, 6, 7, or 8 on any form, the dichotomy and labeling of the subjects was not inappropriate. The effect of the conflict situation on the nonconservers was evident in both experiments from the significant numbers of nonconservers on Pretest Form A who conserved on Posttest Form A, Posttest Form B, and Posttest Form C. In both experiments, the shifts from nonconservation to conservation were all significant at the .001 level by the McNemar test between Pretest Form A and Posttest Form A, between Pretest Form A and Posttest Form B, and between Pretest Form A and Posttest Form C (Table 1).

The effects of the conflict situation upon the nonconservers was also evident in both experiments in the comparison of their mean

TABLE 1

Numbers of Conservers (Cs) and Nonconservers (NCs) Who Shifted or Were Consistent in Experiments I and II between Pretest Form A and Posttests Forms A, B, and C, and the Chi-Square for Each Comparison

Pretest	Posttest					
	Form A		Form B		Form C	
Form A	Cs	NCs	Cs	NCs	Cs	NCs
Exp. I (N = 57)						
Cs	40	0	40	0	38	2
NCs	16	1	15	2	14	3
χ^2	14.06**		13.06**		7.56*	
Exp. II (N = 51)						
Cs	25	0	25	0	24	1
Ns	18	8	19	7	21	5
χ^2	16.06**		17.05**		16.40**	

* $p < .01$.
** $p < .001$.

scores on the pretest with those on the posttests, which are presented in Table 2. The difference between the mean score of these subjects on Pretest Form A and the mean scores of subjects on Posttests Forms A, B, and C were all significant at the .001 level by the t test (Experiment I, $t = 14.79$, $t = 11.57$, and $t = 7.99$, respectively; Experiment II, $t = 6.74$, $t = 7.32$, and $t = 7.51$, respectively).

Of special interest are 11 firm nonconservers in Experiment II who had scores of zero on Pretest Form A. Their mean scores on Posttests Form A, Form B, and Form C are presented in Table 2, and by the t test these differences between the pretest mean and posttest means were significant at the .01 level. The remaining 15 nonconservers in Experiment II (scores between 1 and 6) had a mean score of 2.80 on Pretest Form A. The mean scores of these subjects on Posttests Forms A, B, and C are also presented in Table 2, and the differences between the pretest mean and posttest means were all significant at the .001 level by the t test ($t = 7.11$, $t = 6.98$, and $t = 11.09$, respectively). Gains in conservation from pre-

45

TABLE 2

Mean Scores and Standard Deviations for Pretest A and Posttests A, B, and C for Conservers (Cs) and Nonconservers (NCs) on Pretest A in Experiments I and II, and for Nonconservers Who Scored Zero or More than Zero on Pretest A in Experiment II

Experiment	Pretest A		Posttest A		Posttest B		Posttest C	
	M	SD	M	SD	M	SD	M	SD
Exp. I								
Cs	10.77	1.3	11.90*	.4	11.55*	.8	11.40	1.9
NCs	2.35	1.9	11.41*	1.4	10.18*	1.9	8.82*	2.6
Exp. II								
Cs	10.37	1.8	11.91*	.4	11.87*	.4	11.08	1.9
NCs	1.61	1.8	8.08*	4.4	8.38*	4.2	8.19*	3.9
NCs who scored 0	.00	.0	6.00*	4.9	7.09*	5.1	5.73*	4.7
NCs who did not score 0	2.80	1.6	9.60*	3.2	9.33*	3.1	10.00*	1.8

* Compared to Pretest A, $p < .01$.

test to posttest were compared for those subjects ($N = 11$) who had exhibited no conservation on the pretest and those ($N = 15$) who had exhibited some conservation on it. None of the contrasts was significant (Form A, $t = .54$, $p > .05$; Form B, $t = .24$, $p > .05$; Form C, $t = .89$, $p > .05$).

Another indicator of the effect of the conflict situation upon children's ability to conserve was found in the comparison of their performance on the pretest and posttests with the performance of an appropriate control group on Forms A, B, and C. Since the norms for the standardized sample are separated by sex for the Concept Assessment Kit, the appropriate boy and girl mean scores from the norms are presented in Table 3 for Forms A, B, and C along with the boy and girl mean scores from the experimental subjects for Pretest Form A and Posttests Forms A, B, and C. As they should be, the differences between the norm mean scores

TABLE 3

Comparison of Mean Scores of Experimental Subjects on Pretest A and Posttests A, B, and C with Mean Scores of Standardized Sample on Forms A, B, and C

Group	Pretest Form A		Posttest Form A		Posttest Form B		Posttest Form C	
	Girls	Boys	Girls	Boys	Girls	Boys	Girls	Boys
Standarized	7.15*	5.15*	7.15**	5.15**	7.37**	7.64**	6.82**	5.03**
Experimental	7.72*	6.77*	10.52**	11.25**	10.48**	10.66**	10.38**	10.03**

* $p > .05$.
** $p < .01$.

on Form A and experimental mean scores on Pretest Form A were insignificant by the t test (girls, $t = .48$, $p > .05$; boys, $t = .97$, $p > .05$). However, all other differences between the norm mean scores on Forms A, B, and C and experimental mean scores on Posttests Form A, B, and C were significant at the .01 level (Form A: girls, $t = 3.06$, $p < .01$; boys, $t = 5.00$, $p < .01$; Form B: girls, $t = 2.66$, $p < .01$; boys, $t = 2.29$, $p < .01$; Form C: girls, $t = 4.24$, $p < .001$; boys, $t = 6.02$, $p < .001$).

Not only did the social conflict situation influence the nonconservers' performance on the posttests, it influenced as well the performance of the conservers. The mean scores of the conservers in both experiments on Pretest Form A and Posttests Form A, Form B, and Form C are presented in Table 2. The differences between these mean scores were significant between Pretest Form A and Posttest Form A, between Pretest Form A and Posttest Form B, but not between Pretest Form A and Posttest Form C (Experiment I: $t = 5.17$, $p < .001$; $t = 3.15$, $p < .01$; $t = 1.70$, $p > .05$, respectively; Experiment II: $t = 3.99$, $p < .001$; $t = 3.88$, $p < .001$; $t = 1.29$, $p > .05$, respectively).

In Experiment II, some of the first graders had attended kindergarten where it might be expected that the opportunities for social interaction and conflict would be greater than it would be for those children who had not attended kindergarten. This expectation was not supported by any significant difference in mean performance on Pretest Form A between those who had (6.06) and those who had not (5.81) attended kindergarten ($t = .18$, $p > .05$).

In both experiments there were no significant differences in the proportions of conservers and nonconservers on Pretest Form A between boys and girls (Experiment I, $\chi^2 = .53$, $p > .25$; Experiment II, $\chi^2 = .49$, $p > .25$). However there were the usual differences in these proportions between older and younger children in Experiment I, but not in Experiment II. In Experiment I, there were significantly fewer conservers and more nonconservers in the group below 6.66 years (median age) than in the group above it ($\chi^2 = 6.06$, $p < .02$);

in Experiment II, there were insignificant differences in these proportions between the group above and below the sample's median age of 6.50 years ($\chi^2 = .94$, $p > .25$).

Although the principal findings of Experiment I were replicated in Experiment II, there were significant differences in the proportions of conservers and nonconservers in Experiment I and conservers and nonconservers in Experiment II on Pretest A ($\chi^2 = 4.18$, $p < .05$). The mean score for subjects in Experiment I was 8.16 and the mean score for subjects in Experiment II was 5.85 on Pretest Form A, and the difference in these means was significant ($t = 2.67$, $p < .02$).

Discussion

The issue of whether or not conservation development can be accelerated is complicated in the research literature by theoretical doubts of its possibility, conflicting empirical results, and ambiguity in the criterion of conservation. Theoretically, conservation is taken to be one of many symptoms of concrete operational thought, and in a sense the manipulation of responses which indicate conservation is as trivial as any exercise that manipulates the symptom and not the disease. Although the acceleration of conservation responses without an attending presence of other aspects of operational thought may be an empty accomplishment in developmental theory, it is not one in education. The conservation response, regardless of its theoretical status, is an important behavior in itself for educational psychology. Procedures, like the present social conflict procedure, that induce or facilitate conservation behavior, and also have classroom applications constitute an important part of the psychology of curriculum and instruction.

The data indicate that social conflict or interaction is an important mediator of cognitive growth. Virtually all the children made significant gains in conservation performance after the social conflict situation. Since there were no significant differences in conservation performance between the children in the standardized sample and the children in both experiments on Pretest A, the standardized sample can serve as a control group. Performance on Posttests A, B, C

47

was significantly higher than that of the standardized children on these tests, and indicates that the training effect cannot be attributed to retesting or maturation effects, although the effect may have been due to modeling and not the communication interaction (Waghorn & Sullivan, 1970), or to the efficacy of Lancastrian or peer instruction (Rothenberg & Orost, 1969). In general, conservation training studies have been most successful with nonconservers who were close to the threshold of conservation. However, there were no significant differences in the gains in conservation between those nonconservers who exhibited no conservation on the pretest and those who exhibited some conservation on the pretest. In fact, of 15 children from Experiments I and II who scored 0 on the pretest, 8 had scores of 11 or 12 on the posttests. It should be noted that these gains include the more demanding conservation criterion of an appropriate explanation for the conservation judgment. It should also be noted that there was considerable transfer to different forms of the same concepts and to different concepts.

Brison (1966) was able to induce some form of conservation in one-half of a group of nonconservers with a combination social training procedure and conflict-reversibility instruction. Since there was no deliberate instruction in the present experiments, the data emphasize the effectiveness of social interaction even in the absence of any systematic instructional effort. It was the case that the children often resorted to reversibility explanations to persuade their lagging colleagues, and that in the social situations nonconservers acquiesced and generally gave conservation responses after the third problem ($M = 2.76$) on Form A and generally (80%) did not give a nonconserving response after they had once given a conserving one.

It is not clear what the nonconservers learned in the social situation that sustained them in the individual situation. It probably was not a set to say, "the same," since all forms contained items in which the stimuli were unequal before the conservation transformation. The reversibility explanation for the conservation judgment, although strictly speaking incorrect (Murray & Johnson,

1969), and the invariant quantity explanation ("Your did not add or substract anything"; "they were the same before, and you didn't change the weight, etc.") could be used as rules that would lead to the correct response on all forms if the child had grasped the initial relationship (equal or unequal) between the stimuli before they were transformed. If these rules or algorithms were acquired, and the children's reasons indicate that in some sense they were, they would account for the very high level of performance on the transfer tasks, Forms B and C.

Smedslund (1966) in a review of the research on the many conditions that have been found to be inconsistently related to the acquisition of operational thought concluded that "the occurrence of communication conflicts is a necessary condition for intellectual decentration" and recommended that the key interaction needed for the growth of intelligence was not so much between the individual and the physical environment as it was between the individual and those about him. The present data support his hypothesis and emphasize, as Piaget has (Sigel, 1969), the educational role of social interaction in the transition from egocentrism to operational thought.

REFERENCES

BRISON, D. W. Acceleration of conservation of substance. *Journal of Genetic Psychology,* 1966, **109,** 311-322.

FLAVELL, J. Role-taking and communication skills in children. In W. Hartup & N. Smothergill (Eds.), *The young child.* Washington, D. C.: National Association for the Education of Young Children, 1967.

GOLDSCHMID, M., & BENTLER, P. *Concept assessment kit-conservation manual.* San Diego: Educational and Industrial Testing Service, 1968.

MURRAY, F. B., & JOHNSON, P. E. Reversibility in the nonconservation of weight. *Psychonomic Science,* 1969, **16,** 2£5-287.

NEALE, J. M. Egocentrism in institutionalized and non-institutionalized children. *Child Development,* 1966, **37,** 97-101.

ROTHENBERG, B. B., & OROST, J. H. The training of conservation of number in young children. *Child Development,* 1969, **40,** 707-726.

SIGEL, I. E. The Piagetian system and the world of education. In D. Elkind & J. H. Flavell (Eds.), *Studies in cognitive development. Essays in honor of Jean Piaget.* New York: Oxford University Press, 1969.

SMEDSLUND, J. Les origines sociales de la centra-
tion. In F. Bresson & M. de Montmalin (Eds.),
Psychologie et épistémologie génétiques. Paris:
Dunod, 1966.

WAGHORN, L., & SULLIVAN, E. The exploration of
transition rules in conservation of quantity
(substance) using film mediated modeling.
Acta Psychologica, 1970, **32,** 65–80.

THE VALIDITY OF SOCIAL SCIENCE SIMULATIONS:
A REVIEW OF RESEARCH FINDINGS

William Ray Heitzmann

The last decade has seen numerous confident claims as [1]
to the learning values of educational simulations and games.
These endorsements from salesmen, game designers, teachers,
and professors are unfortunately backed with pitifully little research with which to substantiate such comments.
Walter Cronkite in the CBS television program "The Remarkable Schoolhouse" summed up the state of the art with the
following comment, "By participating, by playing a game, an
otherwise dull subject becomes fascinating and unforgettable
to the students. No more could be asked of any educational
technique." (23)
        Fortunately some have asked more and have had the time
and the courage to test the validity of simulations empirically. A quote from Professors Schran and Kumph, who recently completed a tour of the United States, in which they
observed simulations in action and visited simulation design
and research centers, seems appropriate here. They state:

> Validation studies on environmental games in addition
> to the two already mentioned could not be identified.
> The authors generally found neglect and disinterest in
> validation characterized best in this statement by a
> distinguished gaming practioner: *"I really see that
> considerable efforts are needed in the validation of
> existing games and projects... But I also see that the
> one who undertakes this task will be stoned by the
> others... And I am really not interested in being that
> man."* (26)

        Professor Richard Gross, Stanford University and
former president of the National Council of Social Studies,
remarked in a recent article in *Social Education*, "Are you
interested in simulation? A Gaming bandwagon moves across
the land, yet on this topic we have found practically nothing to report in the realm of doctoral research." (11)
        The most frequent and strongest claim made for simu-
lation is their motivational value. Experimentation does
support this claim with many studies showing high school
interest in games of all kinds. Roger Kaperson (1968),
Charles and Dorothy Christine (1967), Bernard Cohen (1962),
Sarane Boocock and James Coleman (1966) among many others

ORIGINAL MANUSCRIPT, 1973.

have indicated in their research that students enjoy the
gaming and were highly motivated during the game. (13, 4,
5, 2) Some game designers have theorized that some students will not enjoy this type of classroom teaching methodology as children who succeed well in conventional settings will not enjoy the new situation where they might
not excel. While no data is available on this, it is interesting to note that Michael Inbar (1966) has found that
after having thousands of students play the *Disaster Game*
that about twenty percent of the players enjoy the session
very little or not at all. He states that this may be
rectified by "relying less on the 'magic' effect of games
and more on the proper presentation and handling of the
session" (12) Of further interest is the finding of Samuel
Livingstone (1970a) that there was no change in student
motivation to learn subject matter related to the simulation. (18)
      Several research investigations have been conducted
dealing with changes in attitude as a result of simulations.
Samuel Livingstone (1970b) found significant changes in
attitude toward the poor following the playing of *Ghetto*.
That is, the students' attitudes were more favorable toward
the poor following the game. (16) Paul DeKock (1969) found
attitudes changed by the simulation *Sunshine*, which deals
with racial problems. Students, as a result of playing the
games, felt more positive toward black Americans. (7) Additional research on attitude change by Livingstone (1971a)
and Livingstone (1971b), and Livingstone and Kidder (1972)
found similar results concluding beliefs can be changed by
simulation. (14, 17, 20) Professors Garvey and Seiler (1966)
produced findings that challenge the previous studies.
Studying the effects of the *Inter-Nation Simulation* in two
Kansas high schools, they found no significant difference
in attitude between the control group and the experimental
group as a result of playing the game. (10) Livingstone
(1971c) has called into question much of the simulation
attitude-change studies (including his own) in a study in
which he post-tested attitudes four months after students
played *Ghetto* and found no change in beliefs. In previous
studies, he and others post-tested immediately after the
game. (17) From the initial research it seems that there
is little stability of attitudinal change.
      There has been enthusiasm in some quarters over the
possibility that simulations may have a payoff in terms of
increased factual learning. Professor Sarane Boocock (1966a
and 1966b) in a major study involving hundreds of students
and several games, found that students made substantial
gains of cognitive knowledge because of being involved in
a simulation game. (2, 3) This finding was echoed by Eugene
Baker (1966) who concluded after involving eigth grade students in an american history simulation that it was an efficient method for communicating historical.facts and concepts. (19) Livingstone's studies are contradictory on this
topic. In one study (1971a) involving a business simula-

tion, he found that the simulation group out-performed the control group in the area of facts and concepts. (19) However, in another study (1970), using the game *Trade and Develop*, there were no significant differences between groups. (18, 15) Robinson, et. al. in 1966 did an extensive study in which a simulation -- *Inter-Nation Simulation* -- was compared to the case study method in several classrooms at several universities. Robinson found that "no direct and unmediated relations occurred between simulation and fact-mastery or principles learning." On a positive note, he did find that of those who preferred playing simulations showed greater learning than those who preferred case studies but were assigned to *Inter-Nation Simulation*. (24) The most extensive study to date (G. Fennessey, et. al., 1972) has been disappointing to proponents of simulations. Gail Fennessey, in a study entitled *Simulation, Gaming, and Conventional Instruction: An Experimental Comparison* involving 47 schools, 87 teachers, and 4539 students, examined the value of effectiveness of simulations for teaching facts and relationships. The experiment found the control and simulation to be equally effective. (9)

Many advocates of gaming have said that although initial learning may be equal for simulations vis-a-vis other modes of instruction that because of the intensive involvement of the learner in the simulation, retention will be greater. Donna Joan Myer (1967), in a Master's thesis entitled *Long-Term Effects of Simulation* studied the above phenomena. She concluded, "... in this experiment, retention was not improved by use of the simulation method of instruction." (22) This disappointing finding is somewhat mitigated by the work of T. Anotinette Ryan (1968), Oregon State University, whose research study showed that students who had the opportunity to practice simulated problem-solving tasks were able to increase transfer to learning outcomes. (25) This finding is underscored by Professor James L. McKenney's (1962) results following a business game, which are summarized, "The results of the experiment indicate that games do serve a useful purpose when used as a pedagogical device for gaining insight into the process of planning." (21)

At this point it becomes painfully obvious that the research of simulation and gaming abounds in confusion and contradiction. While it is true that this style of instruction is not the panacea that some early advocates had suggested, it would be equally as foolish to disregard the positive claims substantiated by research. An extreme bright note is sounded by Dale Faran (1968) in finding excellent results when working with underachievers using simulations. (8) A similar note is echoed by Karen Cohen (1970), who found that playing the *Consumer Game* with disadvantaged students decreased absences seventeen percent. (6)

Many researchers have concluded their studies with strong advice that the field be subjected to further inquiry. In spite of this, there is a noticeable lack of studies and conclusive results on the role of simulation in learning. Several reasons exist for this phenomena. Educational games are being developed and revised at such a rapid pace, it is difficult to know what is available.[2] This factor, coupled with the diversity or lack of standardization of games, has hindered replication of research findings. As is easily observable, most of the research is scattered, preventing a significant chain of inquiry. In addition to this, the quality of the research varies. For example, some studies have attempted to extrapolate their results from an experimental finding based upon very small and poorly selected research groups. Also the problem of innovation effect seems to be present in some of the studies. In addition, research studies have not been discriminately collected and examined. Results of simulation studies appear in various journals and reports, and it is difficult to keep up with the literature. It is hoped that this paper will be a contribution in this area, that is, summarizing the research findings and the concurrent problems.

It is hoped that teachers and researchers will not be dissuaded from using and experimenting with simulations and games. Anyone who has observed or coordinated a simulation could not help but feel the electricity and excitement of involvement learning. It remains a fertile field with almost infinite research possibilities. Some areas, for example the instructional value of the post-game de-briefing, or the use of a game as a data gathering device, are just beginning to be examined.

Reflective use of simulations analyzing -- in what areas, with what types of students, with what number of students, with what time and financial constraints, and with what objectives -- simulations and games can make a significant and lasting contribution to the American education. I suspect that when the verdict is in, educational simulations will have value in many instructional areas and situations.

FOOTNOTES

1. Those interested in a philosophical argument over the value of simulations should consult James Coleman, "Learning Through Games" and Ivor Kraft, "Pedagogical Futility in Fun and Games", *NEA Journal*, January, 1967.

2. Zuckerman and Horn's recent book, *The Guide to Simulation and Games*, 1973, contains information on over 600 simulations and games.

REFERENCES

1. Baker, Eugene, "A Pre-Civil War Simulation for Teach-
    ing American History": in Sarane Boocock and E.O.
    Schild, *Simulation Games in Learning*, Sage Publica-
    tions, Inc., Beverly Hills, California, 1968.

2. Boocock, Sarane S. and James S. Coleman, "Games and
    Simulated Environments in Learning", *Sociology of Edu-
    cation*, Summer, 1966, pp. 215-236.

3. "An Experimental Study of the Learning Effects of Two
    Games With Simulated Environments". *American Behavioral
    Scientist*, October, 1966, pp. 8-17.

4. Christine, Charles and Dorothy, "Simulation, a Teach-
    ing Tool", *The Elementary School Journal*, May, 1967,
    pp. 396-398.

5. Cohen, Bernard C., "Political Gaming in the Class-
    room", *The Journal of Politics*, 1962, pp. 367-381.

6. Cohen, Karen, *Effects of the Consumer Game on Learning
    and Attitudes of Selected Seventh Grade Students in a
    Target-Area School*, Center for the Social Organization
    of Schools Report #65, Johns Hopkins University, April,
    1970.

7. DeKock, Paul, "Simulations and Changes in Racial Atti-
    tudes", *Social Education*, February, 1969, pp. 181-183.

8. Farran, Dale C., "Competition and Learning for Under-
    achievers", in Boocock and Schild, 1968.

9. Fennessey, Gail and Samuel A. Livingstone, Keith Ed-
    wards, Steven Kidder, and Alice Nafziger, *Simulation
    Gaming, and Conventional Instruction: An Experimental
    Comparison*, Center for the Social Organization of
    Schools Report #128, April, 1972.

10. Garvey, Dale M. and William H. Seiler, *A Study of
    Effectiveness of Different Methods of Teaching*,
    Emporia State College (Kansas), 1966, Monograph.

11. Gross, Richard E. "A Decade of Doctoral Research in
    Social Studies Education", *Social Education*, May, 1972,
    pp. 555-560.

12. Inbar, Michael, "The Differential Impact of a Game
    Simmulating a Community Disaster", *American Be-
    havioral Scientist*, October, 1966, pp. 18-27.

13. Kasperson, Roger E., "Games as Educational Media",
    Journal of Geography, October, 1966, pp. 409-422.

14. Livingstone, Samuel, *Effects of a Legislative Simulation Game on the Political Attitudes of Junior High School Students*, Center for the Social Organization of Schools Report #114, Johns Hopkins University, September, 1971.

15. "Will a Simulation Game Improve Student Learning of Related Factual Material," *Educational Technology*, 1971.

16. Livingstone, Samuel A., *Simulation Games and Attitude Change: Attitudes Toward the Poor*, Center for the Social Organization of Schools Report #63, Johns Hopkins University, April, 1970.

17. *Simulation Games and Attitudes Toward the Poor: Three Questionnaire Studies*, Center for the Social Organization of Schools, Report #118, Johns Hopkins University, July, 1972.

18. Livingstone, Samuel A., *Simulation Games As Advance Organizers in the Learning of Social Science Materials: Experiments 1-3*, Center for the Social Organization of Schools Report #64, Johns Hopkins University, April, 1970.

19. Livingstone, Samuel A., *Two Types of Learning in a Business Simulation*, Center for the Social Organization of Schools Report #104, Johns Hopkins University, June, 1971.

20. Livingstone, Samuel A. and Steven Kidder, *Role Identification and Game Structure: Effects on Political Attitudes*, Center for the Social Organization of Schools Report #134, Johns Hopkins University, July, 1972.

21. McKenney, James L., "An Evaluation of a Business Game in an MBA Curriculum," *The Journal of Business*, 1962.

22. Myer, Donna Jean, *Long-Term Effects of Simulation*, California Western University, November, 1967 (unpublished Master's thesis).

23. Nesbitt, William A., *Simulation Games for the Social Studies Classroom*, New Dimension Series, Foreign Policy Association, New York, 1968.

24. Robinson, James A. and Lee F. Anerson, Margaret G. Hermann, and Richard C. Snyder, "Teaching With Internation Simulation ànd Case Studies," *The American Political Science Review*, March, 1966, pp. 53-65.

25. Ryan, T. Anoinette, "Use of Simulation To Increase Transfer," *The School Review*, June, 1968, pp. 246-252.

26. Schran, Henning and Dieter Kumpf, "Environmental Games in the United States: A Review of A Decade of Confusion," *Simulation and Games*, December, 1972, pp. 464-476.

Game (gaming)

"A technical term denoting a simulation in which the results for one group depend on the actions of their competitors."

E. W. Martin (1959)

"A game is a contest or play activity among opposing players; there is usually the objective of winning and the element of competition."

June R. Chapin (1968)

"Contest (play) among adversaries (players) operating under constraint (rules) for an objective (winning, victory, or payoff)."

Clark C. Abt (1965)

"A game is essentially a simplified slice of reality. Its structure reflects a real-world process that the designer wishes to teach or investigate; the game serves as a vehicle fortesting that process or for learning more about its working..."

Alice K. Gordon (1970)

Simulation

"Essentially, simulation is a means of allowing the student to live vicariously. Furthermore, the simulation has the desirable quality of enabling the teacher to manipulate various courses of action and their consequences without the students suffering physically for wrong choices."

Samuel Brodbelt (1969)

"A simulation is a replica of a real world system worth learning. An educational simulation permits persons to become a working member of the system, to set goals, to develop policies, analyze information."

Ron Klietsch (1970)

"Political games and simulations are models or representations of particular political systems and their associated processes."

C. and M. Hermann (1967)

"Simulation is a model of a situation (social, mathematical, or physical) with reality simplified; it permits the operation upon a specifically devised problem in a time-sequence method."

June R. Chapin (1968)

The Language and Values of Programmed Instruction

Donald G. Arnstine

I

IN THE PAST FEW YEARS, the sponsors of teaching machines and programmed instruction have assaulted with increasing vigor the tradition-bound and barnacled bastions of American schools. A great many educators, with cries of "mechanization" and "long live the unprogrammable child," have stood firm at the gates, but the onslaught has not slackened; the issue is still in doubt. It is the aim of this essay to penetrate the camp of the programmers, count their troops, and assess their strength. As yet, the combatants themselves have not done this: the programmers, because their strategy precludes it, and their opponents, because good reasons are not easily found in the heat of combat.

The claims of the champions of programmed instruction are often magnificent and awe-inspiring. Across their banners might be inscribed the words of one of their doughtiest generals: "Once we have specified the behavior [involved in the act of thinking itself] . . . we have no reason to suppose that it will then be any less adaptable to programmed instruction than simple verbal repertoires."[1]

[1] B. F. Skinner, "Why We Need Teaching Machines," *Harvard Educational Review*, 31:4, p. 397

Optimism for the future of programmed instruction is shared by those who develop the programs; thus Harry F. Silberman, of Systems Development Corporation, writes, ". . . any domain of instruction, including creativity, is fair game for programming."[2] Another enthusiast claims that the program duplicates the work of that "superb teaching mechanism," and human tutor: "Those of us who share the enthusiasm for computer-based teaching machines do so because a computer allows us . . . to approach full simulation of the human tutorial process."[3]

Thus it is clear that confidence is not lacking in the camp of the programmers: "It seems perfectly reasonable," writes Lloyd E. Homme, "to say that the machine teaching enterprise cannot fail."[4] Homme then goes on to elaborate his own vision of the schools of tomorrow:

[2] Silberman, "What Are the Limits of Programmed Instruction?" *Phi Delta Kappan*, XLIV:6, p. 296. The answer to the question in Silberman's title: none.

[3] William R. Uttal, "On Conversational Interaction," in John E. Coulson (ed.), *Programmed Learning and Computer-Based Instruction* (New York: John Wiley, 1962), p. 172.

[4] Homm, "The Rationale of Teaching by Skinner's Machines," in A. A. Lumsdaine and Robert Glaser (eds.), *Teaching Machines and Programmed Learning: A Source Book* (Washington, D.C.: Department of Audiovisual Instruction of the NEA, 1960), p. 136.

THE EDUCATIONAL FORUM, Jan. 1964, vol. 28, pp. 219-226.

"In fact, I will go so far as to predict that classrooms of the future, their walls lined with exotic machines, will resemble nothing so much as the emporiums of Las Vegas. I am even willing to bet that the players will be equally intense in their pursuit of reinforcements."[5]

Unchecked, such enthusiasm is a powerful force. This is important because it is not the programmers themselves, but rather school administrators and boards of education who will ultimately make the decisions about whether to use programmed instruction in the schools and, if so, in what kinds of situations to use it. Since decisions of this sort ought not to be made on the basis of persuasive rhetoric or the results of often carelessly designed research studies, it is the aim of the present essay to assist those who would carefully evaluate the contribution of programmed instruction to the enterprise of education in schools.

Empirical research directed at the efficacy of instructional programs provides little guidance for such careful evaluation. Not only is the design of such research often ill-conceived,[6] but the results of that research when applied to areas within general education are often contradictory when they are not trivial.[7] The discussion that follows, then, will attempt to avoid some of the pitfalls into which empirical investigators have often tripped by examining some of the assumptions that these investigators take for granted *before* conducting their research. Since such an examination is not always a matter of empirical investigation, the focus of the discussion that follows will be on the language and on the implied values on which the theoretical support of programming and the arguments for utilizing programming in schools are predicated.

The phrase "programmed instruction" will be used to refer to any instruction presented by means of a program, and a program "is designed to present material to the learner and to control the student's behavior during his learning by exposing stimulus material, requiring some overt or covert response to this material and providing some form of knowledge of results for each response. It is a program in the sense that it is a list of items, steps, or frames, each of which performs these functions."[8] A "teaching machine" is any device, mechanical or electronic, designed to present the program and facilitate the learner's response to it.

In the subsequent discussion, remarks will be directed to the program, not the

[5] *Ibid.* Other equally sanguine prognostications will be found in Simon Ramo, "A New Technique of Education," *Engineering and Science Monthly*, 21, pp. 17-22, and in James D. Finn, "Automation and Instruction: III, Technology and the Instructional Process," *A V Communication Review*, 8:1, pp. 5-26.

[6] James G. Holland states, "Aside from the over-generalization inevitable from . . . ill-defined variables [selected in research studies], even these relatively uninteresting problems are inadequately treated. Despite the overwhelming recognition of the importance of quality in the program, we are seldom given information for evaluating the program." (New Directions in Teaching Machine Research," in Coulson, *op. cit.*, p. 47.)

[7] See, for example, Lawrence M. Stolurow, *Teaching by Machine* (Washington, D.C.: U.S. Government Printing Office, 1961), Chapter VII.

[8] Joseph W. Rigney and Edward B. Fry, "Programming Techniques," A V *Communication Review*, 9:5, p. 7.

machine, since the machine is only a means for presenting the program to the student. Besides, research has found the program to be equally effective with or without the machine.[9] In order, then, to meet the defense that today's machines are certain to undergo subsequent refinement and improvement, we shall focus on the *program* and assume the possible existence of a computer-based machine of any desired complexity that will present the program to students. Thus the following remarks are not to be considered as limited by present inadequacies of teaching machines.

The analysis of programmed instruction must proceed on two fronts: 1) is the theory of teaching exemplified by programming tenable? and 2) what will be the results of various uses of programming in schools, and are these results desirable?

To judge the desirability of programming for school use, both questions must be considered independently. An affirmative answer to the first question (the theory of teaching *is* tenable) does not preclude rejecting the use of programming in schools on the basis of a negative answer to the second question (the results of using programs in schools are *not* desirable). Conversely, a negative answer to the first question (the theory of teaching is *not* tenable) does not pre-

clude recommending the use of programs in schools on the basis of an affirmative answer to the second question (the results of using programs in schools are desirable on the basis of the empirically *observed results* of their use). These observations serve to indicate that, in the fields of human learning and instruction, there is not yet a necessary connection between theory and practice. Hence an evaluation of one has no necessary implications for the other.

It may be helpful to anticipate, at the outset, some of the conclusions that will be discussed in detail in this essay. In what follows it will be claimed that 1) the so-called principles of programming, allegedly based on reinforcement theory, either suffer from the same defects that have been found in that theory, or bear no relation to the theory at all, and 2) the use of programs in schools, in all but a very few limited applications, leads to results that are incompatible with what has immemorially been called, by both scholars and laymen, education. It is now time to turn to the evidence on which these opinions are based.

II

It is usually claimed that the principles of programming are based on reinforcement theory. Although this theory of behavior and learning will not be called into question here,[10] it stands to

[9] See, for example, Stolurow, "Let's be Informed on Programmed Instruction," *Phi Delta Kappan*, XLIV:6: ". . . there is no objective evidence from research to support the need for a machine to assist student learning. . . . The primary factor that makes instruction effective is the program. . . . Existing programmed materials alone when used in book form will teach as well as when used in a machine." (pp. 255 f)

[10] Standard criticisms of reinforcement theory, succinctly put, may be readily found in Harry Harlow, "Mice, Monkeys, Men, and Motives," *Psychological Review*, 60, pp. 23-32 and Donald Snygg, "The Tortuous Path of Learning Theory," *Audio Visual Instruction*, 7:1, pp. 8-12. A criticism of B. F. Skinner's operant conditioning

reason that at best these principles can be no more valid than the theory on which they are based. We shall find, however, that the relation between the principles of programming and reinforcement theory is not nearly so clear as programmers claim. Although there are many lists of "principles" of programming, we will simply select the four that are presented and explained in a demonstration course published by one of the nation's most active programming firms, TMI-Grolier.[11] The four principles, to be discussed below in order, are those of 1) small steps, 2) active responding, 3) immediate confirmation, and 4) self-pacing.

1. The Principle of Small Steps. The substance of this principle is that the material to be taught, once carefully delimited, must be broken down into very minute teaching units (or "frames" in the program), each closely related to the succeeding one, until all the material has been presented. This, presumably, makes it easy (and relatively errorless) for the student to acquire the entire body of material.[12] This principle is surely reminis-

cent of Descartes,[13] but it bears no relation at all to reinforcement theory—although the claim is usually made that it follows from the notion of "shaping" behavior by a process of successive approximations (i.e. small steps).[14]

Whatever reasons may be adduced for granulating the material to be learned into small steps, they have nothing to do with successive approximations. When a dog's behavior is being shaped such that it will eventually touch a doorknob with its nose, only the movements that more closely approximate doorknob-touching are reinforced. Each previous movement in the wrong direction is extinguished (i.e. not repeated) because it is not reinforced. If this chain of successive approximations were to be a model for an instructional program, we should be embarrassed to find ourselves insisting that the student's responses to each item or frame be extinguished as he proceeds to the next item. Hence the student would learn only the *last* frame in the program.

But this bizarre eventuality need not concern us, for successive approximations cannot possibly be a model for the verbal learning fostered by an instructional program. When the dog was trained to touch the doorknob with his nose, only the *last* successful series of responses was the "correct" (i.e. desired by the experimenter) one; had the other responses

version of reinforcement theory, at once remarkably concise and comprehensive, may be found in Noam Chomsky's review of Skinner's *Verbal Behavior*, in *Language*, 35:1, pp. 26-58.
[11] *The Principles of Programmed Learning* (Albuquerque, N.M.: Teaching Machines Incorporated, 1961). This programmed course on programming actually presents five "principles," but the fifth one, the "principle of student testing," is not a principle of teaching or learning at all, but a technique for revising an instructional program. The other four principles discussed below are mentioned by all workers in the field.
[12] Part of the difficulty in putting this principle into practice stems from the fact that it is not altogether clear just what a "step" refers to—whether it be item length, difficulty, sequence, or what. For further discussion on this point, see A. A. Lumsdaine, "Some Issues Concerning

Devices and Programs for Automated Learning," in Lumsdaine and Glaser, *op. cit.*, pp. 517-539.
[13] Especially Rules V and VI in the "Rules for the Direction of the Mind," in E. S. Haldane and G. R. T. Ross (trans.), *The Philosophical Works of Descartes*, I: (New York: Dover, 1955).
[14] See, for example, B. F. Skinner, "Teaching Machines," *Science*, 128, pp. 969-977.

not been extinguished, the dog would still be wandering around the room days later. Training the dog, then, involved the animal's eventual selection of one complex behavior sequence out of an infinitely varied continuous series of movements. But when a human learner responds to an instructional program, nearly *every* response is "correct" (i.e. desired by the programmer); hence nearly every response is reinforced, and hardly any responses are extinguished. If hardly any responses are extinguished, then there is no shaping of behavior; nothing at all is being successively approximated[15] because every bit of behavior is precisely correct.

The reason for the incompatibility of the training program for Rover and the instructional program for the human student is not far to seek: success for the dog means selection from a continuous series of responses; there is no way to achieve success *but* to shape the dog's series of acts. But for the student, success means selection from a *dis*continuous series of (verbal) responses; there is a finite number of discrete responses available from which he must choose. Thus literally to shape his behavior would be absurd.

We will close this discussion with an example of genuine shaping of a student's verbal behavior. Suppose we want the student to complete the following statement: "All gases are composed of rapidly moving ————." We want the student to say "molecules." The student says, "air." We say nothing. He says "breezes." We say nothing. He says, "movements." We say, "that's good." He says, "emoluments"; we say, "that's good." He says, "moluments," and we say, "you're doing fine." He says, "monuments." We say nothing. He says, "molly's carts"; we say, "now you're getting on the right track." He says, "molly's cubes"; we say, "you're getting warm." He says, "molecules"; we say, "that's right." The student's behavior has been shaped. Q.E.D.

2. The Principle of Active Responding. According to this principle, the student learns best when he is active. When he is passive, he presumably doesn't learn as efficiently. What is needed to test this principle is some specification of how much activity is desirable, and what kind of activity.

For some time, programmers thought that an overt response to an item, such as the filling-in of a blank, or the pressing of a key (indicating selection of a multiple-choice alternative) was "active" and thereby important for learning. However, recent studies indicate that programs allowing only a covert response, or providing no opportunity for a response at all, are just as effective.[16]

The reason for these negative findings

[15] If it is claimed that the student is really successively approximating the "content of the course," it must then be asked, what *is* the content of the course? If the answer is: all the frames in the program, then again, nothing is being successively approximated in the Skinnerian sense; rather, the learner is simply gradually assimilating the program. But if the content of the course is called something *other than* all the frames in the program, then it must be asked, why didn't the frames directly present this other something for the student to acquire?

[16] See John F. Feldhusen, "Taps for Teaching Machines," *Phi Delta Kappan*, XLIV:6, pp. 265-267.

is not far to seek: no one had bothered to define "active." In this respect, the dismal history of "learning by doing" has been repeated. When "learning by doing" was grossly interpreted to mean that children learned *only* when participating in committee work or in construction projects, the absurdity of the notion was clearly seen.[17] By the same token, if "active responses" *means* filling in a blank or pressing a key, this notion, with its arbitrary and restrictive limitation, is equally absurd.

An active response is said to make learning more efficient, but there is no doubt that some people learn efficiently from lectures, broadcasts, books, films, and the like. Have such people been active? Suppose, when they were attending a lecture or reading a book, that they were observed to have been sitting quitely—not even taking notes. They may have been no more "active" than others sitting next to them who did *not* (according to subsequent tests) learn efficiently from the lecture or book. If no *observable* activity was apparent in either the efficient or the inefficient learners, but "activity" is still held to account for better learning, shall we then claim that those who learned efficiently were engaged in some rigorous "mental" activity? If this claim is *allowed*, then the possibility of mental activity would surely weaken the arguments in favor of filling in blanks or punching keys. But if the claim of "mental activity" is *rejected*

as an explanation of observably inactive but efficient learning, then such learning, as it often occurs in response to lectures, films, and books, must remain an anomaly in the light of the principle of active responding.

There is little doubt that learning may occur in some cases when no physical activity is observable, and at other times it may occur under conditions of strenuous and highly articulated physical activity. That the learning of all (or even any particular) verbal materials occurs most efficiently only when the learner completes an unfinished sentence or presses an appropriate key has not been demonstrated. The principle of active responding is no more than a suggestion, and in view of the differences among students, learning materials, and educational objectives, a rather vague one at that.

3. The Principle of Immediate Confirmation. This principle holds that the student learns best when immediately presented with knowledge of the results of his response to an item or frame. If the student makes an error, knowledge of results is not reinforcing and his response, it is said, is extinguished. But if the response is correct, the knowledge of results confirms his judgment and is thus reinforcing. Hence he is likely to repeat that behavior when later presented with the same stimulus situation. (This principle also implies that a program must be written in such a way as to minimize the number of student errors; if this is not done, the student will seldom be reinforced and consequently will learn little.)

The problem with this principle is

---

[17] For an analysis of a closely related conceptual tangle, see John Hanson, "Learning by Experience," in B. O. Smith and Robert H. Ennis (eds.), *Language and Concepts in Education* (Chicago: Rand McNally, 1961), pp. 1-23.

that we have no way of justifying the claim that immediate confirmation is reinforcing to all students in any given school learning situation. Even in carefully designed experiments in which pigeons peck at keys, reinforcement theory does not allow us to *label* food pellets as reinforcers until *after* the sequence of events that includes repeated behavior and eating of the food. Only empirical observation, then, can tell us whether immediate confirmation is really a "principle" of learning, or just a supposition. And researchers have found that when they themselves correctly filled in the blanks in a program and merely asked the students to read the frames, the students learned no less than a comparable group that filled in the blanks themselves and thus received immediate confirmation of their responses.[18] It has also been observed that regularly repeated immediate confirmations became boring for students (the preposterous term used is "pall effect"), and thus remained reinforcers no longer.[19]

Finally, the principle of immediate confirmation begs the question of motivation. It seems hardly deniable that immediate confirmation will have very different effects on students who are interested in the material to be learned and on students who are not. And that people obviously learn from their mistakes is also contrary to the principle of immediate confirmation; this is the basis for the branching-type programs sponsored by Norman Crowder.[20]

We may conclude by saying that some people, when told to learn some sorts of materials, sometimes learn more efficiently when presented with immediate confirmation of their efforts. But this is all the reliable guidance we can get from the principle of immediate confirmation.

4. The Principle of Self-Pacing. It is claimed in this principle that the student spends as much time with the program as he needs to respond to all the items correctly. This much is clear, just as a student spends as much time with an ordinary textbook as he feels he needs to understand it. That everyone learns at his own rate is an analytic statement (that is, true by definition), or else it would make sense to say, "everyone learns at somebody else's rate," or "he learned faster than he could learn." And to say, "he could have learned more quickly" does not mean that the student didn't learn at his own rate. Rather, it means, "he learned (whatever it was he was supposed to learn) *at his own rate* and was then made to do some other things (e.g. work additional problems, wait for others to catch up, etc.) in a period of time in which it is possible that he could have learned something else about the given subject." Of course, the student *did* learn about *something* else: how it feels to be bored, how to sit still when impatient, how to surreptitiously write notes to classmates, etc.

Self-pacing, then, is not at issue in this principle, because learning is always self-paced. The most elaborate teaching device or the best teacher conceivable can only present a student with a situation

[18] Feldhusen, *op. cit.*
[19] *Ibid.*
[20] See Crowder, "Automatic Tutoring by Intrinsic Programming," in Lumsdaine and Glaser (*op. cit.*), pp. 286-298.

that *might* result in his learning;[21] they cannot insure that he will learn what they want him to learn, and it is literally nonsense to claim that they can get him to learn it any faster than he is able to.

Considered in itself, then, the principle of self-pacing is either obvious or implies an absurdity: that in some situations students do not learn at their own rate. The import of this principle, then, must be found elsewhere—namely, in the claim that time is allowed for the student to respond correctly to all the items in the program. This claim, which is quite different from the claim that the student learns at his own rate, is undeniably just, However, it is of value to educators only if "responding correctly to all the items" is what we mean by education, learning, or learning a particular subject.

That students must have immediate confirmation of their own written or key-pressed responses to a sequence of gradually changing items in order to learn *efficiently* has been questioned in the foregoing discussion. It is now time to ask whether the elicitation of such behavior from students has anything at all to do with learning and education as those terms have ordinarily been used in connection with what goes on in schools.

[21] The distinction between "intentional" and "success" uses of the verb "to teach" is relevant to this point. See Israel Scheffler, *The Language of Education* (Springfield, Ill.: Charles C Thomas, 1960), pp. 41f.

Some changing concepts about

LEARNING

AND

MEMORY

JAMES L. McGAUGH

THOSE who study man generally agree that it is our mental capacity that sets us apart from the other animals. Countless centuries ago, we domesticated plants and animals and began other technological achievements which surpass those of all other species. We also developed elaborate forms of communication, including language, which enabled us to transmit acquired knowledge to our offspring. All of these achievements are based, of course, upon our ability to learn: to record experiences and to utilize records of the past in dealing with the present. In adapting to our environment, we have relied upon learning ability to a greater extent than have any other animals. Learning ability is central to the biological and social evolution of man.

NEA JOURNAL, April 1968, vol. 57, pp. 8-9 ff.

In most areas of human enterprise, technological achievements long preceded scientific understanding. Animal husbandry, agriculture, and even medicine antedated recorded history. In each of these areas, however, scientific discoveries of recent decades, in disciplines such as genetics, microbiology, and biochemistry, have so profoundly influenced technological developments and practices that the techniques of the farmer and the physician today bear little resemblance to those used even a few years ago. In areas essential for our survival, we have come to expect our technology to be continuously modified by scientific knowledge.

Although education is clearly essential for survival, the practices of education have been less significantly influenced by basic research findings than have those of agriculture and medicine. Understanding of the nature and biological bases of learning and memory has not, as yet, significantly affected the educational technology. Most of the significant innovations have been concerned either with the *content* of education or with procedures for automating traditional teaching methods; few innovations and varied practices have grown out of basic research concerning the nature of learning and memory.

There are several possible reasons for this state of affairs. First, we simply may not yet know enough about the processes of learning and memory. Second, inadequate traditional views of the nature of learning and memory may have been misleading. Third, we may not have made sufficient effort to examine the implications of recent findings for educational practices. Whatever the reasons for the present situation, it seems clear that if we are to develop effective educational systems, teachers, like farmers and physicians, will need to develop and use more practices which are based on scientific understanding. Society cannot afford the luxury of ignoring this important problem.

The problem is complicated by the fact that at one time educators made a valiant attempt to understand and use· principles of learning theory, but the theory they worked with was neither very good nor very helpful. From the time of Thorndike to the present, the dominant theories have emphasized the learning of stimulus-response connections and have stressed the value of rewards.

It has been difficult to reconcile these emphases with the obvious fact that much, if not most, learning consists of acquiring information or knowledge as a consequence of some sensory impact (watching, listening, reading). Learning may occur *prior to* responding and *prior to* rewards. While overt responding undoubtedly influences learning, it does not do so simply by strengthening stimulus-response connections. Responding provides a repetition or rehearsal of acquired information and, in addition, provides an opportunity for correcting errors if what was remembered was incorrect. But the response cannot occur unless some learning has already occurred.

Understanding of the nature and bases of learning and memory has increased steadily if not dramatically over the past several decades. Unfortunately, we have not yet reached the stage where such information is as relevant for the teacher as the findings of genetics, biochemistry, and microbiology are for the farmer and physician. Nonetheless, the theories and implications emerging from recent findings should not be ignored In this brief essay, I will discuss a few of them, emphasizing three points—the increasing tendency to view learning and memory from a biological perspective, the considerable emphasis being placed on learning and memory as complex processes involved in the storage and utilization of information, and a cautious but increasing interest in considering the educational implications of these emerging facts and theories.

Learning and memory from a biological perspective. Theories of learning have, to a considerable extent, ignored biological factors. The psychologist, John B. Watson, once proposed to take any one of a dozen well-formed, healthy infants and train them to become ". . . any type of specialist . . . doctor, lawyer, artist, merchant, chief . . . even beggar man and thief, regardless of his talents, penchants, tendencies, abilities, vocations. . . ." Beggar man and thief aside, this is, of course, the American Dream—an educational bill of rights that every one of us would like to accept as true.

In evaluating Watson's proposal, much depends upon the meaning of the words *healthy* and *well-formed*. Unfortunately, as far as ability is concerned, all men are not created equal. Because of inborn errors of metabolism, many infants will, regardless of training, never have the ability to become doctors and lawyers. They will be fortunate to learn to speak, feed themselves, and to tie their shoes.

"Normal" variations in intelligence also appear to be at least in part biologically based. Studies of the IQ's of twins have shown that in sets of identical twins the correlation of IQ scores is typically greater than +.80, while that for fraternal twins is usually approximately +.50. The similarity in IQ between pairs of fraternal twins is no greater than that of ordinary brothers and sisters. Numerous studies of this type show that, in general, similarity in IQ varies directly with the genetic similarity. Undoubtedly, heredity influences IQ scores.

Unfortunately, IQ tests were not developed to provide a measure of a psychological process or set of processes. They were developed simply on an empirical basis to provide a score which can be used to predict academic success. As such, IQ tests are used to predict—not to diagnose. They are, of course, not simply tests of learning and memory. They do, however, include subtests which provide measures of learning and memory.

Experimental studies using laboratory rats have shown that it is possible to develop, by selective breeding, strains of rats that are bright and strains that are dull on specific learning tests. Further, numerous different strains of mice specially developed for tumor incidence have been found to differ in learning ability on various tasks. In mice and men, learning ability is genetically influenced.

Learning ability is not, however, completely determined by genetic factors. David Krech and his colleagues at the University of California at Berkeley have found that environmental stimulation influences the learning ability of rats.

Rats reared in an enriched laboratory environment are better learners than rats reared in less stimulating surroundings. Again, however, biological factors appear to play a role; the rats who were better learners differed from the other rats in several morphological and biochemical measures.

We do not yet know in detail how genes and environmental stimulation act to produce normal variations in intelligence and learning ability. The learning tests used with rats and mice provide rather crude measures of learning ability—much in the same way that IQ tests provide crude measures of children's mental capacities. In spite of this crudeness, the tests are able to provide indirect measures of processes which are biologically based.

Learning and memory as complex processes. The processes underlying learning and memory are undoubtedly extremely complicated. Consider what is involved in learning a telephone number. First, the information has to be attended to and received; second, the information must be registered or stored in some way; third, the information must be retained for a period of time; and fourth, it must be retrieved when needed. Learning ability depends upon the efficiency of each of these processes. Since deficiencies in one or more of the systems could cause poor learning, we need to know the nature of the brain processes underlying these systems.

Studies of memory in humans with memory defects have provided some leads. Dr. Brenda Milner at Montreal Neurological Institute has conducted studies of memory in patients with brain lesions in the temporal lobes of both hemispheres of the brain. In some ways, the memory processes of such patients are fairly efficient. Immediate or short-term memory may be normal, and there may be no impairment of the patient's ability to remember events which occurred some time prior to the brain damage. IQ scores are usually unaffected. However, although the patients may appear to be quite normal, they are not. They have completely (or almost completely) lost the ability to acquire and retain new information. The case of one such patient, who received brain damage 10 years ago, illustrates the nature of the defect:

"Ten months after [the occurrence of the brain damage] the family moved to a new house . . . situated a few blocks away . . . on the same street. . . . A year later the man had not yet learned the new address, nor could he be trusted to find his way home alone because he would go to the old house. . . . Moreover, he is unable to learn where objects constantly in use are kept. . . . He will do the same jigsaw puzzles day after day without showing any practice effects and reads the same magazines over and over again without ever finding the contents familiar."

Research in my laboratory and in numerous other laboratories has shown that it is possible to produce amnesia in animals experimentally, by administering treatments including electroshock stimulation and various drugs, after animals are trained on a task. Amnesia results only if the treatments are given within a few

70

minutes or hours after the training. The magnitude of the amnesia decreases as the interval between training and treatment is increased.

Findings such as these suggest that information can be retrieved from at least two memory systems: a short-term system and one for long-term storage. Both brain damage and the treatments such as drugs and electroshock stimulation appear to block storage processes in the long-term memory system.

It seems possible that at least some "normal occurring" deficiencies in learning and memory might be due to impaired functions of the two memory systems. Studies of memory disorders in geriatric patients and retarded children provide some support for this view. For example, W. K. Caird at the University of British Columbia reported results suggesting that, at least in some cases, the memory disorder in elderly patients may be due to a loss of efficiency in the long-term memory storage system.

Millard C. Madsen at UCLA has found that, in comparison with children with high IQ's (an average of approximately 120), children with low IQ's (an average of approximately 60) appear to have poorer short-term memory. Further, the lower-IQ children required longer intervals between training trials for optimal learning. This suggests that mental retardation may be due in part to deficiencies of short-term and long-term memory storage systems. In one study Madsen found that children with low IQ's could learn almost as efficiently as children with high IQ's when a relatively long interval lapsed between repetitions of the material.

Additional evidence that memory storage involves several systems has come from our studies of drug effects on memory storage. We have found in our laboratory that it is possible to enhance learning of laboratory animals by administering certain stimulant drugs shortly after training. These findings indicate that the drugs facilitate learning by enhancing long-term memory storage processes. The effects, like those obtained with memory impairing treatments, are time-dependent. Facilitation is obtained only if the drugs are administered within an hour or two following the training.

A large number of drugs are now known to enhance memory. Many appear to facilitate long-term memory storage in the manner just described. Others appear to act on short-term memory and retrieval systems. Unfortunately, not much is known about the specific ways in which the drugs influence neural functioning to produce memory effects, and we do not yet know whether comparable effects can be obtained with humans.

Implications. Although much has been learned in recent years about the nature and biological bases of learning and memory, we have probably not yet reached the point where such knowledge is of immediate significance for educational technology. All indications are that this point is rapidly being approached, however. Even at the present state of knowledge there are some important implications.

First, it is probably time to discard intelligence tests as we know them now—and time to develop tests designed to assess specific processes of learning and memory. Such tests could be used to diagnose individual differences in learning efficiency and might even prove useful (as IQ tests have not) in helping to develop teaching practices designed to deal with individual differences in learning and memory.

Second, it may be time to anticipate the possibility that, in the future, drugs might be used to correct learning and memory deficiencies in the same way that corrective lenses are now used to correct visual defects. Drug treatment of memory defects could become as common as drug treatment of allergies and emotional disorders. It may be that some day, by these means, educators will be able to fulfill John B. Watson's dream. Perhaps it will be the right of every child to have the opportunity to become a doctor, lawyer, merchant, or chief. The social and economic implications of this possibility are enormous. Perhaps we should begin to give them some thought.

THE CHEMISTRY
OF LEARNING

By DAVID KRECH

AMERICAN educators now talk a great deal about the innovative hardware of education, about computer-assisted instruction, 8 mm cartridge-loading projectors, microtransparencies, and other devices. In the not too distant future they may well be talking about enzyme-assisted instruction, protein memory consolidators, antibiotic memory repellers, and the chemistry of the brain. Although the psychologists' learning theories derived from the study of maze-running rats or target-pecking pigeons have failed to provide insights into the education of children, it is unlikely that what is now being discovered by the psychologist, chemist, and neurophysiologist about rat-brain chemistry can deviate widely from what we will eventually discover about the chemistry of the human brain.

Most adults who are not senile can repeat a series of seven numbers— 8, 4, 8, 8, 3, 9, 9 — immediately after the series is read. If, however, they are asked to repeat these numbers thirty minutes later, most will fail. In the first instance, we are dealing with the immediate memory span; in the second, with long-term memory. These basic behavioral observations lie behind what is called the two-stage memory storage process theory.

According to a common variant of these notions, immediately after every learning trial—indeed, after every experience—a short-lived electrochemical process is established in the brain. This process, so goes the assumption, is the physiological mechanism which carries the short-term memory. Within a few seconds or minutes, however, this process decays and disappears; but before doing so, if all systems are go, the short-term electrochemical process triggers a second series of events in the brain. This second process is chemical in nature and involves, primarily, the production of new proteins and the induction of higher enzymatic activity levels in the brain cells. This process is more enduring and serves as the physiological substrate of our long-term memory.

It would follow that one approach to testing our theory would be to provide a subject with some experience or other, then interrupt the short-term electrochemical process immediately—before it has had an opportunity to establish the long-term process. If this were done, our subject should never develop a long-term memory for that experience.

At the Albert Einstein Medical School in New York, Dr. Murray Jarvik has devised a "step-down" procedure based on the fact that when a rat is placed on a small platform a few inches above the floor, the rat will step down onto the floor within a few seconds. The rat will do this consistently, day after day. Suppose that on one day the floor is electrified, and stepping onto it produces a painful shock. When the rat is afterward put back on the platform—even twenty-

SATURDAY REVIEW, Jan. 20, 1968, pp. 48-50, 68

four hours later—it will not budge from the platform but will remain there until the experimenter gets tired and calls the experiment quits. The rat has thus demonstrated that he has a long-term memory for that painful experience.

If we now take another rat, but this time *interfere* with his short-term memory process *immediately after* he has stepped onto the electrified floor, the rat should show no evidence of having experienced a shock when tested the next day, since we have not given his short-term electrochemical memory process an opportunity to initiate the long-term protein-enzymatic process. To interrupt the short-term process, Jarvik passes a mild electric current across the brain of the animal. The current is not strong enough to cause irreparable harm to the brain cells, but it does result in a very high level of activation of the neurons in the brain, thus disrupting the short-term electrochemical memory process. If this treatment follows closely enough after the animal's first experience with the foot shock, and we test the rat a day later, the rat acts as if there were no memory for yesterday's event; the rat jauntily and promptly steps down from the platform with no apparent expectation of shock.

When a long time-interval is interposed between the first foot shock and the electric-current (through the brain) treatment, the rat *does* remember the foot shock, and it remains on the platform when tested the next day. This, again, is what we should have expected from our theory. The short-term electrochemical process has now had time to set up the long-term chemical memory process before it was disrupted.

SOME well known effects of accidental human head injury seem to parallel these findings. Injuries which produce a temporary loss of consciousness (but no permanent damage to brain tissue) can cause the patient to experience a "gap" in his memory for the events just preceding the accident. This retrograde amnesia can be understood on the as-

sumption that the events immediately prior to the accident were still being carried by the short-term memory processes at the time of the injury, and their disruption by the injury was sufficient to prevent the induction of the long-term processes. The patient asks "Where am I?" not only because he does not recognize the hospital, but also because he cannot remember how he became injured.

Work conducted by Dr. Bernard Agranoff at the University of Michigan Medical School supports the hypothesis that the synthesis of new brain proteins is crucial for the establishment of the long-term memory process. He argues that if we could prevent the formation of new proteins in the brain, then—although the short-term electrochemical memory process is not interfered with— the long-term memory process could never become established.

Much of Agranoff's work has been done with goldfish. The fish is placed in one end of a small rectangular tank, which is divided into two halves by a barrier which extends from the bottom to just below the surface of the water. When a light is turned on, the fish must swim across the barrier into the other side of the tank within twenty seconds— otherwise he receives an electric shock. This training is continued for several trials until the animal learns to swim quickly to the other side when the light is turned on. Most goldfish learn this shock-avoidance task quite easily and remember it for many days. Immediately before—and in some experiments, immediately after—training, Agranoff injects the antibiotic puromycin into the goldfish's brain. (Puromycin is a protein inhibitor and prevents the formation of new proteins in the brain's neurons.) After injection, Agranoff finds that the goldfish are not impaired in their acquisition of the shock-avoidance task, but, when tested a day or so later, they show almost no retention for the task.

These results mean that the short-term memory process (which helps the animal remember from one trial to the next and thus permits him to learn in the first place) is not dependent upon the formation of new proteins, but that the long-term process (which helps the animal remember from one day to the next and thus permits him to retain what he had learned) is dependent upon the production of new proteins. Again, as in the instance of Jarvik's rats, if the puromycin injection comes more than an hour after learning, it has no effect on later memory—the long-term memory process presumably has already been established and the inhibition of protein synthesis can now no longer affect memory. In this antibiotic, therefore, we have our first chemical memory erasure—or, more accurately, a chemical long-term memory preventative. (Almost identical findings have been reported by other workers in other laboratories working with such animals as mice and rats, which are far removed from the goldfish.)

Thus far I have been talking about disrupting or preventing the formation of memory. Now we will accentuate the positive. Dr. James L. McGaugh of the University of California at Riverside has argued that injections of central nervous system stimulants such as strychnine, picrotoxin, or metrazol should enhance, fortify, or extend the activity of the short-term electrochemical memory processes and thus increase the probability that they will be successful in initiating long-term memory processes. From this it follows that the injection of CNS stimulants immediately before or after training should improve learning performance. That is precisely what McGaugh found—together with several additional results which have important implications for our concerns today.

In one of McGaugh's most revealing experiments, eight groups of mice from two different hereditary backgrounds were given the problem of learning a simple maze. Immediately after completing their learning trials, four groups from each strain were injected with a different dosage of metrazol—from none

to five, 10, and 20 milligrams per kilogram of body weight. First, it was apparent that there are hereditary differences in learning ability—a relatively bright strain and a relatively dull one. Secondly, by properly dosing the animals with metrazol, the learning performance increased appreciably. Under the optimal dosage, the metrazol animals showed about a 40 per cent improvement in learning ability over their untreated brothers. The improvement under metrazol was so great, in fact, that the dull animals, when treated with 10 milligrams, did slightly better than their untreated but hereditarily superior colleagues.

In metrazol we not only have a chemical facilitator of learning, but one which acts as the "Great Equalizer" among hereditarily different groups. As the dosage was increased for the dull mice from none to five to 10 milligrams their performance improved. Beyond the 10-milligram point for the dull mice, however, and beyond the five-milligram point for the bright mice, increased strength of the metrazol solution resulted in a deterioration in learning. We can draw two morals from this last finding. First, the optimal dosage of chemical learning facilitators will vary greatly with the individual taking the drug (There is, in other words, an interaction between heredity and drugs); second, there is a limit to the intellectual power of even a hopped-up Southern Californian Super Mouse! .

WE already have available a fairly extensive class of drugs which can facilitate learning and memory in animals. A closer examination of McGaugh's results and the work of others, however, also suggests that these drugs do not work in a monolithic manner on something called "learning" or "memory." In some instances, the drugs seem to act on "attentiveness"; in some, on the ability to vary one's attacks on a problem; in some, on persistence; in some, on immediate memory; in some, on long-term memory. Different drugs work differentially for different strains, different individuals, different intellectual tasks, and different learning components.

Do all of these results mean that we will soon be able to substitute a pharmacopoeia of drugs for our various school-enrichment and innovative educational programs, and that most educators will soon be technologically unemployed—or will have to retool and turn in their schoolmaster's gown for a pharmacist's jacket? The answer is no—as our Berkeley experiments on the influence of education and training on brain anatomy and chemistry suggest. This research is the work of four—Dr. E. L. Bennett, biochemist; Dr. Marian Diamond, anatomist; Dr. M. R. Rosenzweig, psychologist; and myself — together, of course, with the help of graduate students, technicians, and, above all, government money.

Our work, started some fifteen years ago, was guided by the same general theory which has guided more recent work, but our research strategy and tactics were quite different. Instead of interfering physiologically or chemically with the animal to determine the effects of such intervention upon memory storage (as did Jarvik, Agranoff, and McGaugh), we had taken the obverse question and, working with only normal animals, sought to determine the *effects* of memory storage on the chemistry and anatomy of the brain.

Our argument was this: If the establishment of long-term memory processes involves increased activity of brain enzymes, then animals which have been required to do a great deal of learning and remembering should end up with brains enzymatically different from those of animals which have not been so challenged by environment. This should be especially true for the enzymes involved in trans-synaptic neural activity. Further, since such neural activity would make demands on brain-cell action and metabolism, one might also expect to find various morphological differences between the brains of rats brought up in psychologically stimulating and psychologically pallid environments.

I describe briefly one of our standard experiments. At weaning age, one rat from each of a dozen pairs of male twins is chosen by lot to be placed in an educationally active and innovative environment, while its twin brother is placed in as unstimulating an environment as we can contrive. All twelve educationally enriched rats live together in one large, wire-mesh cage in a well lighted, noisy, and busy laboratory. The cage is equipped with ladders, running wheels, and other "creative" rat toys. For thirty minutes each day, the rats are taken out of their cages and allowed to explore new territory. As the rats grow older they are given various learning tasks to master, for which they are rewarded with bits of sugar. This stimulating educational and training program is continued for eighty days.

While these animals are enjoying their rich intellectual environment, each impoverished animal lives out his life in solitary confinement, in a small cage situated in a dimly lit and quiet room. He is rarely handled by his keeper and never invited to explore new environments, to solve problems, or join in games with other rats. Both groups of rats, however, have unlimited access to the same standard food throughout the experiment. At the age of 105 days, the rats are sacrificed, their brains dissected out and analyzed morphologically and chemically.

This standard experiment, repeated dozens of times, indicates that as the fortunate rat lives out his life in the educationally enriched condition, the bulk of his cortex expands and grows deeper and heavier than that of his culturally deprived brother. Part of this increase in cortical mass is accounted for by an increase in the number of glia cells (specialized brain cells which play vital functions in the nutrition of the neurons and, perhaps, also in laying down permanent memory traces); part of it by an increase in the size of the neuronal cell bodies and their nuclei; and part by an increase in the diameters of the blood vessels supplying the cortex. Our postulated chemical changes also occur. The enriched brain shows more acetylocholinesterase (the enzyme involved in the trans-synaptic conduction of neural impulses) and cholinesterase (the enzyme found primarily in the glia cells).

Finally, in another series of experiments we have demonstrated that these structural and chemical changes are the signs of a "good" brain. That is, we have shown that either through early rat-type Head Start programs or through selective breeding programs, we can increase the weight and density of the rat's cortex and its acetylocholinesterase and cholinesterase activity levels. And when we do—by either method—we have created superior problem-solving animals.

What does all of this mean? It means that the effects of the psychological and educational environment are not restricted to something called the "mental" realm. Permitting the young rat to grow up in an educationally and experientially inadequate and unstimulating environment creates an animal with a relatively deteriorated brain—a brain with a thin and light cortex, lowered blood supply, diminished enzymatic activities, smaller neuronal cell bodies, and fewer glia cells. A lack of adequate educational fare for the young animal—no matter how large the food supply or how good the family—and a lack of adequate psychological enrichment results in palpable, measurable, deteriorative changes in the brain's chemistry and anatomy.

Returning to McGaugh's results, we find that whether, and to what extent, this or that drug will improve the animal's learning ability will depend, of course, on what the drug does to the rat's brain chemistry. And what it does to the rat's brain chemistry will depend upon the status of the chemistry in the brain to begin with. And what the status of the brain's chemistry is to begin with reflects the rat's early psychological and educational environment. Whether, and to what extent, this or that drug will improve the animal's attention, or memory, or learning ability, therefore, will depend upon the animal's past experiences. I am not talking about interaction between "mental" factors on the one hand and "chemical" compounds on the other. I am talking, rather, about interactions between chemical factors introduced into the brain by the biochemist's injection or pills, and chemical factors induced in the brain by the educator's stimulating or impoverishing environment. The biochemist's work can be only half effective without the educator's help.

What kind of educational environment can best develop the brain chemically and morphologically? What kind of stimulation makes for an enriched environment? What educational experiences can potentiate the effects of the biochemist's drugs? We don't know. The biochemist doesn't know. It is at this point that I see a whole new area of collaboration in basic research between the educator, the psychologist, and the neurobiochemist—essentially, a research program which combines the Agranoff and McGaugh techniques with our Berkeley approach. Given the start that has already been made in the animal laboratory, an intensive program of research—with animals and with children—which seeks to spell out the interrelations between chemical and educational influences on brain and memory can pay off handsomely. This need not wait for the future. We know enough now to get started.

Both the biochemist and the teacher of the future will combine their skills and insights for the educational and intellectual development of the child. Tommy needs a bit more of an immediate memory stimulator; Jack could do with a chemical attention-span stretcher; Rachel needs an anticholinesterase to slow down her mental processes; Joan, some puromycin—she remembers too many details, and gets lost.

To be sure, all our data thus far come from the brains of goldfish and rodents.

77

But is anyone so certain that the chemistry of the brain of a rat (which, after all, is a fairly complex mammal) is so different from that of the brain of a human being that he dare neglect this challenge—or even gamble—when the stakes are so high?

THE COMMONNESS OF CREATIVITY

BY RALPH J. HALLMAN

THE RECENT UPSURGE OF INTEREST IN CREATIVITY HAS BEEN OCCASIONED BY POST-SPUTNIK PRESSURES UPON EDUCATORS AND PSYCHOLOGISTS, AND IT HAS BEEN AIMED AT IDENTIFYING AND DEVISING APPROPRIATE EDUCATION FOR THE GIFTED CHILD. The research of Getzels and Jackson[1] provides evidence that creativeness exists as a separate form of giftedness, but this study is limited only to the highly gifted individual. The research conferences organized by the University of Utah[2] in 1955, 1957, and 1959 sought to identify creative scientific talent, but again these conferences restricted their investigation to talent of the highest order. The three conferences conducted by the University of Minnesota[3] follow the same pattern. These latter studies were concerned to discover how the gifted child should be taught, how he learns, how he should be grouped for the best results, how he should be administered, and how he should be evaluated.

Though the concept of creativity has been picked up by business and industry as a device for improving management and for increasing profits, the emphasis remains on the specially gifted person. For example, *Harvard Business Review* features an article[4] on the "operational approach" to creativity, and asks whether it might be spelled out so that management can take maximum advantage of it. The three conferences held at Arden House, Harriman, New York in 1956 and 1957[5] were sponsored by thirteen industrial corporations and focused upon ways that creative ideas can be channeled into business and industry. The Carnegie Corporation has been supporting a six-year study of creativity at the University of California at Berkeley. This research to date has been limited to highly gifted people, to novelists, essayists, poets, architects, research scientists, and mathematicians.[6]

The thesis of this paper is that unless creativity can be established as existing commonly in all children, it can never serve as a proper aim of education.

Indeed, some of the recent research recognizes the possibility of the commonness of creativity. For example, the symposia conducted by Syracuse University

---

[1]J. W. Getzels and P. W. Jackson, *Creativity and Intelligence* (New York: John Wiley and Sons, Inc., 1962), chapters 1, 2, and 3.

[2]C. W. Taylor (ed.), *The University of Utah Research Conference on the Identification of Creative Scientific Talent, 1955, 1957, 1959* (Salt Lake City: University of Utah Press, 1956, 1958, 1960).

[3]E. P. Torrance (ed.), *Talent and Education* (Minneapolis: University of Minnesota Press, 1960). See also the multilithed volume, *New Education Ideas*, ed. E. P. Torrance (University of Minnesota Press).

[4]*Harvard Business Review*, November-December, 1956.

[5]Three conferences held at Arden House. Harriman, New York in October, 1956, May and November, 1957 under the sponsorship of the Insti   ontemporary Art, Boston; assisted by W. J. J. Gordon. Three multilithed volumes have be   ..ed entitled, *Creativity as a Process; Intergrating the Creative Process;* and *Motivating the Creative Process.*

[6]*Carnegie Corporation of America Quarterly*, Vol. IX, No. 3 (July 1961).

EDUCATIONAL THEORY, 1963, 13, pp. 132-136.

in 1958 and 1960[7] place emphasis on the need to teach all children creatively. The various papers which were read at this conference speak of "everyone's creative process," of the "democratic values" in the creative arts, of creative enrichment through the arts, and the need for creative teaching.

But the greatest boon to the theory that all children are creative comes from the clinician and psychiatrist, and, following their lead, from the educator. The theory that creativeness characterizes mankind generally is important for both the clinician and the educator. For the former, it provides a broad-based groundwork for a mental health program; for the latter, it transforms professional work into a search for excellences in all human beings. It forces the educator to consider what is the good life and challenges him to devise ways whereby routine classroom activities can contribute to such a life.

Evidence for the theory appears not only in clinical psychology, but in physical science and philosophy as well.

For example, Murray argues strongly for the theory of the commonness of creativity: "And instead of creativity being considered a very rare capacity in man, many of us acknowledge that it is manifested in some way and to some extent in almost everybody."[8] But he goes on to say that he accepts this proposition as an inference from a specific philosophical system, namely, that of the philosopher Whitehead, who "adumbrated a theoretical system of systems in which creativity is a metaphysical ultimate." His is a world view which regards every single fact, event, or occasion of any magnitude as a unique temporal integration of discrete components. Thus, every single occurrence or state of affairs would be a novelty, and creativity would itself constitute the very essence of reality.

Another classical statement of this general position occurs in Bergson's *Creative Evolution*.[9] This volume develops the idea that ultimate reality unfolds in an ever-productive manner, that the present is always greater than the past, that the consequences are greater than the antecedents, that novelty is more than mere rearrangement, and therefore that creativity becomes the normal and even the inescapable. These circumstances, to use Bergson's language, provide for an "absolute originality and unforseeability of forms." He regards personality as undergoing a continuing process of self-formation: "Our personality, which is being built up each instant with its accumulated experience, changes without ceasing. By changing, it prevents any state . . . from ever repeating in its very depth. . . . Thus our personality shoots, grows, ripens without ceasing. Each of its moments is something new added to what was before."[10]

These philosophical systems locate creativity within the final processes which produce the kind of universe which we now experience. Consequently, it should not be surprising to find scientists who share this view and who claim to have discovered empirical evidence for it.

Anderson believes that creativity, defined as the emergence of individuality

---

[7]M. F. Andrews has edited two volumes entitled, *Aesthetic Form and Education* (Syracuse: Syracuse University Press, 1958), and *Creativity and Psychological Health* (Syracuse: Syracuse University Press, 1961). These volumes contain the papers which were read at these two symposia.

[8]H. A. Murray, "Vicissitudes of Creativity," *Creativity and Its Cultivation*, ed. H. H. Anderson (New York: Harper and Brothers, Publishers, 1959), p. 100.

[9]H. Bergson, *Creative Evolution* (New York: The Modern Library, 1944).

[10]*Ibid.*, p. 34.

and of originals, is found in every living cell,[11] and furthermore that this fact accounts for both "the interweaving differences" which characterize creativity on the psychological level and also for the presence of creativity within every one of us. The physiologist, Gerard, argues for the biological basis of the creative imagination,[12] but perhaps Sinnott has presented this argument in its most convincing form.[13] Arguing that life in itself is creative, that it exhibits organizing and self-regulating tendencies, he then suggests that these functions rest upon an even more remote physical process. He holds that the physical and the psychical are much closer together than is commonly believed. This relationship is crucial, he believes, for, "if this can be established, the problem of creativeness at every level may be studied as a biological one, in the widest sense, and against a much broader background than that provided by psychology or philosophy alone."[14] At least, we may validly draw the conclusion that if life as such is creative, then we have grounds for asserting that some degree of creativeness can indeed be found in everyone.

The psychiatrist and clinical psychologist come to the same conclusion, but they deduce it from a particular theory of personality, a theory which selects its evidence from studies of the positively healthy person rather than from pathological data. Maslow provides the classic statement of this position. He dismisses the extremely rare type of creative individual, the genius, and chooses to study "that more widespread kind of creativeness which is the universal heritage of every human being that is born, and which seems to co-vary with psychological health."[15] Thus, he turns to social workers, housewives, athletes, and even psychiatrists for data which proves the normality and commonness of what he calls self-actualizing creativeness.

Fromm and Rogers concur in defining creativeness as capacity for growth in the direction of psychological health, and they therefore support the view that creativity is common to almost everyone. Fromm[16] describes creativeness as the condition of well-being, the ability to be aware, to respond, to be more concerned with being than with having, in short, to become fully human. For Rogers the mainsprings of creativity in man are exactly those curative forces which work toward integration, wholeness, health. The urge to actualize one's potentialities is a therapeutic tendency, and it manifests itself in every human being.

Though recent, this particular formulation of the problem has become very influential. Kelley and Rasey[17] argue that the great volume of creativity is to be found in connection with the small and simple operations of everyday life of ordinary people. Tumin equates the normal, healthy development of human capacities with creativity.[18] Zilboorg's version of this theory allows him to say

---

[11]H. H. Anderson, *Creativity and Its Cultivation* (New York: Harper and Brothers, Publishers, 1959), p. xii, p. 124.

[12]R. W. Gerard, "The Biological Basis of Imagination," *Scientific Monthly*, Vol. 62 (1946), p. 477 ff.

[13]E. W. Sinnott, "The Creativeness of Life," *Creativity and Its Cultivation*, ed. H. H. Anderson (New York: Harper and Brothers, Publishers, 1959), p. 12 ff.

[14]*Ibid.*, p. 14.

[15]A. H. Maslow, *Toward a Psychology of Being* (Princeton, New Jersey: D. Van Nostrand Company, Inc., 1962), p. 127.

[16]E. Fromm, "Value, Psychology, and Human Existence," *New Knowledge in Human Values*, ed. A. H. Maslow (New York: Harper and Brothers, Publishers, 1959), p. 163.

[17]E. C. Kelly and Marie Rasey, *Education and the Nature of Man* (New York: Harper and Brothers, Publishers, 1952), p. 116.

[18]M. M. Tumin, "Education, Development, and the Creative Process," *Aesthetic Form and Education*, ed. M. F. Andrews (Syracuse: Syracuse University Press, 1958), p. 25.

that simple people can be creative,[19] that being a good father, for example, demands a genuine creative effort; for a good father is one who would have his children flourish as unique and independent individuals rather than as copies of his own image. Thurstone worked for several years in an effort to identify the various mental abilities, and he concludes that with respect to the creative factors, these are qualitatively the same at all levels. Guilford's results indicate that all of the primary abilities are found in some degree among the general population.[20]

But a serious problem does arise. If creativity is to be found in all people, then casual observation indicates that the range of creative abilities reaches across such a wide spectrum that the concept of commonness becomes rather useless. To maintain that there are no qualitative differences between a Leonardo da Vinci and a potential delinquent who may occupy our classrooms hardly solves the problem. This issue is perhaps of less concern to the clinician. The therapy which he prescribes may apply equally well to the genius as to the delinquent. The educator's problem becomes more complex if less intense. Instead of individual therapy, or at best therapy in small groups, he must learn to deal with large numbers of individuals as they grope toward some measure of self-fulfillment.

Writers in the field appear to have suggested three possible solutions to the question of range in creative abilities. They argue, (1) that difference in ability is quantitative rather than qualitative, (2) that any difference reduces to a matter of latency as against an overt expression, or (3) that the differential tends to disappear when creativity is defined as a way of conducting one's life rather than in terms of the number and kinds of objects which one may have produced.

I mentioned above that Thurstone subscribes to this first view. He is joined by Jones, who agrees that the creative capacities of the common man differ only quantitatively and not qualitatively from those of genius.[21] Further support can be found from psychologists and educators; examples are Vinacke[22] and Stoddard.[23]

Lowenfeld best exemplifies the second view.[24] Though he believes that all people are creative, some of them remain only potentially so; whereas, others have somehow learned to release into outward expression their latent talents. He distinguishes between potential creativeness and functional creativeness, the former capacity existing as a potential only. Furthermore, the individual may not even be aware of his latent powers. It is easy to inhibit and to neglect these creative potentials in educational systems which place high premiums on formal disciplines, on following directions, and on being told always what to do. This distinction provides Lowenfeld the occasion to identify the educator's prime duty:

---

[19]G. Zilboorg, "The Psychology of the Creative Personality," *Creativity*, ed. Paul Smith (New York: Hastings House, Publishers, Inc., 1959), p. 51 ff.

[20]J. P. Guilford, "Traits of Creativity," *Creativity and Its Cultivation*, ed. H. H. Anderson (New York: Harper and Brothers, Publishers, 1959), p. 158.

[21]E. Jones, "How to Tell Your Friends from Geniuses," *Saturday Review*, Vol. XL (August 10, 1957), p. 9 ff.

[22]W. E. Vinacke, *The Psychology of Thinking* (New York: McGraw-Hill Book Company, Inc., 1952), p. 238 ff.

[23]G. D. Stoddard, "Creativity in Education," *Creativity and Its Cultivation*, ed. H. H. Anderson (New York: Harper and Brothers, Publishers, 1959), p. 187.

[24]V. Lowenfeld, "Basic Aspects of Creative Thinking," *Creativity and Psychological Health*, ed. M. F. Andrews (Syracuse: Syracuse University Press, 1961), p. 130.

"We have to regard it as our sacred responsibility to unfold and develop each individual's creative ability as dim as the spark may be and kindle it to whatever flame it may conceivably develop."[25] Furthermore, the ethical worth of a society must be evaluated in terms of its efforts to develop creative potentials in all members of that society.

The third solution to the problem parallels the general theory of creativity which this paper proposes, namely the theory that creativeness equates with self-actualization processes. It finds support among both clinicians and educators. Dr. Ordway Tead, member of the Board of Education of New York City, believes that creativity refers to a person's health and well-being, to that which is self-fulfilling and rewarding. It is not merely the production of artistic objects, but includes within its meaning the "ongoing process of interpersonal relations such as administering an organization or sharing in directing the affairs of a family."[26]

Perhaps Rogers has developed this conception of creativity in greatest detail. He describes the therapeutic process as movement, as process, as fluidity. It is movement away from such personality structures as defensiveness, facade, and compulsiveness and in the direction of autonomy, acceptance of change, openness, and trust. The movement toward psychological health is the achievement of freedom and of creativeness: "I believe it will be clear that a person who is involved in the directional process which I have termed 'the good life' is a creative person . . . he would be the type of person from whom creative products and creative living emerge."[27]

Rogers is describing a process which can occur not only in geniuses but in any given human being. It is in fact a *human* process. And Rogers is aware of the philosophical significance of this statement. His identification of therapy and creativity means that in its deepest sense an analysis of creativity is a metaphysical analysis, that creativity applies to humanity in its most essential aspects, that being and being creative are identical processes. The fact that only philosophical statements can accurately express the meaning of therapy, and of creativity, does not bother Rogers as a psychologist. "In these days most psychologists regard it as an insult if they are accused of thinking philosophical thoughts. I do not share this reaction," he says.[28] The pattern of movement which he observes in patients takes the form of a movement toward "being," toward the process of his becoming what he inwardly and actually *is*.

These analyses clearly imply that creative capacities exist either potentially or actually in every child and that creativeness is not limited to the very rare talent which we associate with genius. They further imply that these capacities are identical with those which move personality in the direction of psychological health, that they rest upon biological processes and are amenable to environmental influences. Thus, they imply that creativity can serve as a worthy aim of education.

---

[25]*Ibid.*, p. 131.
[26]O. Tead, "The Healthy Person's Creative Outlets," *Creativity and Psychological Health*, ed. M. F. Andrews (Syracuse: Syracuse University Press, 1961), p. 110.
[27]C. R. Rogers, *On Becoming a Person* (Boston: Houghton Mifflin Company, 1961), chapters 8 and 9.
[28]*Ibid.*, p. 163.

IQ:
GOD-GIVEN
OR MAN-MADE?

By GILBERT VOYAT

WHO would have believed that in the declining decades of the twentieth century the antique psychological argument between environment and heredity would garner headlines and rub academic tempers raw? The older, progressive educators scolded each other about the primacy of nurture over nature. The practicing pragmatists insisted that, "You are what you grow up as, not merely what you are born with." The environmentalists declared that slums produce children with more limited intelligence than generous suburbs do. Not so, asserted the genetically persuaded; poor performance in intellectual matters is the result of a shallow gene-pool.

And so the argument continues. In this past winter's issue of the *Harvard Educational Review*, Dr. Arthur R. Jensen, professor of educational psychology at the University of California at Berkeley, suggests that intelligence is a trait not unlike eye color and hardly more susceptible to change. This study presents an interesting renewal of the genetic argument. Although many of the ideas defended have the aura of statistical, scientific work, they are neither new, self-evident, nor irrefutable. The fact that Dr. Jensen's findings are corroborated by statistical evidence does not make them true. It makes them misleading.

His central thesis is simple: Intelligence is a natural trait, inscribed in the genetic pool and unequally distributed among individuals. Theoretically, genius can be found anywhere, regardless of race or social milieu. In practice, however, Jensen insists that in terms of the average IQ, whites are more intelligent than blacks. The average IQ for blacks is, according to his calculation, approximately 15 points below the average for whites. Furthermore, only 15 per cent of the Negro population exceeds the white average. This has been shown, for instance, in a study (cited by Jensen) by Dr. A. M. Shuev, author of *The Testing of Negro Intelligence*, who reviewed 382 previous studies of IQ. Here we have a typical case of validation by quantification. It is impressive, precise, and wrongheaded. The difference in intelligence between whites and blacks is also noticeable among privileged children; upper-status Negro children average 2.6 IQ points below the low-status whites. Jensen makes the further assertion that Indians, who are even more disadvantaged than Negroes, are nevertheless more intelligent. Jensen is very cautious about this differential intelligence. Negro infants, he claims, are more precocious in sensory-motor development in their first year or two than are Caucasian infants. The same holds for motor skills. But, he believes, what is

SATURDAY REVIEW, May 17, 1969, pp. 73-75 ff.

crucially missing among Negroes is what constitutes genuine formal intelligence: conceptual learning and problem-solving ability.

Jensen offers a description of the respective roles of genetic and environmental factors as he defines intelligence. His strategy in demonstrating the roles of inheritance and environment is to utilize exclusively statistical evidence. He discusses extensively the notion of "heritability," which for him is a statistical mean allowing him to state the extent to which individual differences in a trait such as intelligence can be accounted for by genetic factors. He comes to the conclusion that this heritability is quite high in the human species, which means that genetic factors are much more important than environmental factors in producing IQ differences. And *this* relationship is almost entirely displayed in achievement on IQ tests which Jensen sees as related to genetic differences.

THESE analyses lead Jensen to the further conclusion that genetic factors are strongly implicated in the average Negro-white intelligence differences. Given these conclusions, Jensen ascribes the failure of compensatory education and other educational enrichment programs to genetic differences, because any attempt to raise intelligence per se probably lies more in the province of the biological sciences than in that of psychology and education. For example, the magnitude of IQ and scholastic achievement gains resulting from enrichment and cognitive stimulation programs range between 5 and 20 IQ points. But Jensen is inclined to doubt "that IQ gains up to 8 to 10 points in young disadvantaged children have much of anything to do with changes in ability. They are largely the result of getting a more accurate IQ by testing under more optimal conditions."

Nevertheless, Jensen has some positive recommendations. He distinguishes between two genotypically distinct processes underlying a continuum ranging from "simple" associative learning which he calls Level I, to complex conceptual learning which he calls Level II. Level I involves a relatively high correspondence between the stimulus input and the form of the stimulus output. For example, a child will be able to recite, and perhaps remember, a succession of numbers. Object memory, serial rote learning, and selective trial and error learning are other good examples of Level I. In Level II, a child will be able to classify objects according to their similarities. Thus, Level II involves transforming a stimulus before it becomes an overt response. Concept learning and problem-solving in a whole range of experiences are good examples of Level II. Jensen believes that schooling maximizes the importance of Level II. But schools must also be able to find ways of utilizing other strengths in children whose abilities are not of the conceptual variety. In other words, the ideal educational world of Dr. Jensen would provide two types of education: one directed toward the acquisition of basic skills and simple associative learning, which is training rather than education. Given such training, children with only Level I skills will "perfectly" adapt to any society.

Such is Jensen's thesis. It is based mainly upon the validity of IQ tests. What, in fact, do they measure? The crucial question which must be asked concerns the value of IQ tests themselves. Not that Jensen does not discuss their value. He defines intelligence too narrowly as what IQ tests measure: "a capacity for abstract reasoning and problem-solving." How should we define intelligence? Is it useful to define it at all? In short, the very basis of Jensen's findings must be questioned in the light of what experimental psychology can tell us today about the nature of cognitive development and operations.

For example, fifty years ago any textbook of biology would begin by giving a definition of the word "life." Today, such a procedure is not possible because a definition of life is never adequate. The reason probably lies in the dynamic aspects of the concept, which is incompatible with a static and fixed definition. In a like manner, IQ tests essentially quantify static definitions. Therefore, as in biology it is no longer possible to define life statically, so, too, in psychology a static definition of intelligence is impossible. To understand the limitations of Jensen's basic assumptions, it is helpful to consider the point of view of the Swiss psychologist, Dr. Jean Piaget. A brief summary of the Piagetian approach allows us to differentiate between what is measured by standard intelligence tests and what is discovered through the Piagetian technique.

During more than forty years of experimentation, Dr. Piaget has arrived at a formal description of cognitive development and has divided it into four stages. The first one, before the development of language (symbolic function) in the child, deals with the construction of the logic of actions. This has been called "the period of sensory-motor intelligence." Primarily, the process involves the organization of actions into operational patterns, or "schemata of actions," whose main characteristics are to allow the child to differentiate in his actions, between means and goals. Some conditions are necessary in order to achieve this: Space must become organized as a general container; objects must remain permanent; and, in order to anticipate goals, one must assume some acquisition of practical causal processes.

THE main consequence of the appearance of the symbolic function is the reorganization of sensory-motor intelligence. This enables the child to integrate symbols, allowing him to expand the range of his operations. This next stage is called "pre-operational," or "the period of egocentric thinking." Thus, from a response to an event, intelligence is mediated through language, but the child is not yet able to maintain in his mind symbols (abstractions) that lead to ideas whose meanings are constant. Those constancies have to do with those aspects of the "real world," such as measure, mass, motion, and logical categories. In this pre-operational world everything appears to be related to an egocentric point of view. This is a limitation as much as a source of enrichment during this level of intellectual functioning.

The following stage is characterized by the development of concrete operations. From what is essentially a subjective orientation, intellectual functioning moves toward more objectivity in elaborating mental constancies. The child no longer thinks only in terms of himself, but also takes into account the limitations that the external, physical world places upon him. For example, the child no longer believes that the moon follows him down the street. For Piaget, this type of intelligence is called "concrete," because essentially the child is only able to deal with tangible, manipulatable objects. That is, his world is concerned with *necessary* relations among objects.

The final stage of intellectual development deals with the development of formal thinking which permits the formation not only of necessary relations but also *possible* and *impossible* ones. In short, he can "play" with his mind. The child, now an adolescent, can dream things that never were and ask "Why not?" The adolescent is able to make exact deductions, to extract all combinations from a potential or a real situation. He is no longer directed only by concrete relations. He can make hypotheses and elaborate theories. He is able to dissociate the form of his thinking from its content.

Piaget's approach strongly contrasts with Jensen's point of view. In particular, Piagetian "tests" clearly differ from typical IQ tests. Among the major differences, IQ tests are essentially an additive progression of acquired skills. They give a state, a global or overall result for a specific population; their quantitative aspect allows one to place a child among children of his age and development. Piagetian tests, on the other hand, are hierarchical; they describe a progressive organization and individual potentialities. They provide a detailed analysis of the functioning of thinking. In short, they qualify thinking; they do not quantify it. They always respect the intelligence of a specific child.

These differences are important because, given Piaget's theory, we can describe intelligence functionally; we can formalize its structural development. We cannot assign to intelligence a specific, static definition, in terms of properties, for this directly contradicts the idea of development itself. Any static definition reduces intelligence either to exclusively environmental factors or to almost exclusively genetic factors without implying the necessary *equilibrated* interaction between them.

Consider the distinction between Level I and Level II as proposed by Jensen. At first glance, this argument is appealing; transformations are not involved in the process of decoding and understanding information at Level I, whereas transformations are a necessity at Level II.

But what is a transformation? In a fundamental sense, the understanding of *any* transformation is a necessity at both levels of learning. Without distinguishing a transformation in the real world, we would be unable to differentiate one state from another. For instance, we can present to a child glass A of particular width and height and glass B thinner but taller than A. We call the state in which A is filled up and B is empty S-1, and the state in which B is filled and A is empty S-2. We call transformations (T) the pathway from one state to another, that is, in this particular case, the pouring from A to B, as well as the change of level in S-2 since the level of the liquid is higher than in S-1. For the child to understand these two aspects of the transformation, he must be able to understand the operation of conservation because it is this operation which has produced the transformation from one state to another. In other words, the child "makes the discovery" that the amount of water in the short, fat glass is exactly the same when it is poured into the tall, thin glass. Knowledge of the states themselves, however, is only a description of the observable. This point is fundamental. The fact that conservation is achieved by a child around the age of six or seven clearly implies the necessity of mastering invariancies even in order to understand Level I. But, to grasp any invariancy requires the ability to think, even at a very low level, in operational terms.

Thus, the two levels proposed by Jensen are inadequate to provide a clear idea of the development of intelligence itself.

Piaget, on the other hand, never gives a static definition of intelligence; essentially, he gives a functional one. The two functions of intelligence are to understand the external world and to build or discover new structures within it. Therefore, Piaget's experiments would always be culture-fair, because they are involved with a description of a progressive organization directed by logic and not greatly influenced by culture. For example, a whole set of Piagetian experiments have been carried out in Africa, Algeria, Iran, and elsewhere.

The main result is that sequential development, in comparable terms, is observed irrespective of the culture or the race. In other words, the stages are respected in their succession and do not permit, even in a theoretical continuum, division into the type of level differences that Jensen describes, and they most strongly suggest the irrelevance of these genotypically distinct basic processes.

IN contrast, IQ tests have been designed by whites for Western culture.

Thus, their value is limited to the culture within which they were designed. They can never be culture-fair. Therefore, in any testing procedure of intelligence, relativity, not absolutism, should be the criterion, and even the correction of IQ tests for other populations is not valid. Furthermore, IQ tests are simply not adequate to measure processes of thinking. They provide results, they do not lead to an understanding of how intelligence functions. Piaget's approach not only allows an understanding of intellectual functioning but describes it. Furthermore, Piaget's tests allow one to make reliable, individual prognostications. Since their interests lie in a description of the mechanism of thinking, they permit an individual, personalized appraisal of further potentialities independent of the culture. This point is important primarily because it is neglected in IQ tests where the global population is assessed rather than individual potentialities estimated.

If one accepts the premises on which IQ tests are based, then Jensen's point of view could be valid for what concerns the differences in Negro-white performances, and nevertheless remain questionable for ethnic differences based on genetic facts. His approach produces logical fallacies: first, he criticizes and compares the results of IQ tests; next, given differences, he sorts out the environmental and genetic factors; then he minimizes the influence of the milieu, analyzes the remainder in terms of biological implications, and finally compares two ethnic groups and ascribes their differences to genetic factors.

Although Jensen's methodology may have its merits, the problem is that the point of departure is wrong. To decide whether compensatory and other educational programs are failures is an important and responsible act. But, to base a judgment on IQ gains or lack of gains is questionable. Of course, one must have a way to judge such programs. But to decide that the IQ gains are so small that they do not justify the amount of money poured into such educational enterprises, can give people the impression that psychologists and educators know what they are talking about concerning processes of learning. In reality, many factors make it difficult to assess success and failure in educational programs. Of course, any program must be globally appraised and must work for a reasonably large number of children. But one of the problems of education is that very little is known about the underlying processes of learning. Furthermore, pedagogy provides generalized techniques for what must be individualized teaching. Not much is known about how the child grasps and achieves important notions such as conservation, seriation, number, movement, mass, motion, measure, speed, time, and logical categories. This is true regardless of race, color, or creed. Judging educational programs in terms of IQ does not settle the learning problem. On the contrary, psychologists who place their confidence in IQ tests tend to forget the real issue, which is the critical problem of how the child learns.

The tragedy of education lies in the fact that we are still lacking knowledge about learning processes. This situation should make us modest, and we should accept the fact that the nature of cognitive learning remains an open question for experimental and developmental psychology.

One of the major aims in education is to create openness to cognitive contradictions. One does not learn without confusion. One does not learn without feeling some discrepancy between the actual outlook and an imaginable one. One of the major conditions for cognitive development is the resolution of conflicts which leads to adaptation. Therefore, when Jensen states that we should let those who cannot attain his second level of intellectual functioning develop their capabilities within the limitations of his Level I, his position is a dangerous one strictly on cognitive grounds. It prescribes a limitation on experience for the four- or five-year-old who already has an egocentric view of his world. If learning is to take place in the often confusing circumstances of childhood, then the purpose of teaching is precisely to exploit such circumstances, not to limit them.

Briefly stated, the process of cognitive development in logico-mathematical knowledge is a gradual structuring from inside the child rather than a generalization from repeated external events. Dr. C. Kamii from the Ypsilanti Public Schools makes the point relative to her experience in teaching, following Piaget's model, that if we really want children to learn it is the *process* of interacting with the environment which must be emphasized rather than a specific response already decided upon by the teacher. This idea of process is never considered in Jensen's approach to the problem, either in his theoretical position or in his pedagogical evaluation. In Piaget's conception of process, the idea of emphasizing logical conflicts is naturally involved. Jensen's view of process excludes it.

A primary role of the teacher is to be able to follow the process and to provide creative conflicts at appropriate moments. In the long run, the imposition of rules is a less efficient way to teach than influencing the development of underlying cognitive processes that will eventually enable the child to construct his own rules, which will square with physical reality. Thus, teaching must provide methods whereby the child can make his own discoveries. As stated by the Harvard psychologist, Dr. Lawrence Kohlberg, the cognitive developmental view of teaching aims at building broad, irreversible structures rather than the achievement of immediate gains which may be short-term. Immediate gains, and very specific abilities, measured through IQ increments seem to be the only concern of Jensen. But as Piaget states: "The goal in education is not to increase the amount of knowledge, but to create possibilities for a child to invent and discover. . . . When we teach too fast, we keep the child from inventing and discovering himself. Teaching means creating situations where structures can be discovered; it does not mean transmitting structures which may be assimilated at nothing other than a verbal level."

The whole creative aspect of learning and teaching is completely lost in Jensen's point of view. The child is reduced to a ratio. The teaching act becomes a mechanical adjustment of narrowly identified capacities to severely limited learning goals. Education must be more generous than this.

Arthur Jensen and His Critics
The Great IQ Controversy

by *Thomas Sowell*

Professor Arthur R. Jensen is easily the most controversial intellectual figure of our time, perhaps the most controversial intellectual since such nineteenth-century giants as Darwin and Marx. His notoriety erupted three years ago with the publication of an article with the innocuous title "How Much Can We Boost IQ and Scholastic Achievement?" Whatever the scientific merits of that article, it immediately became a classic by the cynical definition "a work that everyone talks about and no one reads." Jensen's new book, *Genetics and Education,*

CHANGE, May 1973, pp. 33-37.

reprints this and other writings on the general theme of hereditary and environmental influences on mental ability, including in particular the question of racial differences in mental ability. The appearance of this book is an appropriate time to reconsider Professor Jensen's work and the critical literature it has provoked.

Those familiar with Jensen's ideas only through the popular press—that is, those unfamiliar with Jensen's ideas—will find this book a valuable initiation into the complex analysis and issues behind the headlines and the furor. Those already familiar with Jensen's work will find little that is new, except for an account of the harassment he has endured since becoming a controversial figure and an elaboration of his views on the sociopolitical implications of his findings. For example, Jensen argues again and again, as he did in his original article, that the educational deficiencies of black children are the fault of the school system and that most black students are perfectly capable of mastering the material in which they are behind their grade levels. Obviously, these are not the conclusions seized upon by the press, and they have been lost in the shuffle of polemics that followed the initial publicity.

Those who expect to find in this book anything like the fireworks that characterize the Jensen controversy as it appears in the media will be disappointed. Instead there is the dry, methodical prose of a learned journal, and the only excitement is the intellectual fascination of seeing a complex subject dissected and an intricate analysis put together piece by piece. Even for one who disagrees, as I do, with the main conclusions of the analysis, it is a thoroughly professional job and clearly a contribution to an evolving understanding of mental tests and mental abilities. It will not be the first time that the development of a whole field has been advanced by the work of someone whose own theories ultimately proved to be wrong.

Jensen's theories are popularly associated with race, but they touch an even rawer nerve. His more fundamental emphasis is on the general role of heredity in mental abilities, which runs counter to a central assumption of the prevailing social philosophy of Western intellectuals for at least the past two centuries. No one today quite expresses Locke's naive faith that each person enters the world as a blank page on which society writes what it will, but that unexpressed assumption is still deeply imbedded in the opinions, emotions and policies of a broad spectrum of Western intellectuals and the Western public generally. Jensen's work undermines the whole structure of beliefs based on that fundamental assumption.

In the area of race and racism, Jensen's impact may be much less than some people assume. In 1961, before Jensen had ever been heard of, James B. Conant noted in his book *Slums and Suburbs* that public school officials in the North as well as the South generally assumed that black children's intelligence was inherently inferior to that of white children. This may shock white liberals, but it should come as no surprise to any black adult whose education was in the hands of whites. The pervasive egalitarianism in the sociological and psychological literature merely indicates the remoteness of intellectual fashions from popular beliefs. In neither case was there anything resembling scientific proof, nor is there today.

The attempt by liberal intellectuals to make racial equality a fact by fiat only set the stage for Jensen's demolition of their position, which is not to be confused with establishing his own conclusions. Indeed, Jensen himself at various places in his writings acknowledges that none of the evidence on either side of this debate is conclusive, though he obviously prefers his own interpretation of the balance of evidence at this point. Jensen's research and analysis contains some of the best evidence *against* his theories. This is a sad commentary on his critics, who have been moralizing or pettifogging instead of confronting Jensen with their own research and alternative analytical models. My suspicion is that some of those who yell loudest against Jensen feel more certain than he that the evidence is all on his side.

Ironically, Jensen's first attraction into the field of mental testing was through one of his students, who observed that low-IQ disadvantaged children seem more intelligent than low-IQ middle-class children. Jensen observed the children for himself, confirmed the student's impression and then devised direct tasks for the children to perform—on which the low-IQ disadvantaged children did better than low-IQ middle-class children. His initial conclusion was that this merely demonstrated the cultural bias of the IQ test, and he thought that the tasks he had devised might constitute a culture-free test. Further and more involved research with a wide variety of tests led him to modify this position. From the contrasting patterns of score distributions on different kinds of tests, Jensen concluded that some kinds of mental abilities are equally distributed among various social groups and other kinds are not.

Still another aspect of disadvantaged students' performances was brought out by Jensen's early research. He retested some low-scoring children from a low socioeconomic background after allowing them several days to become acquainted with him in a play situation, without actually teaching them anything. A rise of eight to ten points in the IQ's of these children was "the rule" according to Jensen, and in fact it "rarely failed." Since the total difference between black and white IQ's is fifteen points, we are talking about the disappearance of from one half to two thirds of that difference by purely psychological means. Jensen did not make that point, but surely some of his critics should have. This evidence has further implications for various "innovative" programs that claim to have "worked" educationally, when in fact they may simply have created a psychological atmosphere in which the students' existing knowledge was better reflected on test scores.

Two separate aspects of the Jensen controversy are often lumped together: the general question of the relationship between heredity and environment, and the specific question of whether black-white differences reflect hereditary or environmental differences. In neither case is it really heredity versus environment, as both Jensen and his more sophisticated critics acknowledge. Heredity and environment each obviously influences "intelligence" (however defined); the unknown to be determined is their respective contributions. Existing evidence indicates that even their relative weights are not fixed. With a sufficiently deprived environment, no hereditary potential can develop into actual ability, and with a sufficiently severe congenital defect, no environment can create mental competence. Since either heredity or environment can have a zero effect in extreme cases and each has some effect in normal cases, the question is really one of estimating their changing weights for different combinations of heredity and environment.

In this context, it is quite conceivable that heredity may explain more of the variation in IQ's (or similar indicators) among the general population, within the usual range of environmental variations, and yet not explain variations where the differences in environment are as extreme as the social difference between being black and white in American society. Attempts have been made to correct for this by comparing blacks and whites of the same income, occupation or educational level. Such studies show that the black-white IQ difference narrows as the other factors are controlled, but that it does not disappear. However, being black in white America is something more than making a few thousand dollars less or averaging fewer years in school.

Some of Jensen's strongest evidence on the role of heredity consists of studies of siblings separated in infancy and reared in different homes. The IQ's of such children correlate much more highly with the IQ's of their biological parents than with the IQ's of the people who raised them, and correlate much more highly with the IQ's of their biological siblings than with the IQ's of the children among whom they are raised. This is clearly a weighty argument for the role of heredity in explaining individual differences, but it is far less convincing as an explanation of group differences where environmental variations between groups are more extreme. How many adopted siblings are likely to be raised in environments as different as the social difference between being black and white? Even among identical twins reared separately, 10 percent had IQ differences equal to or greater than the differences between black and white IQ's, so clearly nonhereditary differences can make a large difference in IQ's.

Another piece of evidence never satisfactorily dealt with by Jensen is the great disparity between males and females among high-IQ black children. In the general population, the sexes are about equally represented among high-IQ individuals, with a slight edge for males. By contrast, various studies of high-

IQ black children show the females outnumbering the males by ratios of from 2.7 to 1 to 5.5 to 1. Since black males and females have the same genetic background, there is clearly some major unexplained influence here. Jensen says that this is a result of black females having a slightly higher mean IQ and both sexes having a normal distribution about their respective means. But this is little more than rephrasing our ignorance and adding a second unexplained phenomenon. Those who support the female-dominance theory of Negro culture have an obvious environmental explanation.

However, there is also an explanation which does not depend upon peculiarities of the black culture and which would simultaneously explain female preponderance among high-IQ black children and the lower black IQ in general. A large volume of research has established a greater female resistance to environmental influences among all races and classes, and indeed in other mammalian species. If the lower black IQ is a result of unfavorable environment, it would be expected to have less of an impact on females. If this is in fact the case, then other severely disadvantaged groups (present or past) would be expected to have similar sex imbalances among high-IQ children. Although most European-immigrant groups arrived long before IQ tests were widely given, preliminary results from early IQ data on late-arriving immigrant children suggest that they may have had a similar pattern.

An example from outside the racial area may illustrate how far we still are from definitive conceptions—much less conclusions—in the heredity-environment controversy. Many studies down through the years have shown that firstborn children are overrepresented among high-IQ students and among a wide variety of both intellectual and career high achievers. Recent studies of National Merit Scholarship finalists show that among two-child through five-child families, more than half of the finalists in each family-size category were the firstborn. Among five-child families, the firstborn constitute 52 percent of the finalists while the fifth-born constitute 6 percent. This 52-to-6 disparity, dwarfing even racial disparities, occurs among children whose heredity and environment are the same, as these are conventionally defined! The point here is that our conventional definitions must obviously miss something crucial, for heredity and environment conceptually exhaust all possible explanations. We recognize of course—in an ad hoc sort of way—that these siblings do not have literally identical heredities or environments, but for research purposes they are at least as similar as the heredities and environment that are statistically "controlled" in most large-scale studies. It might well be, for example, that the environment we need to think about is the psychological environment, hard as that is to research compared to parental income, pupil-teacher ratios, and the like.

The one conclusion that is virtually inescapable from Jensen's *Genetics and Education* is that the whole area of heredity, environment and testing is an almost bottomless pit of complexities. It cannot be reduced to the level of Archie Bunker, who could never make it through one paragraph of Jensen's analysis. Too many of Jensen's critics have tried to reduce the argument to precisely this level, claiming that Jensen "really" set out to promote racism disguised as research, as a means of halting recent black advances and/or justifying the failure of the public school system to educate black children. Crude as it may seem, I recently heard it stated just this baldly by a psychologist whose name would be familiar to any reader of this magazine.

I do not know what is "really" in Jensen's heart of hearts, nor do his critics, and if Jensen himself knows he is more fortunate than most men. What is clear is that the issues raised are important, the complex evidence requires close reasoning and the unresolved problems are enormous. Moreover, the social-policy conclusions that critics assume to follow from Jensen's analysis are not logically entailed by that analysis, nor are they the conclusions that Jensen himself actually derives.

Jensen argues that what we lump together under the general label of "intelligence" is a collection of very different kinds of specific mental abilities, some of which have little or no relationship to others, either structurally or in terms of how they are distributed through the population. He points out that races and social classes differ greatly in their

96

performances on some kinds of mental tests and hardly at all on others. He postulates that one kind of ability — common sense, for lack of a better word — is equally distributed among races and classes. Another kind of reasoning — the manipulation of abstractions — differs greatly among social groups, according to Jensen. The practical educational and social problem is that schools teach through methods which require the second kind of ability, when the same material could be effectively taught to children who have predominantly the first type. The result, according to Jensen, is that many disadvantaged children in high school still lack "basic skills which they could easily have learned years earlier." Repeatedly and insistently, Jensen has argued for a drastic revision of teaching methods. Nowhere has he argued for writing off black children as unteachable. The title of Jensen's controversial article — "How Much Can We Boost IQ and Scholastic Achievement?" — was very significant. His conclusion was that we could boost IQ very little but could boost scholastic achievement a lot.

Whether Jensen is right or wrong about the genetic basis of differences in abstract reasoning, it is an undeniable social fact that children from different backgrounds differ greatly in their facility in handling abstractions. Others explain this by the cultural emphasis of lower-class people (white or black) on immediacy and concreteness, which makes it difficult for the child from such a background to orient himself toward abstractions, much less develop any facility in handling them. This is a fascinating intellectual question, but as a practical social matter Jensen's conclusions are almost indistinguishable from those of many liberal and radical critics of the existing educational system. Indeed some black "militant" teaching programs rely on a nonabstract approach similar to what Jensen advocates.

The fact that Jensen agrees in important ways with the liberals does not, of course, make either of them right. Blacks have long been overrepresented in the abstract field of music and underrepresented in the concrete field of construction work. Jazz music in particular involves the manipulation and transformation of abstract forms. It is ironic that the Negro's main contribution to American culture so closely follows Jensen's definition of the kind of ability in which he is supposed to be deficient. The same is true of the second most notable area of black impact on American culture, the manipulation and transformation of language. Moreover, while blacks are underrepresented in high-level jobs requiring a mastery of abstractions, it is precisely in these areas that they are now making their most rapid advance, while the painful social problems of blacks revolve around getting and keeping jobs of a sort that requires no abstraction.

The great unspoken assumption in the heredity-environment controversy is that if differences between races or classes are genetic, they are less changeable than if they are environmental. Axiomatic as this may seem, the empirical fact is that plant and animal breeders were routinely making substantial biological transformations even before Darwin, and multibillion-dollar environmental social programs have made pathetically few changes in our own time. As long as one generation raises the next, it is hard to see how centralized social engineering can help being as ineffective as an increasing number of studies demonstrate that it is. What progress has occurred has not been a result of raising IQ's or other such indicators but of breaking open employment opportunities.

Jensen's critics have centered their fire on the validity of the IQ test itself, with its demonstrable cultural biases—questions such as "Who wrote *Faust*?"—and have claimed that such tests do not show black children's real ability or predict their academic performance. This criticism has been deliberately left for last because most of the issues do not depend upon these arguments, and because these apparently strong criticisms turn out to miss the point of Jensen's analysis and of the role of testing in general.

Any reasonable person must acknowledge that IQ tests have some culturally biased questions. Jensen acknowledges this several times in *Genetics and Education*. His key argument, however, is that it is precisely in the obviously culturally biased tests that disadvantaged children come closest to middle-class children, and as the tests become more abstract and "culture-free" in content the disadvantaged children's performances fall further behind. In short, Jensen uses the cultural bias of tests—in particular, *differential* cultural bias—as one of his strongest arguments. An environmentalist interpretation of the same facts would be that interest and practice in dealing with intellectual abstractions is one of the most valuable advantages a middle-class child acquires in his home. As the tests move more toward the abstract end of the spectrum, the middle-class child's advantage becomes even greater than when it took the more obvious but less decisive form of better knowledge of certain information. But note that now we are talking about class bias in a different sense than before—namely, in the more accurate reflection of a real difference (even if environmentally determined), rather than in the misrepresentation of actual mental capability. As someone has said, tests are not unfair; life is unfair, and tests measure the results. To construct a culture-free test on which disadvantaged children would score equally well with others would be a romantic deception. One might as well construct a culture-free philosophy in which a starving family in their shack were told that they were really just as well off as a rich family in their mansion. Yet to do one of these things is regarded as liberal, while to do the other is considered conservative, if not reactionary. In either case it is dishonest and ultimately counterproductive.

Because culturally biased tests understate, to some extent, the existing mental capabilities of various disadvantaged groups—as Jensen's own research indicates—many people have concluded that they underpredict their academic performance. This crucial assumption underlies many "special" programs for disadvantaged students, but it is logically a non sequitur and empirically just plain wrong. Low-IQ disadvantaged children outperformed low-IQ middle-class children on tasks that Jensen gave both to perform immediately. But a college education is not a task to be performed immediately on a given occasion. It is years of disciplined application, drawing not only on knowledge and skills acquired earlier but, perhaps even more, on study habits and attitudes built up over a long period. Empirical studies have repeatedly shown that standard test scores predict the academic performances of disadvantaged students just as well as they predict the academic performances of middle-class students. Where there is a bias in prediction, it is, empirically, that disadvantaged students as a group perform slightly less well than their scores would have indicated. By contrast with these empirical studies, there are all sorts of inspirational stories about selected individuals that many college administrators have at their fingertips. But to get access to hard raw data from these same administrators is about as easy as getting membership lists from the Mafia.

It is easy enough to criticize IQ, college entrance examinations and other such tests, and to show that they need much improvement. But the practical question at any given point in time is, what are the alternatives? Other selection devices and criteria have ranged from ineffective to disastrous. Moreover, it is precisely the black students who need IQ tests most of all, for it is precisely with black students that alternative methods of spotting intellectual ability have failed. Dr. Martin Jenkins, who has conducted more studies of high-IQ black children than anyone else, has commented on how frequently even children with IQ's of 150 have not been spotted as outstanding by their teachers. My experiences confirm this. A vivid example is a black mother in Los Angeles who asked a teacher if her child had any special ability, and was told: "Mrs. B., David is just average. He never will be anything more than average." Later, when David was tested, his IQ was 155. I have even more painful memories from my own childhood in Harlem, when I was assigned to a class for backward children, and then—a year later, after taking IQ and other tests—was assigned to a class for advanced children. Anyone familiar with the pathetically inadequate counseling available in most ghetto schools will know that the subjective judgments of the staff are not to be relied on. Here and there, certainly, one finds isolated individuals whose sensitivity and experience enable them to make shrewd assessments of children, but a system of selection cannot depend on such rare persons turning up when needed.

One tragic consequence of the controversy surrounding Jensen has been an anti-IQ feeling among blacks that has even led to the complete banning of IQ tests in New York City and elsewhere. The main beneficiaries of this policy are the school administrators and the main losers the black children.

GOODBYE IQ, HELLO EI (ERTL INDEX)

The national discontent with current modes of intelligence testing has recently culminated in several court decisions and legislative actions banning group tests in factories and in the public schools of certain cities and the state of California. More such decisions are expected. Thus the question of what will replace IQ tests is more vital than ever. John Ertl of the University of Ottawa, inventor of the neural efficiency analyzer, believes he has found a solution to at least some of the problems of testing. He doesn't claim to have a panacea, but perhaps it's a start. A *Kappan* interviewer (William Tracy) talked with Ertl recently in Ottawa about his invention.

KAPPAN: When and how did the concept of a neural efficiency analyzer occur to you?

ERTL: Newspaper reports, which tend to be sensational, happen to be true in this case. In late 1959 I took an "intelligence" test as part of my graduate training in psychology. I scored the equivalent of an IQ of 77. I found this hard to believe. This experience was really my main motivation to find a better, more objective solution to the problem of measuring human intelligence, which at that time I thought — and I still think — is to be found in the electrical activities of the brain.

KAPPAN: How long did it take to perfect the neural efficiency analyzer after the initial concept was formed?

ERTL: The conceptual work was done quite early, in 1961 and 1962. Since then it has been mainly a problem of obtaining sufficient financing to test a large sample of the population. In addition to that, the original concept was one thing; but the development of a usable piece of hardware required two additional inventions following the original one. All of these were unfortunately quite expensive, and the funds were simply not available to do it until lately.

KAPPAN: How many people have been involved with you in developing the machine?

ERTL: All the conceptual work I did myself. On the practical end I have worked with several engineers, in particular Clyde Lee, chief engineer for Associates International.

KAPPAN: Exactly what does the neural efficiency analyzer measure, and how is this measurement related to intelligence?

ERTL: It measures the efficiency and the speed with which information is transmitted from one neuron to another in the brain. This measurement is only peripherally related to intelligence as defined as a score on an IQ test. Our main validation criteria are measures

PHI DELTA KAPPAN, Oct. 1972, vol. 54, pp. 89-94.

outside IQ testing and psychological testing. They are based on the fact that chemical substances known to reduce mental acuity such as thyroid hormone deficiency, alcohol, and a number of drugs all reduce the neural efficiency score obtained on my machine. When these chemical depressants are removed, or the thyroid deficiency is supplemented by hormone injections, the neural efficiency scores become much higher or return to normal. So the criteria I am using for test validity are medically based rather than related to psychological test scores.

KAPPAN: The analyzer measures speed of information transmission, but at this point you have not perfected a way of using it to measure mental power?

ERTL: No. Let me define what I mean by speed, power, and creativity. A person with a high speed factor is the person who is extremely verbally glib, although his thinking processes may be rather shallow. This person would score rather well on the conventional IQ test. A person with a high power factor might take a longer time to assimilate information presented to him, but in the end would likely produce a deep and powerful solution to the problem. Most people have both of these factors in their intellectual makeup to a varying degree, and added to these, some fortunate people also have the factor of creativity. Creativity from a neuro-physiological point of view represents what I call "noise" in the brain, or, put another way, it represents the random interconnections that may occur in response to external stimuli.

KAPPAN: What do you think the most successful uses of the neural efficiency analyzer will be? As you have explained elsewhere, early diagnosis of dyslexia and other kinds of learning disabilities will certainly be an immediate benefit.

ERTL: I think the most useful applica-

tion will be in programs such as Head Start, and in the economical selection of people on whom public funds should be

---

Who Is John Ertl?

John Ertl was born in Budapest, Hungary, but attended secondary school in England and took the B.A. at Carleton University in Canada. He received his doctorate in psychology at the University of Ottawa, where he is now assistant professor of psychology and director of the Center for Cybernetic Studies. The author of numerous articles on intelligence and electrical activity of the brain, he is in demand as a consultant for foundation and government projects. He assisted Phi Delta Kappa's Research Division in developing a 5-year plan for reading research under a U.S. Office of Education contract. Ertl is a member of the Board of Directors of Associates International, the Louisiana-based firm which produces and markets the neural efficiency analyzer.

---

expended to improve their educational level. Perhaps most important, it should permanently dispel the myth of racial inequality in the U.S. I think this will be its major contribution.

KAPPAN: What are your views on the limitations of heredity on intelligence? You say you agree with the 80% heredity, 20% environment theory espoused by William Shockley and Arthur Jensen, among others.

ERTL: Yes, I agree with Shockley and Jensen with respect to the proportions hereditary and environmental factors contribute to the development of intelligence. This does not mean that I agree with their conclusions with respect to racial differences. Mr. Shockley presents a very interesting picture of the high correlation of IQ test scores of monozygotic twins reared apart. I could present an identical graph of the brain-wave activity of monozygotic twins, showing that the brain-wave activity of such twins is consistently more similar than that of the same subject tested twice. There's a very high degree of relationship between parameters of the brain-waves of twins.

Why is it that no tests, including those done by a South African neurophysiologist, have ever shown that there are any brain-wave differences between races? I believe that the existing techniques are sufficiently sensitive to pick up such differences if they are there. They are not there, and the tests of numerous investigators, including the South Africans, show no differences that I know of in the electrical activity in the brains of Negroes, Caucasians, Orientals, and other racial groups. Yet the hereditary component of brain-wave similarities is as strong as the one Mr. Shockley has demonstrated. He ignores scientific facts which do not agree with his theory, and one of them is that no one has ever found any differences in the brain waves of different races; yet the brain-wave activities of identical twins are almost identical, just as their IQ scores are almost identical. Therefore you would expect racial differences in brain-wave parameters (to agree with IQ score differences), but there aren't any. This is a fact that he is now faced with and that he must explain.

KAPPAN: Your reference to tests by the South African neurophysiologist implies that you think that if anyone would go all out to find these differences, he would have. Yet he too failed.

ERTL: Although the 80:20 heredity/ environment ratio has been successfully demonstrated — at least to my mind, and I am not a geneticist — what has not been successfully demonstrated is the effect of this supposedly small percentage over a number of generations. There's no question that the IQ test scores of the Negro population in America are lower than the IQ test scores of the white population. And I emphasize that I said IQ test scores. That does not mean that Negro intelligence is lower; it just means that IQ test scores are lower. No one knows what intelligence is. I certainly don't know what it is. But I do know one thing it's not: It's not a score on an IQ test devised for a white Anglo-Saxon population.

I have no quarrel with Shockley's statistical arguments, most of which are very sound indeed, at least as far as they refer to the genetic component. But it seems to me that the environmental component, although small, when accumulated over a number of generations, in terms of cultural, educational, and dietary insufficiencies, does result in a race of people who through no fault of their own have been reduced in their intellectual capacity, at least as far as IQ tests are concerned.

Furthermore, it seems to me that it should be a frightening thing to Caucasians that in the past few generations the measured intelligence of the Negro population in the U.S. has risen extremely rapidly — much more rapidly than that of the white population, if it has risen at all after 3,000 years of a high level of civilization to which Negroes have been exposed for only 50 to 100 years. In that short period of time they have managed to come, as the literature indicates, within 15 points of the average of the white population. I see no reason why this gap cannot be closed within the next few generations, provided that we expose them to the same environment and cultural heritage that we have had.

KAPPAN: We might add that in this quick rise blacks have been at the added disadvantage of having to play by white rules and be measured by white instruments. Earlier you said that Shockley's statistics were fine, but his basic assumptions were at fault, making the mathematics deceptive.

ERTL: Yes. He assumes that the tests measure intelligence and they don't. They measure an abstract concept of intelligence, and the concept is based on what the Anglo-Saxon culture requires for success. This is not a definition of intelligence. I don't know any more about intelligence than anybody else does, other than to say that it is a subject that is wide open for research. We do not know what the factors of intelligence really are or which ones are important for survival; it may not be the ability to get a B.A. degree from a university.

KAPPAN: So perhaps the IQ test should be called the Success Quotient instead of Intelligence Quotient?

ERTL: That's a very good name for it. It's circular reasoning. To a great extent, IQ tests measure academic achievement; no IQ test could ever be sold that didn't correlate highly with academic achievement.

KAPPAN: Are you saying that no school is going to give a test that shows it's not doing a good job?

ERTL: That's right. The way I hope my test will be used is in selecting people for improved educational opportunities based on this test rather than on tests which are known to be invalid in the case of the culturally deprived population. The whole system of IQ testing makes absolutely no practical sense. It is a well-known fact that current IQ tests have the highest correlation with academic achievement in the previous year.

So I don't see why the government is spending 10 dollars per year per child to measure IQ, when the best test we already have is the past year's academic achievement. Sixty-eight percent of the population has an "average" IQ, and nothing has to be done about it in any case. There's a small percentage, something on the order of 15%, certainly less than 20%, where there is a problem with ability to learn, and it's these people that my machine is specifically designed to assist. The probable reason they're classified as slow learners is that they have a poor socioeconomic background or some language, perceptual, or emotional problem, which certainly has nothing to do with intelligence but has everything to do with IQ test performance. This inability will not reflect itself on the neural efficiency analyzer because the brains of these people are in perfectly good working condition. There's something else wrong with them, and it's important for the psychologist and the school guidance counselor to know this.

KAPPAN: In the time that the machine has been in use so far you have reported several cases of finding children with high potential who have been placed in slow groups for one reason or another. When they were put into the faster groups they were able to adapt very quickly. Have you been able to test this on a widespread basis?

ERTL: No, the machine has not yet been widely used. In the testing we have done, a small but nevertheless important number of children — important especially to the parents — have been misclassified. We have found that those mistakenly placed in slow groups adapt extremely well to the regular classroom.

KAPPAN: What kind of long-term records are you keeping on this sort of test results?

ERTL: I'm afraid that we cannot af-

How Does the Neural Efficiency Analyzer Work?

ERTL: Basically, the test consists of applying electrodes – small silver discs – to the scalp with conductive jelly. There's no pain, of course, and nothing is put into or taken out of the brain. The electrical amplitude of the evoked response is very weak, less than 1/1,000,000 of a volt, and is usually drowned out in the brain's ongoing activity, which is from 5 to 20 times more powerful. The amplifier which enlarges these very minute signals so we can measure them is battery operated; there is no electrical hazard to the subject.

An interesting feature of the neural efficiency analyzer system is that the brain waves themselves control the moment at which the first light will be flashed. This is done by a closed-loop feedback system to ensure that each subject starts the test at the same point in brain-wave phase, avoiding inaccuracies. Exactly 100 flashes of light are delivered by the computer at random intervals, with an average time of one second between flashes. The brain waves are amplified and displayed simultaneously on a monitor oscilloscope. At the same time, the data are fed into the computer, which computes the average time between specific parameters of the evoked response. Thus the test is completed in about 100 seconds and two 3-digit numbers appear on the analyzer screen. Both of these numbers are entered on a table or nomogram, which first gives the neural efficiency score and then predicts what the subject would score on an IQ test if the test were valid.

At the moment, we can't get away from relating to the IQ test system, which has been established for 60 or 70 years. This IQ score is simply our best estimate of what the subject would score on an ideal IQ test. Analyzer test-retest scores over a short period of time are very accurate; over a longer period they are less accurate, but they are still much better than test-retest scores on an IQ test. In my experience with several thousand children's IQ tests, there were differences of as much as 40 points for the same child tested with three different tests, and the tests were given days, not years, apart. I found such discrepancies for perhaps 2 or 3% of the children taking IQ tests.

KAPPAN: With what tests do you generally correlate your scores?

ERTL: Currently, the most popular IQ tests are the Wechsler Intelligence Scale for Children (WISC), the Primary Mental Abilities Test (PMA), and the Otis. We have used these three for our standardization sample.

KAPPAN: The SAT is pretty much a test of achievement, so you wouldn't use that, would you?

ERTL: I don't mind using *any* test, as long as final evaluation is based on which test can predict *future* achievement better. There has been no study on this yet. Unfortunately, it takes time.

KAPPAN: How long does it take to train a person to operate your machine and interpret the scores?

ERTL: It takes no time at all to interpret the scores, because the desired numbers appear on the machine. Machine operation consists of pushing one knob to start the test. This is the total mechanical manipulation required. Brief training, 20 or 25 minutes, is needed to recognize a good EEG, an EEG with the electrodes properly in contact with the head. The subject must not move about. He must be seated in a reasonably relaxed situation. A small monitor oscilloscope is part of the analyzer, to let you view the subject's brain-waves. The training manual provides graphic illustrations of artifacts such as excessive muscle tension or eye blinks or interference from the lights. All of these must be recognized and corrected. Correction is quite easy in most cases. The machine will simply not operate unless conditions are perfect for testing.

ford to keep extensive records at this point. I have followed up seven children that I tested in a large school system in Canada who were misclassified and who were, on my recommendation, put in a regular class. All of these seven in the last two years appear to have done well. That's the only factual information I have on this.

KAPPAN: Is it common to find children seriously misclassified at a particular age?

ERTL: The validity of IQ tests in general tends to be very poor as you go down the scale of age; the younger the child, the less their reliability and predictive ability. So the misclassification would tend to be early rather than late.

KAPPAN: Perhaps this is partially because of the lack of motivation for a very young child to attempt to achieve on the test or to care what marks he gets.

ERTL: Yes, and because of the lack of reliability of the tests themselves. Most of the children who are misclassified in Canada are recent immigrant children who can't speak English, but who are nevertheless given English-language IQ tests. Other children are misclassified because of emotional or other perceptual difficulties which have nothing to do with intelligence. These are the most common kinds of misclassification in Canada. In the States, of course, misclassification based on race and other types of cultural deprivation would be very common.

KAPPAN: So you would say that most of the misclassified children you found were from immigrant or culturally disadvantaged groups?

ERTL: As a matter of fact, the seven I have followed up were not. Mostly, they were simply poorly diagnosed psychologically. One of them was almost totally blind. The others had problems at home. But I am saying that in general

the tendency for misclassification in IQ testing occurs at an early age with people of poor language ability. Or it results from any of the myriad of cultural factors that are known to affect IQ tests.

KAPPAN: Have scores from the neural efficiency analyzer been correlated with IQ scores at various age levels?

ERTL: They have, but our data are still not statistically adequate in that area. It appears, based not so much on my work as on other people's, that full development is reached around the age of 5 or 6 years and after that there is very little change. I have not been able to find any change in the neural efficiency score between the ages of 8 and 14.

KAPPAN: Have you been testing infants and following them up as they develop to 5 years and achieve a mature evoked response?

ERTL: I haven't, but Professor Rudolph Engel, of the University of Oregon Medical School at Portland, has done this from the day of birth and has followed his subjects for two years now. He concurs with my findings that the best at-birth predictor of future IQ existing at this time is the neural efficiency score. There are no IQ tests for newborn infants, as you know. All of this research is based on motor development as a form of IQ test.

KAPPAN: Does he intend to keep on testing the same children for a much longer period of time?

ERTL: Yes, he has already followed them for a considerable period of time and has found that they in fact reach a mature evoked response at around age 2. Some others say that this development continues up to age 5. Others even say it continues up to puberty. This question is not yet totally resolved.

KAPPAN: IQ tests are generally engineered for people up to the age of 18 or 20, but after that they're very unreliable. With your machine there's no age problem. An adult will score just as accurately on the test as a younger person?

ERTL: Yes, that's correct. But I don't want to underestimate developmental changes. They're extremely important, as has been shown, and in fact these are one of the main criteria of validation that I have outside of IQ tests. Both in man and in animals the evoked response changes from long to short as age increases up to a certain point, and if it didn't do that, I would have very little confidence in this measurement in the first place. It's just a question of when the development stops. It appears, at the moment, that this occurs around the age of 5, but this is by no means confirmed as yet.

KAPPAN: I imagine that correlations with standard IQ tests are better at the extremes than they are in the middle, since it's generally thought that IQ tests are too vague in the middle.

ERTL: I would tend to disagree with that one in particular: They *are* poor in the middle, good at the lower end and the middle high end, but they are very poor at the extreme high end.

KAPPAN: And your machine scores correlate better at the lower and middle high areas?

ERTL: Yes, the machine is uninfluenced by problems that IQ tests have in the other areas.

KAPPAN: One way you can try to validate your scores, using what is basically a weak instrument to begin with, is to compare them with IQ scores of people who should be ideally matched to the test. Are there other techniques you can use?

ERTL: When I use that method of validating the scores, the correlations are rather good. When the validation is done against a random group of people with low, middle, high, and very high IQs, the correlations are not all that good, as you would expect. It is impossible to compare a physical measurement, such as a measurement of time, which this machine provides, with what is basically a rubber ruler. An IQ score of 100 could mean 110 or it could mean 90. A score on the neural efficiency analyzer is as precise as you wish to make it. Originally I started out taking people for whom I didn't need any IQ test to know that they were in the top 1% or better of the population. They happened to be colleagues and friends whose intellectual qualities I knew. I took their scores and I also took scores, for example, from a group of people who were unemployed and who had been sent for retraining because of insufficient education or achievement. I personally examined these people and was sure they were of lower intelligence than the group I had been dealing with. The results were extremely good in these cases.

KAPPAN: Do you think the Ertl Index, or whatever your score will be called, will become a household word and be as abused as "IQ" has been?

ERTL: I hope not. I don't believe in the morality of mass IQ testing, whether it's my method or any other method. I do, however, believe in individual testing in situations where it is needed. In these situations the neural efficiency score may be more valuable than the culturally loaded and culturally biased IQ testing we now have.

KAPPAN: There's a current movement in some states and school districts to ban conventional IQ testing. Do you think your machine might be banned, or will it perhaps become an alternative?

ERTL: A very interesting question. I've recently heard that the state of California has banned all group IQ tests. There was a lawsuit by a group of citizens representing the Spanish-speaking population, which is very large in California. They've succeeded in this lawsuit, which refers only to group-given IQ tests. There is presently a senate hearing committee on the subject and the Board of Education of the state of California, to the best of my knowledge, is putting forward the neural efficiency analyzer as an alternative to group IQ testing. It is a test which appears to be culture free and one that the people who opposed the use of IQ tests might accept. In New York City group IQ testing is banned, and I believe this trend is becoming fairly widespread.

KAPPAN: There's no reason this kind of action should be taken against your test, since it is culturally unbiased?

ERTL: I think we have shown that there are no racial differences based on this test. The experimental results are based on relatively small samples, but the early indications are that there are no racial differences at all and that the test is culture free.

KAPPAN: IQ tests are still used in many schools to place children in faster or slower reading groups and for similar purposes. Do you think your machine will have such practical applications?

ERTL: Our initial marketing attempt was to place the neural efficiency analyzer in the hands of professional people only, people who would use it in their own private clinical practice. Or, if requested by a school board to do large-scale testing, they would rent several of our machines and handle the whole thing, financial and otherwise, themselves. Our machine can easily test 50 subjects a day, theoretically 100 in a working day. We don't know what to do about a school board that requests mass testing. I would discourage it, because I don't believe in it. But if they want it there are two ways of going about it: They can rent enough of our analyzers

to do it at the rate they wish, or we can design a mobile unit, a small van or truck which could test maybe 10 people simultaneously with a small computer in the van. This kind of system could test thousands of subjects a day. There's no technical problem whatsoever. We could even do this on a telephone line.

KAPPAN: How will psychologists use the neural efficiency analyzer in their clinical practice?

ERTL: They will use it initially as a supplement to existing tests, especially when they are in doubt because of varying results on two or three different tests. They all have their subjective judgments of the mental level of the patient involved, and they would like to have them confirmed by some independent, objective means. This will be one way they will use it.

Psychologists also have great problems when a child has language disabilities, dyslexia, or comes from a poor socioeconomic background. They can't trust standard tests, because even the makers of the tests tell them the tests aren't valid when used on these subjects. Under these conditions they would probably use the neural efficiency analyzer, and also in cases of severe mental disturbance when tests cannot be given. The machine might be able to determine the degree of deterioration that has occurred. The test is very useful for drug studies. It is also useful for studies of patients who have had brain tumors and operations, to determine how much recovery of the neural efficiency function may or may not have occurred after surgery.

KAPPAN: Have you done considerable testing to determine the effect of drug use on test scores?

ERTL: I have done quite a bit on alcohol, and there's no question that it lowers the score. Fortunately, the next day the score returns to normal. I have tested most mild tranquilizers, anti-depressants, and up-pills – amphetamines and so on. I have not found any drug that improves the score – only drugs that make it worse. I must mention one case, however. My secretary improved her score by 20% by using the vitamin niacinamide. I don't know whether she suffers from some metabolic disorder, but I repeated the test at least 10 times and the results were the same each time. No one else that I have tested with niacinamide shows any change at all. I can't explain it yet.

KAPPAN: Who are some of the psychiatrists and psychologists who are using your test now?

ERTL: One of the main supporters of my point of view is a very distinguished researcher in the field, Dr. Enoch Calloway, director of research at the Langley Porter Institute in San Francisco. He has a Naval Research grant and is approaching the investigation from a substantially different point of view, but he believes he has validated my results. He's after more than just what my machine measures and is interested in several other aspects of intelligence.

KAPPAN: Calloway is looking for some way of really measuring overall intelligence?

ERTL: Yes. Other factors of intelligence that we cannot at this point measure with the neural efficiency analyzer. He is best known for his work on schizophrenia and the electrical activity of the brain. Another psychologist, Rudolph Engel, has done work with new-born babies and has followed them up over a period of years. R. E. Dustman and E. C. Beck have studied different parameters of electrical activity. I am studying time, and they are studying the amplitude or energy content of the brain. They have also found interesting results in terms of high and low IQ subjects. A pediatric neurologist,

Dr. Louis Jacobs of Chappaqua, New York, is using the neural efficiency analyzer. Another psychologist is John Rhodes of Albuquerque, New Mexico.

KAPPAN: Do you have detailed information and test data from the Albuquerque program, where 300 children were tested some time ago?

ERTL: Yes. In that particular sample, the mean IQ derived from a psychological test was 105, which is slightly above average. The subjects happened to be 80% or 90% Mexican-Indian children. Their mean neural efficiency score was almost the same as the score of a random sample of the Ottawa population that I have obtained. I obtained a correlation of .52, which is respectable, between scores on IQ tests given them by the school and the neural efficiency scores. I did not miss a single one of the high and low IQ subjects. On the average subjects, many misclassifications occurred: The scores would say the child was average and sometimes I would say high, sometimes slightly below average. There were no racial differences here, either on the psychological test or on my test. This was not a valid test of the racial hypothesis, because the children didn't even score badly on the IQ test, let alone on mine.

KAPPAN: How do you account for the high mean IQ in this group? Was it the fact that they were a homogeneous high socioeconomic group?

ERTL: Yes, I think that is what it was. My intention was not to test the racial hypothesis there in the first place. All the children in three schools took the test. They just happened to be in a relatively high socioeconomic section.

KAPPAN: Are there any other wide-scale testing programs in progress that will help you fill out your statistical data?

ERTL: We have a project cosponsored by the Canadian government in Honduras where 5,000 Spanish-speaking adults and young adults will be tested. First they will take a battery of psychological tests, whose scores will be compared with our measurements. The main purpose is this: The Honduras government cannot afford to make mistakes in saying, "I want this young man to be a bulldozer operator," and then spend X dollars on him and have him fail to work out. So they hired a psychological testing firm in Montreal to test and predict which would be worthwhile subjects for training in order to reduce their costs. This firm has signed a contract with Associates International to use our machine in their testing.

KAPPAN: Will the psychiatrists and psychologists who will be using the neural efficiency analyzer be following a definite program, or will they be working entirely on their own research?

ERTL: They will be following their separate researches, but we hope to get their evaluations and results when they are available to add to our own statistical data. We decided that in order to increase our data base we could do one of two things: Do it ourselves, on a large scale, or attempt to get controlled results back from customers who are using the machine. Cooperation has been very good so far.

KAPPAN: Is the test what you would call "totally objective"? Is there no way the subject can influence his score?

ERTL: It is totally objective. There are some things – blinking, moving around – which would result in giving the subject a poorer score than if he sat still and followed the instructions, which are very simple: Sit still, watch the flashing light, and try not to blink. That's basically it.

KAPPAN: Can the score be influenced by physical factors which influence standard tests? Factors like mood, poor eyesight, physical condition, or time of day?

ERTL: It cannot be influenced by the first two factors you mentioned. If a subject is totally blind, the test can be done with hearing or touch – even with smell. As I mentioned before, the intake of drugs strongly influences test results. I have not made a study of the time of day other than having retested several hundred subjects on two or three different occasions and found that their scores were highly similar to the test on the first occasion.

KAPPAN: So the same person will score about the same each time he takes the test. There is no wide variation, as there can be on IQ tests?

ERTL: The variation is very small, much smaller than on IQ tests. As I have noted, I have found subjects who when tested on two or three widely used standard tests showed a variation of up to 40 IQ points, placing them everywhere from retarded to well above average, depending on the test used.

KAPPAN: Can a person learn to respond and improve his score?

ERTL: There is a way, but I am not going to tell you what it is.

KAPPAN: Can a subject refuse to respond by, say, closing his eyes?

ERTL: Closing the eyes will not eliminate the response. Nothing short of removing the electrodes or jumping up and down would prevent getting a fairly accurate score.

KAPPAN: Do you think a totally automatic test like this has any 1984 negative connotations or possibilities with regard to mass testing and forced testing?

ERTL: Yes, it has terrible 1984 connotations. I am not clear in my own mind about the morality of the whole thing. The only thing I am sure of at the moment is that IQ tests have been misused absolutely disgracefully based on invalid testing in the first place. I feel that this test is better and that the potential for misuse is less than it is with IQ tests.

KAPPAN: Have you tested animals? Monkeys, horses, rats?

ERTL: I haven't, but other people have. It is difficult if not impossible to make any interspecies comparison. The rat's neural efficiency is much better numerically than the human's. Within rats you can distinguish the bright rats from the dull rats. A rat brain is much smaller than the human brain and therefore the information takes much less time to go from one place to the next. There isn't that much brain there in the first place. For that reason, among others, the rat IQ can't be compared to the human IQ.

KAPPAN: I imagine that your company in Louisiana, Associates International, plans to market the machine widely after testing. Are you marketing the machine now?

ERTL: The initial testing program is now complete and Associates International is in full production of the machine, with the first production run scheduled to be completed by the middle of October.

KAPPAN: Thank you, Mr. Ertl.

CLASSROOM AGGRESSION: DETERMINANTS, CONTROLLING MECHANISMS, AND GUIDELINES FOR THE IMPLEMENTATION OF A BEHAVIOR MODIFICATION PROGRAM[1]

GERALD R. ADAMS

Teachers frequently report that a pupil's conduct in the classroom seemingly influences the extent to which that pupil will learn. Consistently one hears such statements as . . . "he doesn't learn a thing in this class because he's too busy getting into trouble," or "the whole class is disrupted by his aggressive behavior." If such be the case, what can the teacher do to reduce the disruptive effects of classroom misconduct? Hopefully, two avenues are available to most teachers. Ideally, the teacher can turn to the school psychologist for consultation, whereupon the two educational specialists can work as a team to initiate structural change. However, it is well recognized that the school psychologist is not always as available as one would like, nor is he always sufficiently well trained to handle the complex problems that arise in various educational settings. Therefore, the teacher may need to turn to applied oriented reviews of psychological literature for possible answers.

This paper will concentrate on one principal disruptive behavior—aggression. First, an attempt will be made to examine some of the major determinants of aggression; second, some methods of effective control will be reviewed; third, guidelines for the implementation of a behavior modification program will be presented. It may be noted that by no means will this paper exhaust potential modifying procedures, rather it will concentrate on some of the simpler and more pragmatic techniques.

———
[1]Publication costs were supported by the University of Nebraska Senate Research Committee.

PSYCHOLOGY IN THE SCHOOLS, April 1973, pp. 155-168.

Frustration

Parke (1969) has suggested that the most influential statement of causation for aggression has hinged upon the now classic frustration-aggression hypothesis. This position originally assumed that the existence of frustration always led to some form of aggressive behavior (Dollard, Doob, Miller, Mowrer, & Sears, 1939). However, this dogmatic statement quickly was revised when Barker, Dembo, and Lewin (1941) demonstrated that some children regressed rather than aggressed when placed in frustrating situations. Hence, the new revision of the frustration-aggression hypothesis (Miller, 1941) stated that aggression is not the sole reaction to frustration, but that nevertheless the occurrence of aggression always is initiated by some form of frustration. Davitz (1952) substantiated the necessity for the new revision by demonstrating that aggression was the reaction to frustration only for those persons who held this reaction as a dominant response pattern and that reward training for constructive responding under a frustration condition could change this dominance of aggressive responding to a frustration-constructive response pattern.

Based upon such research (Barker, *et al.*, 1941; Davitz, 1952), some writers have concluded that aggression is the result of aggression training. To many, aggression is the product of previous learning experiences, with the exclusion of the possibility of an innate predisposition toward assertive behavior as suggested by a frustration-aggression hypothesis. Berkowitz (1965) recognizes the possibility of a coexistence between learning and instinct and therefore provides us with a second revision of the original version presented in 1939. Three alterations are proposed: the first component suggests that frustration results in an emotional response that initiates a readiness tendency toward aggressive reactions. Second, this readiness tendency will result in aggressive behavior only when appropriate cues are available. The appropriate cue property is based upon a mental connection or association between an object and some former determinant of aggression. Finally, Berkowitz (1965) concludes,

"Instead of postulating that all aggression 'presupposes the existence of frustration,' . . . suitable cues may lead to aggressive behavior by arousing previously learned but latent aggressiveness habits. Furthermore, these habits can probably be formed without the learner being frustrated. He can, for example, learn by observing the behavior of some aggressive model . . . [p. 308-309]."

Observation

Several laboratory experiments have found that observation of film-mediated aggression increases the aggressiveness of the viewers (Bandura, Ross, & Ross, 1963; Lovass, 1961; Mussen & Rutherford, 1961). Hicks (1965) has demonstrated that one-time exposures can have long-range effects up to 6 months. Furthermore, Adams and Hamm (1971) found that the observation of film-mediated aggression results in a generalization effect in which the viewer not only imitates the behaviors observed, but also produces a significant amount of nonobserved aggressive behavior. However, Feshbach and Singer (1970) have questioned these findings on the grounds that laboratory research is not always indicative of what is found in a natural viewing environment.

Reinforcement

The research literature repeatedly has verified that selective reinforcement for specific aggressive behaviors increases the occurrence of these behaviors (Bandura & Walters, 1959; Patterson, Littman, & Bricker, 1967; Walters & Brown, 1963). To use a Hullian framework (Bugelski, 1964) based on the concept referred to as the "habit-family hierarchy," it may be said that selective reinforcement of behavior that has a low probability of occurrence due to its historically low frequency of reinforcement will increase the probability of occurrence due to the rearrangement of the behavior's relative position in the hierarchy. That is to say, the occurrence of a behavior in a given situation is based upon the frequency of reinforcement that historically has occurred upon the emission of that behavior. Therefore, the importance of reinforcement cannot be minimized, as Feshbach and Feshbach (1971) state in a comprehensive review of children's aggression:

> "Selective reinforcement of aggressive behavior is a significant determinant of aggression, perhaps the most important single process influencing the acquisition and performance of an aggressive response . . . [p. 368]."

Both Feshbach and Feshbach (1971) and Patterson, *et al.* (1967) have emphasized the importance of the social and familial environment as reinforcing agents for aggressive behavior. The latter have assumed a position not dissimilar to that of Hull's habit-family hierarchy. These investigators treat aggressive behavior as a relatively rare, high-amplitude behavior that is only one of many subclasses of a broader heading referred to as assertive behavior. Furthermore, they contend that these assertive behaviors, of which aggression is a member, are acquired and maintained primarily through the reactions that occur in the social environment. The acquisition process is a function of two major factors. First, acquisition of assertive behaviors is dependent upon the social environment dispensing positive reinforcement for such behaviors; *i.e.*, by the use of social reinforcers, parents and peers shape the response repertoires of children to include high frequencies of assertive-aggressive behaviors; and second, frequent emotionally aversive encounters within the social environment result in the acquisition of assertive-aggressive behaviors. Hence, certain social stimuli are associated with various emotionally motivating states (hunger, fear, anger, deprivation, etc.) and thus through a conditioning process become eliciting stimuli for assertive-aggressive behavior. Furthermore, the termination of these aversive emotional states by the use of assertive-aggressive behaviors results in a reinforcing effect that strengthens the probability of their recurrence.

The Social Environment

Several investigators also have examined the social nature of the situation as a determinant of aggression. In an often-cited experiment, Bandura (1965) had children observe a film-mediated model perform some very unique physical and verbal aggressive behavior. Each child was placed in one of three experimental conditions: (1) the model was rewarded after aggression, (2) the model was punished after aggression, or (3) the model received no consequences after aggression. The children were tested for the amount of aggressive behavior that they imitated subsequent to their observation of the three experimental conditions. One of the major findings was that the amount of imitated aggression by the viewer was based in part on the social consequences received by the model for aggression. As was predicted, the model-rewarded group imitated more types of responses, followed by the no-consequence group and then the model-punished group.

Further research has analyzed the effects of permissiveness of adults toward aggressive behavior in a social situation. In general, it has been hypothesized that a permissive adult reduces the amount of anxiety felt from fear of punishment for aggression. However, Parke (1969) cites research literature that questions such an interpretation. He contends that

"Permissiveness represents more than mere neutralization of adult control; rather the nonreaction of the permissive adult in a situation where the child anticipates punishment may serve as a cue indicating tacit approval for aggressive play behavior. . . [p. 397]."

Thus, it might be suggested that in many cases adults unintentionally are providing social cues that serve as elicitors of aggressive behavior within the context of a normal social interaction with children.

The acquisition of aggression through interaction with peers also has been investigated. Patterson, et al. (1967) used a field observation technique to examine aggressive exchanges between nursery school children. Their main discovery was that the reaction of the victim to the aggressor was a major determinant of future aggression. When the victim reacted with submissive behaviors (crying, with-drawing, etc.) toward the aggressor, he served as a positive reinforcer for these assertive actions and increased the probability that this same action would be directed toward him at a later date. However, retaliatory counterattacks by the victim served as a negative reinforcer that decreased the occurrence of aggressive behavior toward the victim. Hence, the nature of the social interaction that occurs in the environment, be it consequences to the observed model, interaction between the adult and child, or peer reactions and/or nonreactions for aggression, is a sig-nificant determinant of aggressive-assertive behavior.

METHODS OF CONTROL

It is well recognized among progressive educators that theory plays an im-portant role in educational advancement. However, most remain pragmatists, not theoreticians. The consensus seems to be that one should employ that which is practical and useful and discard that which is not. This seems to be an admirable approach—retain that aspect of a method that attains the desired objective, cast aside all ineffective elements, and build further on that which is operationally sound. Perhaps then, the following mechanisms of control should be used. In attempting to apply these mechanisms to a particular classroom situation, try one method; if it fails, try another.

Stimulus Control.

Stimulus control is based on the assumption that behavior is lawful, *i.e.*, that there is a direct relationship between behavior and environmental cues. Thus, the more we know about the relevant stimuli that elicit aggression, the easier the task of manipulating and controlling such behavior.

If it is assumed that Berkowitz's assumptions as to the presence of latent aggressiveness are correct, one may contend that even though "readiness for aggression" exists due to some form of frustration, aggressive behavior will not occur until the appropriate cue is present. In most cases of classroom misconduct, close observation by the teacher will uncover certain situational factors that contain cue properties that stimulate aggression. Therefore the teacher can control certain forms of aggression by confining the student to activities and social situations that do not contain the aggression-eliciting cue properties.

Punishment

Perhaps the easiest method of control for the teacher to use is punishment. The question we must ask, however, is related to the effectiveness of such a procedure. Does the use of punishment control aggression immediately and, furthermore, inhibit its recurrence at a later date?

Holland and Skinner (1961) describe two forms of punishment based on the use of pleasant (positive) and aversive (negative) reinforcers. These writers conceptualize punishment as (1) withdrawal of pleasant reinforcers or (2) the presentation of an aversive stimuli. The emphasis of their definition centers around events that immediately follow a response. The authors clearly state the difference between punishment and reinforcement. Once again, punishment has occurred when a response has been followed by withdrawal of a pleasant reinforcer or the presentation of an aversive stimuli, while the presentation of a pleasant reinforcer after a response is reinforcement.

In a classic study, Hollenberg and Sperry (1951) examined the effects of punishment on inhibition of aggression. The experiment demonstrated that verbal punishment subsequent to aggression decreased that behavior, but only temporarily. This is a frequent finding. Azrin (1960) reports that punishment merely suppresses the undesired behavior and that the behavior recovers when punishment is discontinued. Not only does the behavior reoccur, but often at much higher frequencies than were observed prior to the initiation of punishment.

Then, too, Parke (1969) presents research literature that suggests that punishment for aggression in one situation actually may increase aggression in a milieu distinctly dissimilar to that in which punishment originally was received. Furthermore, correlational research by Sears, Maccoby, and Levin (1957) and Bandura and Walters (1959) reports that parental use of punishment is correlated positively with the frequency of aggressive behavior in children. Bandura and Walters (1963) contend that this phenomenon is due to the counter-effect of a child's observation of an aggressive model who is severely punitive and that this modeling effect counteracts or inhibits the effects of punishment.

In general, the evidence to date suggests that aversive punishment alone does not suppress behavior permanently unless severe intensities are used (Reese, 1966). However, punishment combined with other procedures has been found to be much more effective in terms of durational effect. One such technique can be found in the clinical literature. Lovaas, Schaeffer, and Simmons (1965) demonstrated that aversive punishment for self-stimulation and aggression can eliminate pathological behaviors in autistic children for as long as 9 months. In their experimental sessions the autistic children received a shock each time they engaged in self-stimulatory or tantrum behavior (punishment). This procedure terminated only when the child would approach the experimenter (escape-avoidance training). This combination of punishment and escape-avoidance training suppressed self-stimulation and aggression while it instated social behaviors for an extended period of time.

Perhaps the most easily applied method to control behavior is withdrawal of reinforcement or denial of the opportunity to acquire reinforcement. For example, Baer (1962) used a response-contingent withdrawal of reinforcement technique to control thumbsucking in preschoolers. An animated cartoon was used as the reinforcer. The children were allowed to watch the cartoon; however, each time a child put his thumb in his mouth the cartoon was turned off. This technique quickly decreased the amount of thumbsucking by these children.

The withdrawal of the S from a situation in which reinforcement normally occurs is referred to as "time out." Reese (1966) states that the child can be removed from the reinforcing situation in a number of ways: (a) remove the opportunity to respond (e.g., place the child in temporary isolation); (b) turn out the lights (this is frequently called "blackout"), or (c) introduce a stimulus that has been correlated with nonreinforcement (e.g., introduce an activity that does not allow reinforcement for aggression to occur, perhaps individual seat work). He cites an interesting experiment that compared the effectiveness of verbal reprimands and time-out procedures to control assertive-aggressive behaviors in delinquent boys (Tyler, 1965). Tyler found that misbehavior in a recreation area was controlled most effectively by time-out periods immediately after any undesirable behavior and that verbal reprimands were ineffective, which demonstrates that punishment can be effective when it is applied appropriately.

Resistance to Deviation

Furthermore, investigators have examined the function of punishment on the moral development of children and adolescents. Extensive research has been completed on resistance to deviation. Resistance to deviation typically is defined as the ability to withstand pressure or temptations to deviate from a set behavior standard in the absence of a social agent's surveillance, *i.e.*, parents, teachers, relatives, etc. Therefore, one has another body of literature to tap for effective methods to establish and maintain social conduct.

Research has tended to center on the importance of punishment as a determinant of resistance to deviation. Leading investigators in the area, such as Walters, Parke, and Cane (1965), have substantiated that punishment is an important determinant of resistance. Parke (1969) has collected a wealth of readings on this area of social development. Some of the more germane findings are as follows:

Walters, Parke, and Cane (1965) have demonstrated that punishment is an effective means to internalize social rules in children, the effectiveness being a function of timing. Punishment has been found to be more effective when it is delivered to the child upon initiation, rather than termination, of the act. However, Aronfreed (1965) has shown that punishment after termination of the act can be as effective a method as early-timed punishment when it is accompanied by a verbal rationale; *i.e.*, a reason not to commit the act. Furthermore, Parke and Walters (1967) have demonstrated the need for positive interaction with children and its effects on resistance to deviation. These investigators found that experimenters who had a positive interaction (friendly, warm) with children prior to the use of punishment developed in the children a greater resistance to deviation than experimenters who had impersonal contact. This finding suggests that the personality of the punishing agent may be an important determinant in the effective use of punishment. Warm and friendly teachers may find that they can use punishment effectively and efficiently, while cold and distant teachers may not be able to do so. Perhaps the cognitive interpretation by the student may go as follows: the warm teacher really likes me and is not punishing me just for the fun of it, but to help make me a better person; while the cold, unfriendly teacher either does not care about me or dislikes me and is punishing me because of it.

Induction

Teachers also may find that techniques used by parents can be used in the classroom. For example, Hoffman and Saltzstein (1967) have examined three disciplinary techniques used by parents: (a) power assertion (power and authority are used to dominate the child); (b) love withdrawal (a nonphysical expression of disapproval); and (c) induction, which centers on the consequences of a person's acts. The results suggested that induction is the only technique that is highly related to guilt feelings after transgression, as measured by such factors as confession, willingness to accept responsibility for one's own actions, consideration of others, etc. Therefore, the technique proposed by Dreikurs and Grey (1968) in their text, *Logical consequences: a handbook of discipline,* may be a beneficial practice to incorporate into one's classroom discipline procedures.

In logical consequences, the emphasis is placed on the resulting consequences that occur due to the child's own acts (Dreikurs & Soltz, 1964). The term "logical" consequence is used over "natural" consequence because the parent or teacher is defining the consequence in a rational and logical manner. The child is granted freedom of choice. He can inhibit or terminate his behavior or continue and shoulder the consequences of his actions. The following example may clarify what is being said:

> A young child in grade school decided to play a prank on his teacher. Thinking it would be funny to let the air out of two tires on her car, he did so. Upon being caught, what were the logical consequences of his behavior, why pump the tires back up, of course. Unfortunately, a tire pump was unavailable, what was the alternative? Wisely, the teacher had the boy blow up 30 large balloons consecutively.

Thus, the boy was confronted with the logical consequence of such a prank.

One may contend that logical consequences are merely a form of punishment. However, Dreikurs and Grey (1968) provide a number of criteria that distinguish the two. These writers contend that logical consequences express the reality of the social order (the rules that govern effective functioning within a society); *i.e.,* punishment, the power of a personal authority. Then, too, punishment involves a moral judgment, while logical consequences emphasize the experiences that result as a function of the act. When the consequences are pleasant the act will more likely to recur; if unpleasant, the action probably will be avoided. Hence, in reality logical consequences are capitalizing on the effects of positive and negative reinforcement that occur subsequent to an act in the social environment. Furthermore, logical consequences are concerned with what happens now, while in general punishment is imposed on children for past transgressions. Finally, the tone of the voice used in logical consequences is friendly; in punishment it is angry and denotes pressure, demands, or even retaliation.

Social Reinforcement

As noted previously, Davitz (1952) has demonstrated that reward training can be used to alter a person's dominant response pattern. Adams and Hamm (1971) also have shown experimentally that the S's history of reinforcement for imitation may determine the extent to which the S will imitate observed aggression. Other investigations on children's behavior (Baer, Peterson, & Sherman, 1967; Baer & Sherman, 1964; Gewirtz & Stingle, 1968) have shown that the effects of reward training not only affect the specific responses that have been reinforced, but also generalize to other nonrewarded and unrelated behaviors.

The effects of reinforcement on two different classes of aggression have been examined by Lovaas (1961). His research clearly demonstrates that reinforcement effects can generalize from verbal to motor aggression; i.e., reinforcement for verbal aggression can increase nonverbal aggression even though nonverbal aggression was not reinforced directly. This suggests that the assertive-aggressive response classes are interrelated in some fashion. Hence, it may be possible for teachers to decrease and/or regulate motor aggression by means of reinforcement manipulations of verbal behavior.

Perhaps the most direct means to decrease the strength of an undesired behavior is to strengthen a more desirable response. Just as Davitz has demonstrated, Brown and Elliott (1965) have shown that teachers can decrease aggression effectively by ignoring aggressive responses while they encourage more prosocial behavior such as cooperation. In a clinical setting, Lovass, et al. (1965) have reported that when appropriate reactions to music (hand clapping, singing, rocking in time, etc.) were socially reinforced in a 9-year-old autistic girl these reactions gained in response strength, while self-destructive aggression decreased.

Successive Approximations

A major tool for the control and alteration of behavior is the technique of "shaping." Behavior shaping is simple and easily used in the classroom. Many times the teacher wants to increase prosocial behavior in overly aggressive children, but the child seldom emits prosocial behaviors that can be reinforced. Rather than just wait for the appropriate response to occur for the teacher to reinforce, one can shape the response.

Shaping consists of reinforcing closer and closer approximations of the desired act. At first, one may reinforce any behavior remotely related to the final form. Gradually, shape behavior that appears successively closer to the desired one. Finally, deliver reinforcement only when the appropriate behavior is given. This shift in criterion, from a general form of behavior to a specific one for reinforcement, is referred to as successive approximation.

Catharsis

The catharsis hypothesis of aggression states that observational exposure to an aggressive model results in a reduction of emotionally expressed aggression performed by the observer. That is, the observation of aggression has a tension-releasing property that reduces the need to express aggression directly. Therefore, one would predict that observation of aggression on television or the cinema would decrease the degree of aggression displayed by the observer.

Interestingly enough, when one reviews laboratory research one finds that the results contradict a catharsis hypothesis (Bandura, Ross, & Ross, 1963; Berkowitz & Gleen, 1966; Lovass, 1961; Mussen & Rutherford, 1961; Walter & Thomas, 1963). It has been demonstrated that exposure to aggression on film increases rather than decreases aggression by the viewer. However, Feshbach and Feshbach (1971) have criticized this work on grounds that laboratory research is not always indicative of what occurs in a natural setting. Furthermore, it may be suggested that the brief film sequences used in laboratory research may not be lengthy enough for the cathartic effect to occur. Perhaps the initial or immediate reaction to exposure of aggression is an increase in displayed aggression, but is it not possible that prolonged viewing results in a decrease through some cathartic or saturation effect?

In an early investigation of total time spent in viewing aggression and its effects on displayed aggression, Eron (1963) found that there was a negative relationship between total viewing time and aggressive behavior as rated by parents. The greater the number of hours spent in observing favorite aggressive films, the less aggression the children displayed. In a more recent study that used male Ss aged 10 to 17, Feshbach and Singer (1970) systematically controlled television exposure at seven different institutions. The program lasted for 6 weeks, and the amount of time spent in viewing aggressive programs was manipulated experimentally. A minimum of 6 hours' viewing a week was required.

Measures of aggressive values, fantasies, and personality attributes were recorded. Behavioral ratings on the Ss were completed by supervisors each day. The results, as a whole, have provided support for the catharsis hypothesis, which suggests that television viewing of aggressive programs may help to control and modify the expression of aggression.

GUIDELINES FOR THE IMPLEMENTATION OF A CLASSROOM BEHAVIOR MODIFICATION PROGRAM

Ideally, the teacher should consult and work with the school psychologist in the initial stages of implementing a behavior modification program. The school psychologist brings to the classroom a broad theoretical background that helps the teacher to establish programs that will optimally benefit the long-term interests of the child. In the course of weekly events the teacher may need to modify some ongoing educational practices (Fine, 1970). An outside trained observer may be able to pinpoint certain specific behaviors by teachers that initiate and maintain undesirable responses on the part of the student.

Unfortunately, at this time in our educational history the role of the school psychologist remains rather vague in terms of what services he is to provide to the school community. Currently the school psychologist basically is functioning as a psychological tester. Until the day arrives when the school psychologist is relieved of the burdensome primary duty of testing so that he can practice his other professional skills, the classroom teacher will be, to a large extent, on his own. For that reason, the following guidelines may be helpful to the teacher who wishes to establish a behavior modification program.

Philosophy

Inasmuch as philosophy determines our educational emphasis and practices, it also will subordinate the preferred method of behavior control. For example, the philosophical approach referred to as "Realism" defines the ontological question of being, or what is real, as a world of things. Subject matters for a Realist are the mathematics and science of the physical world. The basic educational methods are recitation and mastery of factual information. Disciplinary emphasis is placed upon the acquisition of rules of conduct. Therefore, one who holds this educational philosophy may investigate behavior modification techniques that examine effective means of internalizing social rules in children; *e.g.*, Walters, Parke, and Cane's (1965) study on the use of punishment as a determinant of resistance to deviation.

On the other hand, the Idealist sees reality as a world of mind. The curriculum is more abstract and intellectually oriented. Heavy emphasis is placed on lectures and discussions of such subject matters as literature, philosophy, and religion. Character development is established according to "Idealism" through the imitation of exemplars. This philosophical approach will find an abundance of useful behavior modification material in the literature that concerns imitation and observation learning; *e.g.*, Bandura, Ross, and Ross (1963); Feshbach and Feshbach (1971); or Gewirtz and Stingle (1968).

Another educational philosophy is "Neo-Thomism." This approach gravitates epistemologically toward logical reasoning and revelation. Subject matter is of a spiritual and intellectual nature with the primary method of education formal catechistic drill. The education of character is defined as the disciplining of behavior to reason. With such a strong emphasis upon reason, an educator who assumes this philosophy should find the research literature on induction and logical consequences most helpful for behavior modification implication (Dreikurs & Grey, 1968; Hoffman & Saltzstein, 1967).

A philosophy currently popular, as verified by the abundance of educational literature on behavioral objectives, is referred to as "Experimentalism." For the Experimentalist, reality is a world of experience. Subject matter focuses on social experience, and the acquisition of knowledge is established by systematic testing and retesting. Problem solving is the basic learning strategy to be acquired by the student; decision making and the consequences that follow a decision are the key elements in character development. Relevant research applicable to this approach is so abundant that only a few sources need to be named (Bugelski, 1964; Davitz, 1952; Holland & Skinner, 1961; Patterson, Littman, & Bricker, 1967; Reese, 1966).

FURTHER GUIDELINES

The remaining section of this article presents further guidelines for the implementation of a classroom behavior modification program. The basic structure is founded in the scientific method of Experimentalism.

Observation

The first step in the establishment of a structured behavior modification program is to define the basic problem, describe the situation in which the problem exists, and create a convenient classification system that will be useful as a communication and recording tool.

For example, the classroom teacher may find himself in a socioeconomic stratum in which aggression ranks excessively high as a dominant classroom behavior and reduces potential learning efficiency of the students. What should the teacher do? First, he should observe the problem carefully. Some basic questions upon which the teacher may wish to concentrate are the following: Does the problem exist in my classroom only? Does it generalize to other teachers (substitute teachers, for example), or does it seem to exist only in my presence? Are the children aggressive in every classroom activity or in a selected few? Do specific children initiate most of the aggression? Are one or two children in the classroom the target for most of the aggressive behavior observed? Are there obvious specifiable stimuli that elicit the aggressive behavior?

Once questions of this type are answered tentatively, the teacher can make a systematic description of the problem and build a classification system that describes the basic type of aggressive responses observed. The following classification system has been found to be relatively inclusive with preschoolers: (a) verbal aggression: toward teacher, toward peer, and toward self; (b) physical aggression: toward teacher, toward peer, and toward self; and (c) object aggression. Each of these categories has been broken down into further subcategories such as pushing, pinching, kicking, kneeing, etc.

Hypothesis

When the casual observations have been completed the teacher can make statements as to the determinants and possible controlling mechanisms of aggression. By careful analysis of the observational material the teacher can propose specific hypotheses related to the main determinants of aggression and attempt systematically to test and retest possible controlling methods. It should be kept in mind that the hypotheses made are nothing more than speculations based on limited information or even an intuitive feeling for the situation.

Experimentation

Where the teacher has assessed the situation and proposed a hypothesis of control based upon his philosophical approach to education, he must attempt to validate the effectiveness of his hypothesized controlling mechanism through systematic experimentation. To determine whether the proposed technique is effective to reduce aggression, the teacher needs to establish a base rate; i.e., the average number of aggressive responses observed over several observation periods for each child. Next, the teacher initiates the behavior modification program. Observational ratings must be taken intermittently over a period of time. When compared to the base rate the scores on these ratings should show a reduction in the frequency of aggression observed. If not, back to the drawing board. Try one program for awhile; if it shows no reduction in aggression, alter the one in use or initiate another.

An Illustration

The following example was experienced by the author during his second year of public school teaching. A dual problem existed in this particular classroom: low academic motivation and a high frequency of classroom aggression. Casual observation suggested that the low motivation was due mainly to a historical lack of rewards for attempted academic endeavors, while the high frequency of aggression appeared to be chiefly the result of a number of teachers in successive years labeling several children as behavior problems. These aggressive children, therefore, appeared to be fulfilling the expectations of their former teachers.

In this example, the teacher desired to resolve both problems at the same time, that is, to increase motivation while lowering the classroom aggression level. A search of the literature on classroom control suggested that the best method would be to establish a program based on a "token" model. A token model focuses on the use of positive reinforcement, whereby students can earn tokens for desirable behaviors and at an appropriate time exchange them for a reward or some enjoyable object. This method is analogous to earning money to purchase a desired toy.

The general procedure for this method went as follows: base rates for each child were recorded on academic successes and frequency of aggression in the classroom. This was followed by asking students to make a list of those things that they enjoyed most at school. The students were instructed to list only those activities that could be completed by all the class in 30 minutes. This list included such activities as free reading time, classroom games, current event quizzes, spell-downs, extended recess, etc.

After completion of the list by the students, the teacher informed the class that they were going to play a new game that would extend over a lengthy part of the semester. He instructed the class that each student would play for himself. A small chip would be given for a grade or action that the teacher felt was desirable. The student with the largest total of chips on each Friday would choose from the list the activity that he (and the rest of the class) would pursue for 30 minutes that day.

Verbal praise by the teacher in front of the class was given to each student as he earned a chip. Those students with lesser abilities were rewarded according to their own ability level. Physical and verbal aggression were ignored, whereas cooperative prosocial behavior was rewarded. Both qualitative and quantitative reinforcement were used. Qualitative reinforcement was the selection of the game on Friday by the winner. Quantitative reinforcers were the verbal praises expressed to the student in front of the class by the teacher.

Assessment of the program was determined periodically. Scores on academic tasks, as well as behavioral ratings, were compared with the base rate scores over a 2-month period. The results showed that responses or actions that were undesirable and were not rewarded were extinguished (forgotten) and disappeared. Those actions that were reinforced were strengthened. Furthermore, the frequency of reinforcement determined the frequency of the occurrence of the action that was rewarded.

SUMMARY

Several of the basic determinants of aggression have been summarized in this paper. A review of the educational and developmental psychology literature provides one with ample starting points for possible procedures to serve as a structural foundation upon which a behavior modification program can be constructed. An attempt was made to demonstrate the possibility of the initiation of a behavior modification program within several philosophical approaches to education; the emphasis, however, has been placed upon the use of the experimental model in education.

REFERENCES

ADAMS, G. R. & HAMM, N. H. A test of the "contiguity" and "generalized imitation" theories of imitation learning. Paper presented at the biennial meeting of the Society for Research in Child Development, Minneapolis, April 1971.

ARONFREED, J. Punishment learning and internalization: some parameters of reinforcement and cognition. Paper presented at the biennial meeting of the Society for Research in Child Development, Minneapolis, March 1965.

AZRIN, N. H. Sequential effects of punishment. *Science*, 1960, *131*, 605-606.

BAER, D. M. Laboratory control of thumbsucking by withdrawal and representation of reinforcement. *Journal of Experimental Analysis of Behavior*, 1962, *5*, 525-528.

BAER, D. M., PETERSON, R. F., & SHERMAN, J. A. The development of imitation by reinforcing behavioral similarity to a model. *Journal of Experimental Analysis of Behavior*, 1967, *10*, 405-416.

BAER, D. M., & SHERMAN, J. A. Reinforcement control of generalized imitation in young children. *Journal of Experimental Child Psychology*, 1964, *1*, 37-49.

BANDURA, A. Influence of models' reinforcement contingencies on the acquisition of imitative responses. *Journal of Personality and Social Psychology*, 1965, *1*, 589-595.

BANDURA, A., ROSS, D., & ROSS, S. Vicarious reinforcement and imitative learning. *Journal of Abnormal and Social Psychology*, 1963, *67*, 601-607.

BANDURA, A., & WALTERS, R. H. *Adolescent aggression.* New York: Ronald Press, 1959.

BANDURA, A., & WALTERS, R. H. *Social learning and personality development.* New York: Holt, Rinehart & Winston, 1963.

BARKER, R. G., DEMBO, T., & LEWIN, K. Frustration and regression: an experiment with young children. *University of Iowa Studies in Child Welfare*, 1941, *18*, No. 1.

BERKOWITZ, L. The concept of aggressive drive: some additional considerations. In L. Berkowitz (Ed.), *Advances in experimental social psychology.* (Vol. 2) New York: Academic Press, 1965.

BERKOWITZ, L., & GLEEN, R. G. Film violence and the cue properties of available targets. *Journal of Personality and Social Psychology*, 1966, *3*, 525-530.

BROWN, P., & ELLIOTT, R. Control of aggression in a nursery school class. *Journal of Experimental Child Psychology*, 1965, *2*, 103-107.

BUGELSKI, B. R. *The psychology of learning applied to teaching.* Indianapolis: Bobbs-Merrill, 1964.

DAVITZ, J. R. The effects of previous training on post-frustration behavior. *Journal of Abnormal and Social Psychology*, 1952, *47*, 309-315.

DOLLARD, J., DOOB, L. W., MILLER, N. E., MOWRER, O. H., & SEARS, R. R. *Frustration and aggression.* New Haven: Yale University Press, 1939.

DREIKURS, R., & GREY, L. *Logical consequences: a handbook of discipline.* New York: Meredith Press, 1968.

DREIKURS, R., & SOLTZ, V. *Children: the challenge.* New York: Ducee, Sloan, & Pearce, 1964.

ERON, L. D. Relationship of TV viewing habits and aggressive behavior in children. *Journal of Abnormal and Social Psychology*, 1963, *67*, 193-196.

FESHBACH, N., & FESHBACH, S. Children's aggression. *Young Child*, 1971, *26*, 364-377.

FESHBACH, S., & SINGER, R. *Television and aggression.* San Francisco: Jossey-Bass, 1970.

FINE, M. J. Some qualifying notes on the development and implementation of behavior modification programs. *Journal of School Psychology*, 1970, *8*, 301-305.

GEWIRTZ, J. J., & STINGLE, K. G. Learning of generalized imitation as the basis for identification. *Psychological Review*, 1968, *75*, 374-397.

HICKS, D. J. Imitation and retention of film-mediated aggressive peer and adult models. *Journal of Personality and Social Psychology*, 1965, *2*, 97-100.

HOFFMAN, M. L., & SALTZSTEIN, H. D. Parent discipline and the child's moral development. *Journal of Personality and Social Psychology*, 1967, *5*, 45-57.

HOLLAND, J. G., & SKINNER, B. F. *The analysis of behavior.* New York: McGraw Hill, 1961.

HOLLENBERG, E., & SPERRY, M. Some antecedents of aggression and effects of frustration in doll play. *Personality*, 1951. *1*, 32-43.

LOVAAS, O. I. Effect of exposure to symbolic aggression on aggressive behavior. *Child Development,* 1961, *32,* 37-44.

LOVAAS, O. I., SCHAEFFER, B., & SIMMONS, J. Q. Building social behavior in autistic children by use of electric shock. *Journal of Experimental Research in Personality,* 1965, *1,* 99-109.

MILLER, N. E. The frustration-aggression hypothesis. *Psychological Review,* 1941, *48,* 337-342.

MORRIS, V. C. *Philosophy and the American schools.* Boston: Houghton-Mifflin, 1961.

MUSSEN, P. H., & RUTHERFORD, E. Effects of aggressive cartoons on children's aggressive play. *Journal of Abnormal and Social Psychology,* 1961, *62,* 461-464.

PARKE, R. D. (Ed.) *Readings in social development.* New York: Holt, Rinehart and Winston, 1969.

PARKE, R. D., & WALTERS, R. H. Some factors influencing the efficacy of punishment training for inducing response inhibition. *Monograph of the Society for Research in Child Development,* 1967, *32,* No. 1, (Serial No. 109).

PATTERSON, G. R., LITTMAN, R. A., & BRICKER, W. Assertive behavior in children: a step toward a theory of aggression. *Monographs of the Society for Research in Child Development,* 1967, *32,* No. 5, (Serial No. 113).

REESE, E. P. *The analysis of human operant behavior.* Dubuque: Wm. C. Brown, 1966.

SEARS, R. R., MACCOBY, E., & LEVIN, H. *Patterns of child rearing.* New York: Harper, 1957.

TYLER, V. O., JR. Exploring the use of operant techniques in the rehabilitation of delinquent boys. Paper read at the annual meeting of the American Psychological Association, Chicago, September 1965.

WALTERS, R. H., & BROWN, M. Studies of reinforcement of aggression: III. Transfer of responses to an interpersonal situation. *Child Development,* 1963, *34,* 563-572.

WALTERS, R. H., PARKE, R. D., & CANE, V. A. Timing of punishment and the observation of consequences to others as determinants of response inhibition. *Journal of Experimental Child Psychology,* 1965, *2,* 10-30.

WALTERS, R. H., & THOMAS, E. Enhancement of punitiveness by visual and audiovisual displays. *Canadian Journal of Psychology,* 1963, *16,* 244-255.

Intent, Action and Feedback:
A Preparation for Teaching

NED A. FLANDERS

The Problem

The point is that much of what is learned in education courses is neither conceptualized, quantified, nor taught in a fashion that builds a bridge between theory and practice. Education students are only occasionally part of an exciting, systematic, exploration of the teaching process, most infrequently by the instructor's example. How can we create, in education courses, an active, problem-solving process, a true sense of inquiry, and a systematic search for principles through experimentation? At least one factor favors change and that is the lack of solid evidence that anything we are now teaching is clearly associated with any index of effective teaching, with the possible exception of practice teaching.

A great many factors resist curriculum change in teacher education. Perhaps the most important is that genuine curriculum innovation, to be distinguished from tinkering with content and sequence, would require that existing faculty members, old and new alike, think differently about their subject matter, act differently while teaching, and relate differently to their students. For some this is probably impossible, for all it would be difficult. Yet changes do occur when enough energy is mobilized and convictions are strongly held.

It is a serious indictment of the profession,

however, to hear so many education instructors say that their students will appreciate what they are learning *after* they have had some practical teaching experience. What hurts is the obvious hypocrisy of making this statement and then giving a lecture on the importance of presenting material in such a way that the immediate needs and interests of the pupils are taken into consideration. Such instances reveal a misunderstanding of theory and practice. To be understood, concepts in education must be verified by personal field experiences; in turn, field experiences must be efficiently conceptualized to gain insight. With most present practices, the gorge between theory and practice grows deeper and wider, excavated by the very individuals who are pledged to fill it.

One stumbling block is our inability to describe teaching as a series of acts through time and to establish models of behavior which are appropriate to different kinds of teaching situations. This problem has several dimensions. First, in terms of semantics, we must learn how to define our concepts as part of a theory. We also need to organize these concepts into the fewest number of variables necessary to establish principles and make predictions. Too often we try to teach the largest number of variables; in fact, as many as we can think of for which there is some research evidence. Second, in terms of technology, we must develop procedures for quantifying the

THE JOURNAL OF TEACHER EDUCATION, Sept. 1963, vol. 14, pp. 251-260.

qualitative aspects of teaching acts so that our students will have tools for collecting empirical evidence. Third, in terms of philosophy, we must decide whether our education students are going to be told about teaching in lectures and read about it in books or if they are going to discover these things for themselves. This paper will be devoted to these three issues, in reverse order.

A Philosophy of Inquiry

When Nathaniel Cantor (5) published his nine assumptions of orthodox teaching, there was little evidence to support his criticisms. Must pupils be coerced into working on tasks? In what way is the teacher responsible for pupils' acquiring knowledge? Is education a preparation for later life rather than a present, living experience? Is subject matter the same to the learner as it is to the teacher? The last decade has provided more evidence in support of Cantor's criticism than it has in defense of existing practice.

H. H. Anderson and his colleagues (1,2,3,4) first demonstrated that dominative teacher contacts create more compliance and resistance to compliance, that dominative teacher contacts with pupils spread to the pupil-to-pupil contacts even in the absence of the teacher, and that this pattern of teaching creates situations in which pupils are more easily distracted and more dependent on teacher initiative.

Flanders and Havumaki (8) demonstrated that dominative teacher influence was more persuasive in changing pupil opinions but that such shifts of opinion were not stable since inner resistance was so high.

A research team in Provo, Utah (9) believes that patterns of spontaneous teacher action can be identified and that more effective patterns can be distinguished from less effective patterns. The difference is that more dominative patterns are less effective.

Our own eight-year research program which involved the development of interaction analysis as a tool for quantifying patterns of teacher influence lends further support to Cantor. The generalizations to follow are

based on all teachers observed in our different research projects. This total is only 147 teachers, representing all grade levels, six different school districts in two countries; but these teachers came from the extremes of a distribution involving several thousand teachers. The total bits of information collected by interaction analysis are well in excess of 1,250,000.

The present, average domination of teachers is best expressed as the rule of two-thirds. About two-thirds of the time spent in a classroom, someone is talking. The chances are two out of three that this person is the teacher. When the teacher talks, two-thirds of the time is spent by many expressions of opinion and fact, giving some direction and occasionally criticizing the pupils. The fact that teachers are taking too active a part for effective learning is shown by comparing superior with less effective classrooms. A superior classroom scores above average on constructive attitudes toward the teacher and the classwork. It also scores higher on achievement tests of the content to be learned, adjusted for initial ability. In studies (7) of seventh grade social studies and eighth grade mathematics, it was found that the teachers in superior classrooms spoke only slightly less, say 50 to 60 per cent of the time, but the more directive aspects of their verbal influence went down to 40 to 50 per cent. These teachers were much more flexible in the quality of their influence, sometimes very direct, but on more occasions very indirect.

To describe the classrooms which were below average in constructive pupil attitudes and in content achievement (they are positively correlated), just change the rule of two-thirds to the rule of three-fourths plus.

The foregoing evidence shows that no matter what a prospective teacher hears in an education course, he has, on the average, been exposed to living models of what teaching is and can be that are basically quite directive. After fourteen or so years he is likely to be quite dependent, expecting the instructor to tell him what to do, how to do it, when he is finished, and then tell him how well he did it. Now it is in this general context that we turn to the question of how we can develop a spirit of inquiry with regard to teaching.

Thelen (10) has described a model of personal inquiry, as well as other models, and the question is whether teacher education can or should move toward this model. He describes this model as follows (*ibid.*, p. 89) :

> . . . (personal inquiry) is a process of interaction between the student and his natural and societal environment. In this situation the student will be aware of the process of which he is a part; during this process he will be aware of many choices among ways he might behave; he will make decisions among these ways; he will then act and see what happens; he will review the process and study it with the help of books and other people; he will speculate about it, and draw tentative conclusions from it.

Returning to the education course, the student will be aware of the learning process of *that* classroom, he will confront choices, he will make decisions among the choices, he will act and then evaluate his actions, and then he will try to make some sense out of it with the help of books, the instructor, and his peers. This is a tall order, but who knows, it may be the only route to discovery and independence for the prospective teacher.

Occasionally we hear of exciting learning experiences in which education students attain a sort of intellectual spirit of inquiry. A unit on motivation can begin with an assessment of the motivation patterns of the education students. The same assessment procedures can then be used at other grade levels, permitting comparisons and generalizations. Principles of child growth and development can be discovered by observation and learned more thoroughly, perhaps, than is possible with only lecture and reading. But this is not what is meant by inquiry.

Inquiry in teacher education means translating understanding into action as part of the teaching process. It means experimenting with one's own behavior, obtaining objective information about one's own behavior, evaluating this information in terms of the teacher's role; in short, attaining self-insight while acting like a teacher.

Procedures for obtaining self-insight have been remarkably improved during the last decade in the field of human relations training. Two characteristics of these training methods seem relevant to this discussion. First, information and insights about behavior must become available in a way that can be accepted and in a form that is understood. Second, opportunities to utilize or act out these insights must be provided. Our ability to accept information about ourselves is a complex problem, but it helps if we believe the information is objective, valid, and given in an effort to help rather than hurt. Our understanding of this information will depend a great deal on our ability to organize the information conceptually. Freedom to act at least requires freedom from threat or embarrassment.

From all of these things, a spirit of inquiry develops.

The Technique of Interaction Analysis

Interaction analysis is nothing more and nothing less than an observation technique which can be used to obtain a fairly reliable record of spontaneous verbal statements. Most teacher influence is exerted by verbal statements, and to determine their quality is to approximate total teacher influence. This technique was first developed as a research tool, but every observer we ever hired testified that the process of learning the system and using it in classrooms was more valuable than anything else he learned in his education courses. Since interaction analysis is only a technique, it probably could be applied to teacher education in a fashion that is consistent or even totally inconsistent with a philosophy of personal inquiry. How it is used in teacher preparation is obviously as important as understanding the procedure itself.

The writing of this manuscript followed the completion of a terminal contract report of a U.S. Office of Education-sponsored, in-service training program based on interaction analysis as a tool for gathering information. How we used interaction analysis is illustrated by the conditions we tried to create for the fifty-five participating teachers, most of whom represented about one-half of the faculties of two junior high schools:[1]

1) Teachers developed new (to them) concepts as tools for thinking about their behavior and the consequences of their behavior. These concepts were used to discover principles of teacher influence. Both types of concepts were necessary: those for describing actions and those for describing consequences.

2) Procedures for assessing both types of concepts in practical classroom situations were tried out. These procedures were used to test principles, to modify them, and to determine when they might be appropriately applied.

3) The training activities involved in becoming proficient in the assessment of spontaneous behavior, in and of themselves, increased the sensitivity of teachers to their own behavior and the behavior of others. Most important, teachers could compare their intentions with their actions.

4) By avoiding a discussion of right and wrong ways of teaching and emphasizing the discovery of principles of teacher influence, teachers gradually became more independent and self-directing. Our most successful participants investigated problems of their own choosing, designed their own plans, and arranged collaboration with others when this seemed advantageous.

Five filmstrips and one teacher's manual have been produced and written. These materials would have to be modified before they could be used with undergraduate students. Before asking how interaction analysis might be used in teacher preparation, we turn next to a description of the procedures.

The Procedure of Observation

The observer sits in a classroom in the best position to hear and see the participants. At the end of each three-second period, he decides which category best represents the com-

communication events just completed. He writes this category number down while simultaneously assessing communication in the next period and continues at a rate of 20 to 25 observations per minute, keeping his tempo as steady as possible. His notes are merely a series of numbers written in a column, top to bottom, so that the original sequence of events is preserved. Occasionally marginal notes are used to explain the class formation or any unusual circumstances. When there is a major change in class formation, the communication pattern, or the subject under discussion, a double line is drawn and the time indicated. As soon as the total observation is completed, the observer retires to a nearby room and completes a general description of each separate activity period separated by the double lines, including the nature of the activities, the class formation, and the position of the teacher. The observer also notes any additional facts that seem pertinent to an adequate interpretation and recall of the total visit.

The ten categories that we used for interaction analysis are shown in Table 1.

The numbers that an observer writes down are tabulated in a 10 × 10 matrix as sequence pairs, that is, a separate tabulation is made for each overlapping pair of numbers. An illustration will serve to explain this procedure.

Teacher: "Class! The bell has rung. May I have your attention please!"[6] During the next three seconds talking and noise diminish.[10]

Teacher: "Jimmy, we are all waiting for you." [7] Pause.

Teacher: "Now today we are going to have a very pleasant surprise, [5] and I think you will find it very exciting and interesting. [1] Have any of you heard anything about what we are going to do?" [4]

Pupil: "I think we are going on a trip in the bus that's out in front." [8]

Teacher: "Oh! You've found out! How did you learn about our trip?" [4]

By now the observer has written down 6, 10, 7, 5, 1, 4, 8, and 4. As the interaction proceeds, the observer will continue to write

[1] Interaction analysis as a research tool has been used ever since R. F. Bales first developed a set of categories for studying groups. Most of our research results can be found in the references at the end of this paper. Its use as a training device is more recent. Projects have taken place in New Jersey, Philadelphia, Chicago, and Minneapolis. Systematic evaluation is available in only the Minneapolis project.

TABLE 1

CATEGORIES FOR INTERACTION ANALYSIS

Teacher Talk	Indirect Influence	1.* Accepts Feeling: accepts and clarifies the feeling tone of the students in a nonthreatening manner. Feelings may be positive or negative. Predicting or recalling feelings are included. 2.* Praises or Encourages: praises or encourages student action or behavior. Jokes that release tension, not at the expense of another individual, nodding head or saying, "um hm?" or "go on" are included. 3.* Accepts or Uses Ideas of Student: clarifying, building or developing ideas suggested by a student. As teacher brings more of his own ideas into play, shift to category five. 4.* Asks Questions: asking a question about content or procedure with the intent that a student answer.
	Direct Influence	5.* Lecturing: giving facts or opinions about content or procedures; expressing his own ideas, asking rhetorical questions. 6.* Giving Directions: directions, commands, or orders with which a student is expected to comply. 7.* Criticizing or Justifying Authority: statements intended to change student behavior from nonacceptable to acceptable pattern; bawling someone out; stating why the teacher is doing what he is doing; extreme self-reference.
Student Talk		8.* Student Talk—Response: talk by students in response to teacher. Teacher initiates the contact or solicits student statement. 9.* Student Talk—Initiation: talk by students which they initiate. If "calling on" student is only to indicate who may talk next, observer must decide whether student wanted to talk. If he did, use this category.
		10.* Silence or Confusion: pauses, short periods of silence and periods of confusion in which communication cannot be understood by the observer.

* *There is no scale implied by these numbers. Each number is classificatory; it designates a particular kind of communication event. To write these numbers down during observation is to enumerate, not to judge a position on a scale.*

down numbers. To tabulate these observations in a 10×10 matrix, the first step is to make sure that the entire series begins and ends with the same number. The convention we use is to add a 10 to the beginning and end of the series unless the 10 is already present. Our series now becomes 10, 6, 10, 7, 5, 1, 4, 8, 4, and 10.

These numbers are tabulated in a matrix, one pair at a time. The column is indicated by the second number, the row is indicated by the first number. The first pair is 10-6; the tally is placed in row ten, column six cell. The second pair is 6-10; tally this in the row six, column ten cell. The third pair is 10-7, the fourth pair is 7-5, and so on. Each pair overlaps with the next, and the total number of observations, "N," always will be tabulated by N-1 tallies in the matrix. In this case we started a series of ten numbers, and the series produced nine tallies in the matrix.

Table 2 shows our completed matrix. Notice that in a correctly tabulated matrix the sums of the corresponding rows and columns are equal.

The problem of reliability is extremely complex, and a more complete discussion can be found in two terminal contract reports (6,7) one of which will be published as a research monograph in the 1963 series of the Cooperative Research Program. Education students can learn how to make quick field checks of their reliability and work toward higher reliability under the direction of an instructor.

The Interpretation of Matrices

A matrix should have at least 400 tallies, covering about twenty minutes or more of a homogeneous activity period, before attempting to make an interpretation.

TABLE 2

Category	1	2	3	4	5	6	7	8	9	10	Total
1				1							1
2											0
3											0
4								1		1	2
5	1										1
6									1		1
7						1					1
8			1								1
9											0
10					1	1					2
Total	1	0	0	2	1	1	1	1	0	2	9

Certain areas within the matrix are particularly useful for describing teacher influence. Some of these areas will now be discussed by making reference to Table 3.

The column totals of a matrix are indicated as Areas "A," "B," "C," and "D." The figures in these areas provide a general picture by answering the following questions: What proportion of the time was someone talking compared with the portion in which confusion or no talking existed? When someone was talking, what proportion of the time was used by the students? By the teacher? Of the time that the teacher talked, what proportion of his talk involved indirect influence? Direct influence?

The answers to these questions form a necessary backdrop to the interpretation of the other parts of the matrix. If student participation is about 30 or 40 per cent, we would expect to find out why it was so high by studying the matrix. If the teacher is particularly direct or indirect, we would expect certain relationships to exist with student talk and silence.

The next two areas to consider are areas "E" and "F." Evidence that categories 1, 2, and 3 were used for periods longer than three seconds can be found in the diagonal cells, 1-1, 2-2, and 3-3. The other six cells of Area E indicate various types of transitions between these three categories. Sustained praise or clarification of student ideas is especially significant because such elaboration often involves criteria for praise or reasons for accepting ideas and feelings. The elaboration of praise or student ideas must be present if the student's ideas are to be integrated with the content being discussed by the class.

Area F is a four-cell combination of giving directions (category 6) and giving criticisms or self-justification (category 7). The transition cells 6-7 and 7-6 are particularly sensitive to difficulties that the teacher may have with classroom discipline or resistance on the part of students. When criticism follows directions or direction follows criticism, this means that the students are not complying satisfactorily. Often there is a high loading on the 6-9 cell under these circumstances. Excessively high frequencies in the 6-6 cell *and* 7-7 cells indicate teacher domination and supervision of the students' activities. A high loading of tallies in the 6-6 cell alone often indicates that the teacher is merely giving lengthy directions to the class.

The next two areas to be considered are Areas G and H. Tallies in these two areas occur at the instant the student stops talking and the teacher starts. Area G indicates those instances in which the teacher responds to the termination of student talk with indirect influence. Area H indicates those instances in which the teacher responds to the termination of student talk with direct influence. An interesting comparison can be made by contrasting the proportion G to H versus the proportion A to B. If these two proportions are quite different, it indicates that the teacher tends to act differently at the instant a student stops talking compared with his overall average. Often this is a mark of flexible teacher influence.

There are interesting relationships between Area E and Area G and between Area F and Area H. For example, Area G may indicate that a teacher responds indirectly to students at the instant they terminate their talk, but

131

an observer may wish to inspect Area E to see if this indirect response is sustained in any way. The same question with regard to direct influence can be asked of Areas F and H. Areas G and H together usually fascinate teachers. They are often interested in knowing more about their immediate response to student participation.

Area I indicates an answer to the question, What types of teacher statements trigger student participation? Usually there is a high tally loading in cells 4-8 and 4-9. This is expected because students often answer questions posed by the teacher. A high loading on 4-8 and 8-4 cells alone usually indicates classroom drill directed by the teacher. The contrast of tallies in columns 8 and 9 in this area gives a rough indication of the frequency with which students initiate their own ideas versus respond to those of the teacher.

Area I is often considered in combination with Area J. Area J indicates either lengthy student statements or sustained student-to-student communication. An above-average frequency in Area C, but not in Area J, indicates that short answers, usually in response to teacher stimulation, have occurred. One would normally expect to find frequencies in Area E positively correlated with frequencies in Area J.

We turn next to concepts and principles of teacher influence before speculating about how this technique can be applied to teacher education.

Concepts and Principles of Teacher Influence

It may be too early to determine what are the *fewest* number of concepts which, if organized into logically related principles, can be used by a teacher to plan how he will use his authority. Surely he will need concepts that refer to his authority and its use. He will need concepts to describe learning goals and pupil tasks. He will need concepts to classify

TABLE 3

MATRIX ANALYSIS

Category	Classification		Category	1	2	3	4	5	6	7	8	9	10	Total
Accepts Feelings	Teacher Talk	Indirect Influence	1	Area E										
Praise			2											
Student Idea			3											
Asks Questions		Direct Influence	4	"Content Cross"							Area I			
Lectures			5											
Gives Directions			6							Area F				
Criticism			7											
Student Response	Student Talk		8	Area G						Area H	Area J			
Student Initiation			9											
Silence			10											
			Total	Area A			Area B			Area C	Area D				
				Indirect Teacher Talk			Direct Teacher Talk			Student Talk					

132

the responses of students. He may also need concepts to characterize class formations and patterns of classroom communication. These concepts are at least the minimum.

Concepts That Refer to Teacher Behavior

Indirect influence:—Indirect influence is defined as actions taken by the teacher which encourage and support student participation. Accepting, clarifying, praising, and developing the ideas and feelings expressed by the pupils will support student participation. We can define indirect behavior operationally by noting the per cent of teacher statements falling into categories 1, 2, 3, and 4.

Direct influence:—This concept refers to actions taken by the teacher which restrict student participation. Expressing one's own views through lecture, giving directions, and criticizing with the expectation of compliance tend to restrict pupil participation. We can define direct behavior operationally by noting the per cent of teacher statements falling into categories 5, 6, and 7.

Other concepts which we do not have the space to discuss include: flexibility of teacher influence, dominance or sustained direct influence, and intervention.

Concepts That Refer to Learning Goals

Clear goals:—Goal perceptions are defined from the point of view of the pupil, not the teacher. "Clear goals" is a state of affairs in which the pupil knows what he is doing, the purpose, and can guess at the first few steps to be taken. It can be measured by paper-and-pencil tests, often administered at different points in a problem-solving sequence.

Ambiguous goals:—"Ambiguous goals" describes a state of affairs in which a pupil is not sure of what he is expected to do, is not sure of the first few steps, or is unable to proceed for one reason or another. It can be measured as above.

Other concepts in this area include: attractive and unattractive clear goals, pupil tasks, task requirements, and similar concepts.

Concepts That Refer to Pupil Responses

Dependent acts:—Acts of dependence occur when a pupil not only complies with teacher influence but solicits such direction. A pupil who asks a teacher to approve of his work in order to make sure that it is satisfactory, before going on to the next logical step, is acting dependently. This type of response can be measured by observation techniques and by paper-and-pencil tests on which he indicates what kind of help he would like from the teacher.

Independent acts:—Acts of independence occur when the pupils react primarily to task requirements and are less directly concerned with teacher approval. The measurement of this concept is the same as for dependent acts.

Other concepts include: dependence proneness—a trait, compliance, conformity, counterdependence, and similar concepts.

Some Principles That Can Be Discovered

We discovered in our research (7) that, during the first few days of a two-week unit of study in seventh grade social studies and when introducing new material in eighth grade mathematics, superior teachers (as previously defined, page 252) are initially more indirect, becoming more direct as goals and associated tasks become clarified. We also suspect that these same teachers are more indirect when helping pupils diagnose difficulties, when trying to motivate pupils by arousing their interest, and in other situations in which the expression of pupil perceptions is helpful. On the other hand, the average or below average teacher did exactly the opposite.

Now the problem in teacher education is not only to create a situation in which education students could verify these relationships but could practice controlling their own behavior so as to become indirect or more direct at will. One place to begin is to have two, six-man groups work on a task under the direction of a leader. One task is something like an assembly line; it has a clear end product and sharp role differentiation. The other task is much more difficult to describe and does not have clear role differentiation. Now let the class superimpose different patterns of leader influence. Let them interview the role players, collect interaction analysis data by some simplified system of categories, and discuss the results. When undergraduate students first try to classify verbal statements, it sometimes helps to use only two or three categories. In one instance, the issue was the effect of using broad questions versus narrow questions. A broad question was one to which it was hard to predict the type of answer. A narrow question was one to which it was easy to guess at the type of answer. Which type of question was more likely to increase pupil participation? The students role-played this and kept a record of broad questions, narrow questions, and the length of the response. The fact that they verified their prediction correctly for this rather superficial problem was much less important compared with the experience that they gained. They learned how to verify a prediction with empirical evidence, and some had a chance to practice control of their own behavior for professional purposes.

There is no space here to list a complete set of principles that can be investigated by systematic or intuitive data-collecting procedures. The following questions might stimulate useful learning activities. Does dependence always decrease as goals become clear? Is the final level of dependence determined by the pattern of teacher influence when goals are first formulated? Are measures of content achievement related to the pupils' attitudes toward the teacher and the schoolwork? What effects can you expect from excessive and pedantic clarification of pupil ideas and feelings? And many others.

Applications of Interaction Analysis to Teacher Education

Suppose that before education students were given their practice teaching assignment, they had been exposed to a variety of data-collecting techniques for assessing pupil perceptions, measuring achievement, and quantifying spontaneous teacher influence. Suppose, further, that these skills had been taught in a context of personal inquiry as described earlier. What effect would this have on their approach to practice teaching?

One of their suggestions might be that two students should be assigned as a team to the first assignment. While one took over the class the other could be collecting information; the next day or so, the roles could be reversed. Together they would work out a lesson plan, agree on the data to be collected, go over the results with the help of the supervising teacher who might also have the same data-collecting skills. This situation could approach the inquiry model described earlier. The practice teacher might discover that his failure to clarify the pupils' ideas restricted the development of curiosity or that his directions were too short when he was asked for further help; both of these inferences can be made from an interaction matrix with reasonable reliability and objectivity.

Later on a student may wish to take a practice teaching assignment by himself and turn to the supervising teacher for aid in feedback. In either case, the requirement is that the learner be able to compare his intentions with feedback information about his actions and analyze this information by using concepts which he found useful in his earlier courses in education.

There are some precautions that can already be stated with regard to the use of interaction analysis in such a situation.

First, no interaction analysis data should be collected unless the person observed is familiar with the entire process and knows its limitations.

Second, the questions to be answered by inspecting the matrix should be developed before the observation takes place.

Third, value judgments about good and bad teaching behavior are to be avoided. Emphasis is given to the problem being investigated so that cause-and-effect relationships can be discovered.

Fourth, a certain amount of defensive behavior is likely to be present at the initial consultation; it is something like listening to a tape recording for the first time.

Fifth, a consultation based on two observations or at least two matrices helps to eliminate value judgments or at least control them. Comparisons between the matrices are more likely to lead to principles.

Just how experiences of the type we have been discussing will fit into the present curricula is difficult to know. If activities of the sort described in this paper are valuable, are they to be superimposed on the present list of courses or is more radical surgery necessary?

Perhaps this is the point to risk a prediction, which is that teacher education will become increasingly concerned with the process of teaching itself during the next few decades. Instead of emphasizing knowledge which *we think* teachers will need in order to teach effectively, as we have in the past, we will turn more and more to an analysis of teaching acts as they occur in spontaneous classroom interaction. We are now at the point in our technology of data collecting at which procedures for analyzing and conceptualizing teaching behavior can be developed. Systems for doing this will become available regardless of whether they are similar or dissimilar to the procedures described in this paper. When this fine day arrives, the role of the education instructor will change, and the dichotomy between field and theory will disappear. The instructor's role will shift from talking about effective teaching to the rigorous challenge of demonstrating effective teaching. The process of inquiry will create problem-solving activities that will produce more independent, self-directing teachers whose first day on the job will be their worst, not their best.

These changes will be successful to the extent that the graduates of teacher education can learn to control their own behavior for the professional purpose of managing effective classroom learning. It will be the responsibility of the education instructor to help prospective teachers discover what their teaching intentions should be and then create training situations in which behavior gradually matches intentions with practice. Teaching will remain an art, but it will be studied scientifically.

REFERENCES

1. Anderson, Harold H. "The Measurement of Domination and of Socially Integrative Behavior in Teachers' Contacts with Children." *Child Development* 10: 73-89; June 1939.
2. ———, and Brewer, Helen M. *Studies of Teachers' Classroom Personalities, I: Dominative and Socially Integrative Behavior of Kindergarten Teachers.* Applied Psychology Monographs of the American Psychological Association. No. 6. Stanford California: Stanford University Press, July 1945.
3. ———, and Brewer, Joseph E. *Studies of Teachers' Classroom Personalities, II; Effects of Teachers' Dominative and Integrative Contacts on Children's Classroom Behavior.* Applied Psychology Monographs of the American Psychological Association. No. 8. Stanford, California: Stanford University Press, June 1946.
4. ———; Brewer, J. E., and Reed, M. F. *Studies of Teachers' Classroom Personalities, III: Follow-up Studies of the Effects of Dominative and Integrative Contacts on Children's Behavior.* Applied Psychology Monographs of the American Psychological Association. No. 11. Stanford, California: Stanford University Press, December 1946.
5. Cantor, Nathaniel. *The Teaching-Learning Process.* New York: Dryden Press, 1953. pp. 59-72.
6. Flanders, N. A. A terminal contract report on using interaction analysis for the inservice training of teachers. To be submitted to the U.S. Office of Education, N.D.E.A., Title VII. Available from the author, University of Michigan, after April 1963.
7. ———. *Teacher Influence, Pupil Attitudes, and Achievement.* Dittoed manuscript to be published in 1963 as a Research Monograph, Cooperative Research Program, U.S. Office of Education. Available from author, University of Michigan, 1962. 176 pp.
8. ———, and Havumaki, S. "Group Compliance to Dominative Teacher Influence." *Human Relations* 13:67-82.
9. Romney, G. P.; Hughes, M. M.; and others. *Progress Report of the Merit Study of the Provo City Schools.* Provo, Utah, August 1958. XIX + 226 pp. See also *Patterns of Effective Teaching: Second Progress Report of the Merit Study of the Provo City Schools.* Provo, Utah, June 1961. XII + 93 pp.
10. Thelen, H. A. *Education and the Human Quest.* New York: Harper Brothers, 1960. pp. 74-112.

135

Systematizing Teacher Behavior Research

By Allan C. Ornstein

Status of the Research

The research on teacher behavior is voluminous and contradictory. Biddle (1964), Eisner (1963), Flanders (1964), and Johnson (1969) maintain that the problem is so complex that no one knows or agrees upon what a competent teacher is. Broudy (1969) contends that we "can define good teaching any way we like" [p. 583]. Morris (1969) affirms that since we are unable to define a good teacher, it is injudicious to formulate scientifically based generalizations about good teacher behavior. Eisner (1963) and Macdonald and Zaret (1968) believe that we lack the ability to evaluate the symbolic aspects of teaching. Cronbach (1966) and P. W. Jackson (1968) maintain that we lack sufficient knowledge about learning to evaluate teacher behavior or instruction adequately. Goheen (1966) points out that teacher behavior cannot be defined and analyzed, and therefore, "there will always be teachers who will break all the rules and yet be profoundly successful" [p. 221]. Kerlinger (1967) asserts that no single teacher can possibly possess all the traits listed in several studies. Eisner (1963) and P. W. Jackson (1968) contend that teachers are relatively unaffected by teacher behavior research. Flanders (1960) and French (1961) affirm that research findings are not applicable to a specific classroom situation — teachers or students. Gage (1967, 1968) alleges that teacher behavior research does not make good sense or "hang together" in a comprehensible way. Guba and Getzels (1955) aver that teacher behavior research has failed "to produce generally meaningful and useful results" [p. 330]. Wall (1969) declares that the "findings . . . are either confirmations of 'common sense' or manifestly absurd" [p. 163]. Biddle and Ellena (1964) state that acceptable findings are often later repudiated. P. W. Jackson (1966) believes that the few discoveries up to now are "pitifully small" in proportion to the outlay in time and effort. Tanner (1969) is of the opinion that "emphasis on teacher behavior has gone to excess" [p. 366], and Biddle (1964) claims it is "becoming unmanageable" [p. 2]. Elsewhere, Biddle (1967) affirms that investigators themselves do not know what to make of [their] findings" [p. 348]. Berelson and Steiner (1964) summed up and dismissed research on teacher behavior in five words: "There are no clear conclusions" [p. 441]. Why? One reason involves the "theoretical framework" whereby the investigator *systematizes* the concepts of the research.

PHI DELTA KAPPAN, May 1971, pp. 551-555.

Systematizing the Research

Methods for organizing teacher behavior research generally fall into one of three categories: 1) model systems, 2) instructional processes, and 3) teacher behavior characteristics. Of the three, the model-systems approach is the most sophisticated, and it may include instructional processes and/or teacher behavior characteristics, along with other inputs or outputs. The instructional-processes approach, next in sophistication, views teaching as a continuous interaction process between teacher and students, and evaluates this interaction, namely teacher and student behavior, by observation. The teacher-behavior-characteristics approach is the least sophisticated, either constituting a study in itself or comprising, in part, one of the two more sophisticated approaches.

Model systems. According to Ryans (1963b), the model system is an identifiable scheme of complex but organized and interrelated elements and/or subelements which function as a coordinated prototype. The model directs attention to the systematic nature of teaching and learning. A few examples of the model system are: 1) Flanders (1960), involving the teacher's authority, goals, interaction, and flexibility; 2) Jensen (1955), comprising seven categories of class productivity and class cohesiveness: problem solving, authority-leadership, power, friendship, personal prestige, sex, and privilege; 3) Getzels and Thelen (1960), who view the classroom as a social system governed by institutional roles and individual needs and three teaching styles — namely, nomothetic, idiographic, and transactional — which indicate to what extent the teacher gravitates toward the institution or the individual; 4) Ryans' (1963b) communication of informational model, constituting classifying, evaluating, decision making, ordering, and transmitting; and 5) Biddle (1964), embracing seven cause-and-effect factors for teacher effectiveness: formative experiences, teacher properties, teacher behaviors, immediate effects, long-term consequences, classroom situations, and school and community contexts.

The model system tends to be all-embracing, attempting to include every variable, and, according to Gage and Unruh (1967), making it too unwieldy for effective research. If the model system includes every variable, or nearly every variable — which is still difficult to imagine — it follows, then, that the model, without the investigator's knowledge or ability to make subtle distinctions, may often manipulate insignificant variables and/or inconsequential events. Moreover, it may assign them equal weights. Even if the investigator discerns which variables are more important, the validity can be questioned, and even assuming different weights are assigned, they, too, can be questioned.

Gage and Unruh (1967) and Siegel and Siegel (1967) assert that the number of combinations makes the model approach unmanageable; likewise, Cronbach (1967) and Stolurow (1965) affirm that teacher-student interactions are too many and too complex to simplify into a model. Atkin (1967-68) contends that the model system erroneously reinforces a fragmented view of teaching and that such a view transmutes the model into trivia. P. W. Jackson (1966, 1968) maintains that teacher behavior cannot be processed into a model; it is too spontaneous and uncontrollable. Atkin (1967-68) declares that there are too many subleties inherent in teaching, making the model illogical — though its appeal is based on logic. Also,

Atkin affirms that the model approach is based on precise calculations of inputs and specifications of performance; however, teacher behavior inputs and specifications are obscure and vary with different researchers — producing, according to this investigator, a distorted, deficient, and/or inconceivable model. Gage and Unruh (1967) aver the model system to be merely "metaphorical, not to be taken literally" [p. 361]. In this connection, none of the five model specimens seems to utilize empirical data or has been put to the test or consummated in a classroom situation.

Instructional processes. Approaches to the study of the instructional process may be divided into two groups. One group tends to be descriptive and based on nonsystematic observations. The observer usually enters the classroom, takes notes, develops insights, and is at liberty to analyze nearly any facet of the teaching-learning process; nonempirical data are forthcoming. Exemplifying this type of teacher behavior analysis are Eddy (1967), Henry (1955), Holt (1964), and P. W. Jackson (1968). These observers tend to be indicative of the anti-teacher syndrome; one might hypothesize that they have preconceived, negative notions about the teacher and what goes on in the classroom, and since this approach does not call for reliability or validity, their observations coincide with their biases. Since this method ignores research methodology, it is not elaborated upon in this paper — merely noted so as to distinguish the second type of study of the instructional process.

The second approach tends to be analytical and based on systematic observation in which the observer tests preconceived hypotheses, teacher-student interaction, and/or teacher behavior characteristics.

The second type of study of the instructional process, according to Biddle (1967), is usually described and evaluated by a defined, but abstract, unit of measurement, varying in size and involving a sequence of responses, or, according to this investigator, some kind of distinct or prescribed behavior by the teacher and student(s): "moves" (Bellack, 1966; Meux and B. O. Smith, 1964); "acts" (Flanders, 1965; Macdonald and Zaret, 1968); or "messages" (Galloway, 1962). A series of responses or behaviors usually constitutes a separate set: "episode" (Meux and B. O. Smith, 1964; B. O. Smith, 1964); "cycle" (Bellack, 1966); "pattern" (Flanders, 1965); "incident" (Macdonald and Zaret, 1968); or "communication" (Galloway, 1962).

A few examples of this instructional process suffice; they are the work of: 1) Meux and B. O. Smith (1964) and B. O. Smith (1964), who devised 13 categories for placing teacher-student "moves" into "episodes" or "monologues"; 2) Bellack (1966), who classified a set of four "moves" by teachers and students — structuring, soliciting, responding, and reacting — into a "cycle"; 3) Flanders (1965), who devised a nine-point interaction scale involving statements or "acts" by teachers and students, thereby classifying "indirect" and "direct" teacher behavior or "patterns"; 4) Macdonald and Zaret (1968), who classified verbal "acts" into "opening" teacher-student behavior or "incidents," leading to productive learning, and "closing" teacher-student behavior, leading to reproductive learning; and 5) Galloway (1962), who classified three kinds of "messages" — facial expressions, actions, and vocal language — into seven possible categories of nonverbal "communication" toward students. The point is, however, that it is not sufficient to divide the variance into teacher and student behaviors, for in this way we lose the most important part of the variance — the teacher-student interaction.

Since the instructional process is usually dependent, at least in part, on categorizing teacher behavior characteristics (and observing teacher and student behaviors), the discussion below of the limitations of teacher behavior characteristics is applicable, too, to the approach to the study of the instructional process.

Teacher Behavior Characteristics. Among the reams of research on teacher behavior, there are many options for choosing teacher behavior characteristics (Flanders, 1965; Ryans, 1963a). This in itself causes a problem; that is, Barr, Eustice, and Noe (1955); Gage (1967, 1968); Ryans (1960, 1964); B. O. Smith (1967); and Start (1966) contend that our inability to define or agree upon which teacher behaviors constitute "good" teacher behavior or "effective" teaching has confused researchers and/or caused inconsistencies among the research findings. Flanders (1964) affirms that a particular pattern of teacher behavior cannot be advocated, and Broudy (1969) and Eisner (1963) contend that these behavior patterns cannot be reduced to a formula or rule. Also, Berelson and Steiner (1964), Biddle (1964), and Rosencranz and Biddle (1964) point out that there is no consistent relationship between teacher behavior and teaching.

Some investigators, for example, Bettelheim (1961), Hargadon (1966), Rogers (1959), Sheviakov and Redl (1956), and Stavsky (1957), contend — either directly or indirectly — that it is fruitless to try to identify "good"

teacher behavior because teaching involves an interpersonal relationship — human behavior — between teacher and student which must be described and analyzed. Nevertheless, these investigators fail to provide an empirical method for evaluating their recommendations or for conducting research.

According to a committee of the American Educational Research Association (1952) and Biddle (1964), confusion over a variety of terms, such as "teacher traits," "teacher personality," "teacher competence," "teacher performance," etc., adds to the general problem. Even worse, according to the present investigator, the definition and usage of these terms vary among different researchers.

AERA (1952), Biddle and Ellena (1964), Gage (1967, 1968), Ryans (1964), and Wehling and Charters (1969) maintain that there are too many teacher behaviors to analyze or assess. AERA (1952), Getzels and Jackson (1963), Rosencranz and Biddle (1964), and Ryans (1964) are of the opinion that there is a lack of agreement upon a common method for evaluating teacher behavior. Biddle (1964, 1967), Foa (1965), Gage and Unruh (1967), and Hyman (1968) affirm that there are no clear or acceptable methods for categorizing and/or identifying teacher behaviors. Allon (1970), Carroll (1964), Klein (1969), and Withall (1951) assert that teacher behavior categories are vague and ill-defined. Ryans (1963a) believes that teacher behaviors are not generalizable to other teachers. Hyman (1968) and Meux and B. O. Smith (1964) allege that there is difficulty in classifying teacher behaviors into proper or valid dimensions; teacher behavior from one study often cannot be categorized into the same dimension in another study. However, Meux and B. O. Smith (1964), Ryans (1960), and Wehling and Charters (1969) affirm that different teacher behaviors categorized into a specific dimension, despite their "independence," are often related either logically or statistically. Carroll (1964), Flanders (1964), Hyman (1968), B. O. Smith (1967), and Tanner (1969) believe that the validity or "independence" of teacher behaviors which are categorized into dimensions is likely to decrease with the increase of dimensions: overlapping increases, while mutual exclusiveness decreases. Yet most of the aforementioned investigators point out that if the teacher behavior dimensions are decreased, the findings are oversimplified and little worthwhile data are forthcoming. Thus, Flanders (1964) and Klein (1969) question whether an adequate set of criteria can be developed for classifying teacher behaviors.

Allon (1970), Biddle (1967), and Perkins (1964) maintain that there are too many "similarities" and "dissimilarities" among the different teacher behavior categories, causing serious and confusing analytical problems, making it nearly impossible to determine the differences within a teacher behavior classification. For example, a teacher who "gives directions" would be considered as exhibiting "direct behavior" by Flanders (1965), "controlling behavior" by Hughes (1962, 1965), as well as by this investigator,[1] "routine" behavior by Gallagher and Aschner (1963), "directing and managing" behavior by Meux and B. O. Smith (1964), and "responsible" behavior by Ryans (1960). These different teacher behavior categories, although somewhat similar, tend to invalidate comparisons between different studies. Meux and B. O. Smith

(1964) allege that a particular teacher behavior judged to be "effective" in one study can be judged "ineffective" in another study. According to Getzels and Jackson (1963), the only consistencies are the obvious teacher behaviors; for example, "friendly" behavior is indicative of a "good" teacher and hostile (the opposite-type) behavior is indicative of a "poor" teacher.

Biddle (1964) points out that there are thousands of descriptive words that may be applied in describing and classifying teacher behavior. For example, dealing with one category of teacher behavior alone, verbal behavior, Flanders (1965) employed seven different examples while Zahorik (1968) used 175 different examples. Assuming acceptable content validity was established in both cases, who is right, and who determines who is right? Judges are biased; so is the reader. Into how many different components can verbal behavior or, for that matter, any type of teacher behavior be subdivided? Granted, categorizing teacher behavior may depend on one's purposes; however, no one really seems to know or agree upon how many ways it can be subdivided. Similarly, Meux and B. O. Smith (1964), Ryans (1964), and Turner (1964) are of the opinion that linguistic usage, confusion over words, and/or interchangeability of words cause difficulties concerning agreement on operational or behavioral meanings of teacher behavior categories, or, according to Jenkins (1960) and Perkins (1964), in the way in which teacher behavior occurs, as well as the nature and scope of the behavior. For example, this investigator uses "welcomes and is respectful of views other than own" as a behavior phrase to help describe *affective teacher behavior*.[2] A similar teacher behavior, "sincere sympathy with a pupil's viewpoint" [p. 88], is categorized by Ryans (1960) under *understanding behavior*. Dumas (1966) classified "sympathy with pupil viewpoint" [p. 24] with *empathy*. Medley and Mitzel (1963) identified "tried to see pupil point of view" [p. 276] with *teacher climate*. Remmers (1963), reviewing different rating scales, reported "accepted students' viewpoint with open mind" [p. 342] under *adequacy of relations with students*. Sontag (1968) itemized "shows interest in the viewpoint of pupils" [p. 395] with *concern for students*. Jersild (1940) linked "permitted expression of opinion" [p. 144] with *teacher performance*. This type of discrepancy, this inability to agree upon operational terms, causes a lack of generalizability in the findings; it often causes the research and related literature to be misleading, too.

Even when there is agreement on "good" teacher behavior, it is wrong to assume that there is a commonly agreed-upon meaning regarding the words used to describe such behavior. Teacher behavior concepts and definitions have different meanings among different groups of subjects — for example, students, teachers, supervisors — in part because of their different roles (Bellack, 1966; Rosencranz and Biddle, 1964; L. M. Smith and Geoffrey, 1965); moreover, this is true even within the same group of subjects (Cliff, 1968; McCallon and Dumas, 1967; McNeil, 1967).

As a result, these concepts and definitions vary among the different investigators, too, even though they often attempt some kind of acceptable validity. For example, this investigator used 14 items for classifying cognitive teacher behavior.[3] Gallagher and Aschner (1963) organized the same teacher behavior into four dimensions, based

on the Guilford (1966) model of intellect, along with 11 subdimensions and 14 illustrative items. Masia (1965) organized cognitive teacher behavior into six dimensions, based on the Bloom (ed.), Englehart, Furst, Hill, and Krathwohl (1956) taxonomy of educational objectives, along with 17 items to illustrate the six dimensions. Warren (1968) presented 40 items to evaluate the same teacher behavior. Almost all the specific items differ among these investigators, even though, with the exception of Gallagher and Aschner, the other investigators solely (Masia and Warren) or largely (this investigator) refer to Bloom for purposes of defining cognitive teacher behavior and use similar definitions. In this connection, Biddle (1964) remarks that the investigators have their own vocabulary for defining specific teacher behaviors.

Biddle (1967), J. M. Jackson (1960), and Turner (1964) maintain that judgments about teacher behavior are socially biased. Atkin (1967-68), Glaser (1963), Gibb (1960), and Stake (1967) believe that teacher behavior varies with the nature of goals; however, according to this investigator, most studies fail to take this into account, and therefore are misleading. Also, Atkin (1967-68) maintains that teacher behaviors involve values and social outcomes which cannot be quantified.

According to AERA (1952), Biddle (1964), Broudy (1969), Gage (1968), Hearn (1953), and Ryans (1964), there is no adequate single criterion against which a list of teacher behaviors can be validated. According to B. O. Smith (1967), it is "inappropriate to ask whether . . . a system is a true classification of the relevant phenomena." The most we can hope is that the selection and classification of teacher behaviors are "wise" and "useful" and that the method for classifying them is relatively clear – bearing in mind that "this condition may never be completely satisfied by any system" [p. 67].

[1]See A. C. Ornstein, "Selected Teacher Behavior Attributes Rated as Desirable by Ninth-Grade Disadvantaged Students and Ninth-Grade Teachers of the Disadvantaged," unpublished doctoral dissertation, New York University, 1970, Appendix C.

[2]*Ibid.*

[3]*Ibid.*

BIBLIOGRAPHY

Allon, N. R. "Systems of Classroom Interaction Analysis: A Discussion of Structural Limitations." *Journal of Experimental Education* 38 (1969): 1-3.

American Educational Research Association. "Report of the Committee on the Criteria of Teacher Effectiveness." *Review of Education Research* 22 (1952): 238-63.

Atkin, J. M. "Research Styles in Science Education." *Journal of Research in Science Teaching* 5 (1967-68): 338-45.

Barr, A. S.; Eustice, D. E.; and Noe, E. J. "The Measurement and Prediction of Teacher Efficiency." *Review of Educational Research* 25 (1955): 261-69.

Bellack, A. A., *et al. The Language of the Classroom.* New York: Teachers College, Columbia University, 1966.

Berelson, B., and Steiner, G. A. *Human Behavior: An Inventory of Scientific Findings.* New York: Harcourt, 1964.

Bettelheim, B. "The Decision to Fail." *School Review* 69 (1961): 377-412.

Biddle, B. J. "The Integration of Teacher Effectiveness Research." In *Contemporary Research on Teacher Effectiveness,* edited by B. J. Biddle and W. J. Ellena, pp. 1-40. New York: Holt, 1964.

Biddle, B. J. "Methods and Concepts in Classroom Research." *Review of Educational Research* 37 (1967): 337-57.

Biddle, B. J., and Ellena, W. J., eds. *Contemporary Research on Teacher Effectiveness,* preface. New York: Holt, 1964.

Bloom, B. S. (ed.); Engelhart, M. D.; Furst, E. J.; Hill, W. H.; and Krathwohl, D. R. *Taxonomy of Educational Objectives, the Classification of Educational Goals. Handbook I: Cognitive Domain.* New York: McKay, 1956.

Broudy, H. S. "Can We Define Good Teaching? *Record* 70 (1969): 583-92.

Carroll, J. B. "Words, Meanings, and Concepts." *Harvard Educational Review* 34 (1964): 178-202.

Cliff, N. "Adjective Check List Responses and Individual Differences in Perceived Meaning." *Educational and Psychological Measurement* 28 (1968): 1063-77.

Cronbach, L. J. "The Role of the University in Improving Education." *Phi Delta Kappan* 47 (1966): 539-45.

Cronbach, L. J. "How Can Instruction Be Adapted to Individual Differences?" In *Learning and Individual Differences,* edited by R. M. Gagné, pp. 23-39. Columbus, Ohio: Merrill, 1967.

Dumas, W. W. "Strengths and Weaknesses of Student Teachers in English." *Journal of Experimental Education* 35 (1966): 19-27.

Eddy, E. M. *Walk the White Line: A Profile of Urban Education.* Garden City, N.Y.: Doubleday, 1967.

Eisner, E. W. "Qualitative Intelligence and the Act of Teaching." *Elementary School Journal* 63 (1963): 299-307.

Flanders, N. A. "Diagnosing and Utilizing Social Structures in Classroom Learning." In *The Dynamics of Instructional Groups,* edited by N. B. Henry, pp. 187-217. National Society for the Study of Education, part 2. Chicago: University of Chicago Press, 1960.

Flanders, N. A. "Some Relationships Among Teacher Influence, Pupil Attitudes, and Achievement." In *Contemporary Research on Teacher Effectiveness,* edited by B. J. Biddle and W. J. Ellena, pp. 196-231. New York: Holt, 1964.

Flanders, N. A. *Teacher Influence, Pupil Attitude, and Achievement.* Monograph No. 12. Washington, D.C.: U.S. Department of Health, Education, and Welfare, 1965.

Foa, U. G. "New Developments in Facet Design and Analysis." *Psychological Review* 72 (1965): 262-74.

French, R. L. "Research as a Basis for Creative Teaching." *Educational Horizons* 39 (1961): 28-34.

Gage, N. L. "An Analytical Approach to Research on Instructional Methods." *Journal of Experimental Education* 37 (1967): 119-25.

Gage, N. L. "An Analytical Approach to Research on Instructional Methods." *Phi Delta Kappan* 49 (1968): 601-06.

Gage, N. L., and Unruh, W. R. "Theoretical Formulations for Research on Teaching." *Review of Educational Research* 37

(1967): 358-70.

Gallagher, J. J., and Aschner, M. J. "A Preliminary Report on Analysis of Classroom Interaction." *Merrill-Palmer Quarterly* 9 (1963): 183-94.

Galloway, C. M. "An Exploratory Study of Observational Procedures for Determining Teacher Nonverbal Communication." Ph.D. dissertation, University of Florida, 1962.

Getzels, J. W., and Jackson, P. W. "The Teacher's Personality and Characteristics." In *Handbook of Research on Teaching*, edited by N. L. Gage, pp. 506-82. Chicago: Rand McNally, 1963.

Getzels, J. W., and Thelen, H. A. "The Classroom Group as a Unique Social System." In *The Dynamics of Instructional Groups*, edited by N. B. Henry, pp. 53-82. National Society for the Study of Education, part 2. Chicago: University of Chicago Press, 1960.

Gibb, J. R. "Sociopsychological Processes of Group Instruction." In *The Dynamics of Instructional Groups*, edited by N. B. Henry, pp. 115-35. National Society for the Study of Education, part 2. Chicago: University of Chicago Press, 1960.

Glaser, R. "Instructional Technology and the Measurement of Learning Outcomes: Some Questions." *American Psychologist* 18 (1963): 519-21.

Goheen, R. F. "The Teacher and the University." *American Scientist* 54 (1966): 221-25.

Guba, E. G., and Getzels, J. W. "Personality and Teacher Effectiveness: A Problem in Theoretical Research." *Journal of Educational Psychology* 46 (1955): 330-44.

Guilford, J. P. "Intelligence: 1965 Model." *American Psychologist* 21 (1966): 20-26.

Hargadon, B. K. "Transference: A Student-Teacher Interaction." *School Review* 74 (1966): 446-52.

Hearn, A. C. "The Relationship Between Specific Traits and General Teaching Competence." *Educational Administration and Supervision* 39 (1953): 500-03.

Henry, J. "Docility, or Giving the Teacher What She Wants." *Journal of Social Issues* 2 (1955): 33-41.

Holt, J. *How Children Fail*. New York: Pitman, 1964.

Hughes, M. M. "What Is Teaching? One Viewpoint." *Educational Leadership* 19 (1962): 251-59.

Hughes, M. M., *et al.* "Development of the Means for the Assessment of the Quality of Teaching in Elementary Schools." In *Development of School-University Programs for the Pre-Service Education of Teachers for the Disadvantaged Through Teacher Education Centers*, edited by M. D. Usdan and F. Bertolaet, pp. 159-67. Research Project No. F-068. Washington, D.C.: U.S. Department of Health, Education, and Wel-

fare, 1965.

Hyman, R. T., ed. *Teaching: Vantage Points for Study*, introduction. Philadelphia: Lippincott, 1968.

Jackson, J. M. "Structural Characteristics of Norms." In *The Dynamics of Instructional Groups*, edited by N. B. Henry, pp. 136-63. National Society for the Study of Education, part 2. Chicago: University of Chicago Press, 1960.

Jackson, P. W. "The Way Teaching Is." In *The Way Teaching Is*, edited by O. Sand and L. J. Bishop, pp. 7-27. Washington, D.C.: Association for Supervision and Curriculum Development, 1966.

Jackson, P. W. *Life in Classrooms*. New York: Holt, 1968.

Jenkins, D. H. "Characteristics and Functions of Leadership in Instructional Groups." In *The Dynamics of Instructional Groups*, edited by N. B. Henry, pp. 164-84. National Society for the Study of Education, part 2. Chicago: University of Chicago Press, 1960.

Jensen, G. E. "The Social Structure of the Classroom Group: An Observational Framework." *Journal of Educational Psychology* 46 (1955): 362-74.

Jersild, A. T. "Characteristics of Teachers Who Are 'Liked Best' and 'Disliked Most'." *Journal of Experimental Education* 9 (1940): 139-51.

Johnson, D. W. "Influences on Teachers' Acceptance of Change." *Elementary School Journal* 70 (1969): 142-53.

Kerlinger, F. N. "The Factor Structure and Content of Perceptions of Desirable Characteristics of Teachers." *Educational and Psychological Measurement* 27 (1967): 643-56.

Klein, J. T. "Presuppositions of Teaching." *Educational Theory* 19 (1969): 299-307.

Macdonald, J. B., and Zaret, E. "A Study of Openness in Classroom Interactions." In *Teaching: Vantage Points for Study*, edited by R. T. Hyman, pp. 197-208. Philadelphia: Lippincott, 1968.

Masia, B. B. "Evaluating Educational Outcomes by Means of Formal Behavioral Science Instruments." In *Development of School-University Programs for the Pre-Service Education of Teachers for the Disadvantaged Through Teacher Education Centers*, edited by M. D. Usdan and F. Berto-laet, pp. 214-51. Research Project No. F-068. Washington, D.C.: U.S. Department of Health, Education, and Welfare, 1965.

McCallon, E. L., and Dumas, W. "A Factorial Comparison of Three Teacher Interpersonal Perception Measures." *Journal of Educational Research* 61 (1967): 19-21.

McNeil, J. D. "Concomitants of Using Behavior Objectives in the Assessment of Teacher Effectiveness." *Journal of Experimental Education* 36 (1967): 69-74.

Medley, D. M., and Mitzel, H. E. "Measuring Classroom Behavior by Systematic Observation." In *Handbook of Research on Teaching,* edited by N. L. Gage, pp. 247-328. Chicago: Rand McNally, 1963.

Meux, M., and Smith, B. O. "Logical Dimensions of Teaching Behavior." In *Contemporary Research on Teacher Effectiveness,* edited by B. J. Biddle and W. J. Ellena, pp. 127-64. New York: Holt, 1964.

Morris, S. "Teaching Practice: Objectives and Conflicts." *Educational Review* 21 (1969): 120-29.

Perkins, H. V. "A Procedure for Assessing the Classroom Behavior of Students and Teaching." *American Educational Research Journal* 1 (1964): 249-60.

Remmers, H. H. "Rating Methods in Research on Training." In *Handbook of Research on Teaching,* edited by N. L. Gage, pp. 329-78. Chicago: Rand McNally, 1963.

Rogers, C. R. "Significant Learning: In Therapy and in Education." *Educational Leadership* 16 (1959): 232-42.

Rosencranz, H. A., and Biddle, B. J. "The Role Approach to Teacher Competence." In *Contemporary Research on Teacher Effectiveness,* edited by B. J. Biddle and W. J. Ellena, pp. 232-63. New York: Holt, 1964.

Ryans, D. G. *Characteristics of Teachers.* Washington, D.C.: National Council on Education, 1960.

Ryans, D. G. "Assessment of Teacher Behavior and Instruction." *Review of Educational Research* 33 (1963): 415-41. (a)

Ryans, D. G. "Teacher Behavior Theory and Research: Implications for Teacher Education." *Journal of Teacher Education* 14 (1963): 274-93. (b)

Ryans. D. G. "Research on Teacher Behavior in the Context of the Teacher Characteristics Study." In *Contemporary Research on Teacher Effectiveness,* edited by B. J. Biddle and W. J. Ellena, pp. 67-101. New York: Holt, 1964.

Sheviakov, G. V., and Redl, F. *Discipline for Today's Children and Youth.* 2d ed. Washington, D.C.: Association for Supervision and Curriculum Development, 1956.

Siegel, L., and Siegel, L. C. "The Instructional Gestalt." In *Instruction: Some Contemporary Viewpoints,* edited by L. Siegel, pp. 261-90. San Francisco: Chandler, 1967.

Smith, B. O. "Recent Research on Teaching: An Interpretation." *High School Journal* 51 (1967): 63-74.

Smith, B. O., *et al. A Tentative Report on the Strategies of Teaching.* U.S. Department of Health, Education, and Welfare, Research Project No. 1640. Urbana, Ill.: University of Illinois Press, 1964.

Smith, L. M., and Geoffrey, W. *Toward a Model of Teacher Decision-Making in an Urban Classroom.* U.S. Department of Health, Education, and Welfare, Final Report, Project No. S-048. St. Louis: Washington University Press, 1965.

Sontag, M. "Attitudes Toward Education and Perception of Teacher Behaviors." *American Educational Research Journal* 5 (1968): 385-402.

Stake, R. E. "The Countenance of Educational Evaluation." *Teachers College Record* 68 (1967): 523-40.

Start, K. B. "The Relationship of Teaching Ability to Measures of Personality." *British Journal of Educational Psychology* 36 (1966): 158-65.

Stavsky, W. H. "Using the Insights of Psychotherapy in Teaching." *Elementary School Journal* 58 (1957): 28-35.

Stolurow, L. M. "Model the Master Teacher or Master the Teaching Model." In *Learning and the Educational Process,* edited by J. D. Krumboltz, pp. 223-47. Chicago: Rand McNally, 1965.

Tanner, L. N. "Teacher Behavior and the Destructive Critics." *School and Society* 97 (1969): 366-67, 370.

Turner, R. L. "Teaching as Problem-Solving Behavior: A Strategy." In *Contemporary Research on Teacher Effectiveness,* edited by B. J. Biddle and W. J. Ellena, pp. 102-26. New York: Holt, 1964.

Wall, W. D. "The Future of Educational Research." *Educational Research* 10 (1968): 163-69.

Warren, P. B. "A Study of Lower Class and Middle-Upper Class Students' Perceptions of the Behavioral Traits of the Effective Teacher." Ed.D. dissertation, New York University, 1968.

Wehling, L. J., and Charters, W. W., Jr. "Dimensions of Teacher Beliefs About the Teaching Process." *American Educational Research Journal* 6 (1969): 7-30.

Withall, J. "The Development of the Climate Index." *Journal of Educational Research* 45 (1951): 93-100.

Zahorik, J. A. "Classroom Feedback of Teachers." *Journal of Educational Research* 62 (1968): 147-50.

People Poll

THE QUESTION:

What's your idea of a good teacher?

WHERE ASKED:

Broad and Locust sts.

Arthur Pressman, lawyer, Germantown: "A good teacher is someone who is more concerned about how much his students learn rather than being solely concerned about the exercise of teaching."

Pressman

Samuel Horowitz, printer, Balwyn Park: "Someone who knows how to handle children, especially in elementary school. Someone who knows when to be tough or easy on the kids, when to smile and when to coddle them."

Horowitz

Kelly Jomains, unemployed, Center City, looking for a job as a child care worker: "Someone that you can go to and talk to — not just about your problems, but about everyone. Someone who cares about you and will help you. Someone who can give little children a motherly kind of affection."

Jomains

Patricia Gray, clerk, West Philadelphia: "A good teacher must have the ability to explain something to you so you can understand. She must also have a good personality, a good attitude, be able to get along with people and control her temper, too."

Gray

PHILADELPHIA DAILY NEWS, Feb. 28, 1972, p. 22.

Victor Tilden, appliances, sales and service, Powelton Village: "A good teacher is concerned with discipline in schools more than most teachers are today. There should be more of the hickory stick, especially in the Philadelphia schools, which are too permissive with children.

Tilden

This carries over with their home life, their social life and their contact with other people."

Mike Delmonte, Temple University electronics student, Center City: "A good teacher is someone who can get the idea of information across. He must have a good imagination of what he's talking

Delmonte

about and the ability to simplify even the most complex subject."

Martha Mayo, keypunch operator, Camden: "Someone who takes interest in the children as far as the classroom is concerned. There should be more homework and more

Mayo

discipline in the classroom. Too many teachers are too lenient and children don't concentrate as much as they could."

Barbara Leafy, computer retriever, Center City: "Someone that's fair, and doesn't lean so much toward favoritism as the teachers do in Catholic Schools like the one I went to. A teacher should give you credit

Leafy

for doing your work, and if you don't do it, you shouldn't get any credit. A teacher should also know her subject well and enjoy what she's doing."

146

'BEST' TEACHERS 'DEMAND,' 'CARE'

By Ellen Ellick

Who gets the good report cards when teenagers "grade" their teachers?

Teachers who let you sleep through class, maybe? Those who assign the least homework?

Not necessarily so, said several Midlands' teens.

"A good teacher," said Benson High School senior Robin Pilus, 17, "is one who is interested in the student and isn't just there to teach school."

"A bad teacher is one who comes at 7:30 a.m. and leaves at 3:15 p.m. and doesn't have anything to do with the clubs or isn't interested in anyone personally," she added.

Others had different descriptions of "good" and "bad" teachers, but all agreed that the "best" teachers are usually those who demand a lot of their students, make the subject interesting, and care about the students personally.

A dozen Midlands' teens interviewed by The World-Herald had views that coincided with findings of a study made by Michigan State University for the American College Testing Program.

'Like an Individual'

In the Michigan sampling of 1,600 high school students, the two characteristics mentioned most often as typical of a "best" teacher were "demanding" and "caring."

This is the way Julie Iselin, 17, also a Benson High senior, described American government teacher Charles Davey:

"He treats you like an individual. You're a person, not just another student. He also expects quite a bit from you. He wants you to get involved in today, and after you leave his class you want to."

South High School senior Sandra Franklin, 17, said of algebra teacher Richard Wolfarth and Spanish teacher Mrs. Helia Rico:

"Their classes were hard but they made them fun. You worked hard but you were willing to work."

OMAHA WORLD-HERALD, Aug. 13, 1971, p. 13.

147

Others didn't name specific teachers but described traits of their favorites.

Mercy High senior Judy Jankowski, 16, said a good teacher is "understanding."

Stephen Letak, 16, a Gross High junior, described one teacher:

"She's not like the normal teacher. She gets a good laugh about what we do, instead of scolding all the time."

'Something to Think About'

And Pat Beran, a 17-year-old Ord, Neb., High School senior, said: "The best teachers are those who communicate with you. You can go up after class if you have a problem, and they'll help without making you feel like they don't have time for you."

He added: "I like a teacher who works me hard better than one who just lets me get by with little effort."

According to recent Westside High School graduate Vince Boucher, 18, the best teachers are "those who give students something to think about but don't tell them what to think."

Vince added that he has had several good teachers and it would be hard to single out one.

What about the teachers who get poor ratings from their students?

In the Michigan study, the poor teachers were described as "not caring," "lazy," "unprepared in class," "boring" and "hard to get along with."

Midlands' teens described such teachers in various ways. For example:

"Some spoon-feed you from the book but don't give you anything to think about or grow on," said Monica Brazeal, 18, recent graduate of Council Bluffs Thomas Jefferson High.

'Hard to Talk To'

Said Julie: "They never give anyone a break. They stick to the subject all the time and are never interested in you. It's like they are saying, 'You stay in your world, and I'll stay in mine.' "

"The worst teachers," said Vince, "are hard to talk to. You can't ever get help from them."

"Some could care less if you pass or fail," said Judy.

Sandra described one teacher: "He never asked for assignments. There was no pressure. Nobody did anything all year long, and nobody knew anything at the end of the year."

148

Pat said the worst teachers "have closed minds" and "are too busy to talk to you."

Jim Dunker of Strange, Neb., criticized teachers who "show favoritism to a few, then never have time for the poorer students."

Stephen concluded that while good teachers had a lot in common — interest in students, knowledge of subject — the bad teachers were all different.

But he had one special dislike — "blackboard teachers. They stand there with their back to you and expect you to memorize everything they write."

TEACHERS' EXPECTANCIES: DETERMINANTS OF PUPILS' IQ GAINS[1]

ROBERT ROSENTHAL   AND   LENORE JACOBSON

Summary.—Within each of 18 classrooms, an average of 20% of the children were reported to classroom teachers as showing unusual potential for intellectual gains. Eight months later these "unusual" children (who had actually been selected at random) showed significantly greater gains in IQ than did the remaining children in the control group. These effects of teachers' expectancies operated primarily among the younger children.

Experiments have shown that in behavioral research employing human or animal *S*s, *E*'s expectancy can be a significant determinant of *S*'s response (Rosenthal, 1964, in press). In studies employing animals, for example, *E*s led to believe that their rat *S*s had been bred for superior learning ability obtained performance superior to that obtained by *E*s led to believe their rats had been bred for inferior learning ability (Rosenthal & Fode, 1963; Rosenthal & Lawson, 1964). The present study was designed to extend the generality of this finding from *E*s to teachers and from animal *S*s to school children.

Flanagan (1960) has developed a nonverbal intelligence test (*Tests of General Ability* or *TOGA*) which is not explicitly dependent on such school-learned skills as reading, writing, and arithmetic. The test is composed of two types of items, "verbal" and "reasoning." The "verbal" items measure the child's level of information, vocabulary, and concepts. The "reasoning" items measure the child's concept formation ability by employing abstract line drawings. Flanagan's purpose in developing the TOGA was "to provide a relatively fair measure of intelligence for all individuals, even those who have had atypical opportunities to learn" (1960, p. 6).

Flanagan's test was administered to all children in an elementary school, disguised as a test designed to predict academic "blooming" or intellectual gain. Within each of the six grades in the school were three classrooms, one each of children performing at above average, average, and below average levels of scholastic achievement. In each of the 18 classes an average of 20% of the children were assigned to the experimental condition. The names of these children were

[1]This research was supported by Research Grants GS-177 and GS-714 from Division of Social Sciences of the National Science Foundation. We thank Dr. Paul Nielsen, Superintendent, South San Francisco Unified School District, for making this study possible; Dr. David Marlowe for his valuable advice; and Mae Evans, Nancy Johnson, John Laszlo, Susan Novick, and George Smiltens for their assistance. A more extended treatment of this material will be published by Holt, Rinehart and Winston as a chapter in a book tentatively entitled *Social Class, Race, and Psychological Development.*

PSYCHOLOGICAL REPORTS, 1966, vol. 19, pp. 115-118.

given to each teacher who was told that their scores on the "test for intellectual blooming" indicated that they would show unusual intellectual gains during the academic year. Actually, the children had been assigned to the experimental condition by means of a table of random numbers. The experimental treatment for these children, then, consisted of nothing more than being identified to their teachers as children who would show unusual intellectual gains.

Eight months after the experimental conditions were instituted all children were retested with the same IQ test and a change score was computed for each child. Table 1 shows the mean gain in IQ points among experimental and con-

TABLE 1
MEAN GAINS IN IQ

Grade	Controls		Experimentals		Diff.	t	p†
	M	σ	M	σ			
1	12.0	16.6	27.4	12.5	15.4	2.97	.002
2	7.0	10.0	16.5	18.6	9.5	2.28	.02
3	5.0	11.9	5.0	9.3	0.0		
4	2.2	13.4	5.6	11.0	3.4		
5	17.5	13.1	17.4	17.8	−0.1		
6	10.7	10.0	10.0	6.5	−0.7		
Weighted M	8.4*	13.5	12.2**	15.0	3.8	2.15	.02

*Mean number of children per grade = 42.5.
**Mean number of children per grade = 10.8.
†p one-tailed.

trol Ss in each of the six grades.[2] For the school as a whole those children from whom the teachers had been led to expect greater intellectual gain showed a significantly greater gain in IQ score than did the control children ($p = .02$, one-tail). Inspection of Table 1 shows that the effects of teachers' expectancies were not uniform across the six grade levels. The lower the grade level, the greater was the effect ($rho = −.94$, $p = .02$, two-tail). It was in the first and second grades that the effects were most dramatic. The largest gain among the three first grade classrooms occurred for experimental Ss who gained 24.8 IQ points *in excess* of the gain (+16.2) shown by the controls. The largest gain among the three second grade classrooms was obtained by experimental Ss who gained 18.2 IQ points in excess of the gain (+4.3) shown by the controls.

An additionally useful way of showing the effects of teachers' expectancies on their pupils' gains in IQ is to show the percentage of experimental and control Ss achieving various magnitudes of gains. Table 2 shows such percentages

---

[2]There were no differences in the effects of teachers' expectancies as a function of Ss' initial level of educational achievement; therefore, the three classrooms at each grade level were combined for Table 1. In one of the three classrooms at the fifth grade level, a portion of the IQ test was inadvertently not re-administered so that data of Table 1 are based on 17 instead of 18 classrooms.

TABLE 2

PERCENTAGES OF EXPERIMENTAL AND CONTROL Ss GAINING 10, 20, OR 30
IQ POINTS (FIRST AND SECOND GRADE CHILDREN)

IQ Gain	Control Ss*	Experimental Ss**	χ^2	p†
10 points	49	79	4.75	.02
20 points	19	47	5.59	.01
30 points	5	21	3.47	.04

*Total number of children = 95.
**Total number of children = 19.
†p one-tailed.

for the first and second grades only. Half again as many experimental as control Ss gained at least 10 IQ points; more than twice as many gained at least 20 IQ points; and more than four times as many gained at least 30 points.

An important question was whether the gains of the experimental Ss were made at the expense of the control Ss. Tables 1 and 2 show that control Ss made substantial gains in IQ though they were smaller than the gains made by experimental Ss. Better evidence for the proposition that gains by experimental Ss were not made at the expense of control Ss comes from the positive correlation between gains made by experimental and control Ss. Over the 17 classrooms in which the comparison was possible, those in which experimental Ss made greater gains tended also to be the ones where control Ss made greater gains ($rho =$ .57, $p = .02$, two-tail).

Retesting of the children's IQ had been done in classroom groups by the children's own teacher.[3] The question arose, therefore, whether the greater gain in IQ of the experimental children might have been due to the teacher's differential behavior toward them during the retesting. To help answer this question three of the classes were retested by a school administrator not attached to the particular school. She did not know which children were in the experimental condition. Results based on her retesting of the children were not significantly different from the results based on the children's own teachers' retesting. In fact, there was a tendency for the results of her retesting to yield even larger effects of teachers' expectancies. It appears unlikely, then, that the greater IQ gains made by children from whom greater gains were expected could be attributed to the effect of the behavior of the teacher while she served as an examiner.

There are a number of possible explanations of the finding that teachers' expectancy effects operated primarily at the lower grade levels, including: (a) Younger children have less well-established reputations so that the creation of expectations about their performance would be more credible. (b) Younger children may be more susceptible to the unintended social influence exerted by the expectation of their teacher. (c) Younger children may be more recent

[3]Scoring of the tests was done by the investigators, not by the teachers.

arrivals in the school's neighborhood and may differ from the older children in characteristics other than age. (d) Teachers of lower grades may differ from teachers of higher grades on a variety of dimensions which are correlated with the effectiveness of the unintentional communication of expectancies.

The most important question which remains is that which asks how a teacher's expectation becomes translated into behavior in such a way as to elicit the expected pupil behavior. Prior research on the unintentional communication of expectancies in experimentally more carefully controlled interactions suggests that this question will not be easily answered (Rosenthal, in press).

But, regardless of the mechanism involved, there are important substantive and methodological implications of these findings which will be discussed in detail elsewhere. For now, one example, in question form, will do: How much of the improvement in intellectual performance attributed to the contemporary educational programs is due to the content and methods of the programs and how much is due to the favorable expectancies of the teachers and administrators involved? Experimental designs to answer such questions are available (Rosenthal, in press) and in view of the psychological, social and economic importance of these programs the use of such designs seems strongly indicated.

REFERENCES

FLANAGAN, J. C. *Tests of general ability: technical report.* Chicago, Ill.: Science Research Associates, 1960.

ROSENTHAL, R. The effect of the experimenter on the results of psychological research. In B. A. Maher (Ed.), *Progress in experimental personality research.* Vol. I. New York: Academic Press, 1964. Pp. 79-114.

ROSENTHAL, R. *Experimenter effects in behavioral research.* New York: Appleton-Century-Crofts, in press.

ROSENTHAL, R., & FODE, K. L. The effect of experimenter bias on the performance of the albino rat. *Behavioral Science,* 1963, 8, 183-189.

ROSENTHAL, R., & LAWSON, R. A longitudinal study of the effects of experimenter bias on the operant learning of laboratory rats. *Journal of Psychiatric Research,* 1964, 2, 61-72.

THE SELF-FULFILLING PROPHECY

THOMAS L. GOOD *and* **JERE E. BROPHY**

Publicity about "Pygmalion in the Classroom" [a 1968 Holt publication by Robert Rosenthal and Lenore Jacobson that describes the now-famous study in which the authors found that teacher expectations affect pupil achievement] has aroused much interest and created a good deal of confusion. Some popularized accounts of the book have been misleading, seeming to imply that the mere existence of an expectation will automatically and mysteriously guarantee its fulfillment. Teachers rightly recognize this idea as utter nonsense and reject it. Unfortunately, however, they sometimes then reject completely the concept of the self-fulfilling prophecy.

During the second semester of the 1969-70 school year, we carried out research that leads us to say that sometimes teachers' expectations do, indeed, function as self-fulfilling prophecies. But we wish to make clear that when we say this, we do *not* mean that any expectation is, ipso facto, going to come true. We *do* mean that teachers' expectations can affect their behavior and that their behavior will in turn affect the children by communicating these expectations to them.

In our study, we observed four first grade classrooms after the teachers had had time to get to know their children well. We made no attempt to influence the expectations of the teachers; instead we simply asked them to rank the children in their class in order of achievement. In each of the four rooms, we selected from these lists for special observation three boys and

NEA JOURNAL, April 1971, pp. 52-53.

154

three girls who ranked high and three boys and three girls who ranked low. Our interest was in discovering whether or not the teachers treated the highs and the lows differently in ways that were predictable from the self-fulfilling prophecy hypothesis. The findings were quite clear: Differential treatment of the two groups consistent with the hypothesis occurred in all four classrooms.

Particularly instructive are certain findings concerning the teachers' behavior when the children were reading aloud in the reading group or attempting to answer teacher questions. In both situations, the teachers tended to treat the two groups of children differently when they were "stuck" or when they had given a wrong answer. When dealing with high expectation pupils in such instances, the teachers tended to repeat the question, rephrase the question, give a clue, or ask another question—reactions that involve working with the child and giving him a second chance to respond to the same question or to a related one. With the low expectation pupils, the teachers tended to give the answer or call on someone else, thereby closing off the interaction.

There were also striking differences in the teachers' reactions to the children's responses. Even though the highs gave many more right answers and fewer wrong ones than the lows, they were twice as likely to receive praise for a correct response and only one-third as likely to receive criticism for an incorrect response. And there was a clear difference in the frequency with which the teachers failed to give any kind of reaction to the child. This absence of teacher reaction occurred in only 3 percent of the interactions with the highs, whereas it occurred in 18 percent of those with the lows.

Teacher behavior flowing from low expectations interferes with progress in two ways.

First, it limits the amount of material that a child can learn—partly because his teachers do not try to teach him as much and partly because they give up much more easily and quickly in teaching him the things they do try to teach.

Second, such behavior stifles a pupil's motivation and gives him a feeling of alienation. (Not surprisingly, the highs in our study sought out the teacher to discuss their work about five times as often as the lows.) If anything, we might expect the teacher to be on the lookout for chances to encourage the lows by praising the success that they do attain and would, at the same time, be slow to criticize them in view of their greater learning difficulty.

The sad state of affairs we observed in these four classrooms apparently is the end result of a gradual process that, in all probability, begins when initial difficulties in teaching the lows erode the teacher's confidence in his ability to teach them. This leads him eventually to adopt the attitude that these children are unable to learn like the others. As the attitude becomes more firmly established, failure expectations likewise become firmly established.

Gradually, things get to the point where the teacher "knows" in advance that certain children will not learn the lesson. He no longer expects to teach the lows in the sense of working with them until they master the material. Instead, unconsciously abandoning serious teaching efforts, he halfheartedly goes through the motions of teaching just long enough to reassure himself that the children indeed cannot learn.

Under such circumstances, the teacher is naturally more tuned to evidence of failure than of success in the lows. He may not notice when these children *are* doing good work or when they *are* paying attention. Consequently, he misses opportunities to encourage them and to stimulate new learning. He focuses attention on their failures and finally functions as a carping critic rather than as an encouraging instructor.

None of this process is deliberate. The teachers we observed were surprised and distressed when we told them what we had found. They were open to suggestion and correction, realizing that even the best teachers need and benefit from feedback.

Unfortunately, however, because expectations guide both perceptions and behavior, their self-perpetuating capacity is very strong. Being human, all teachers are much more likely to see what they expect to find than what they don't expect to find. And all too frequently they fail to test their assumptions in the classroom, which often leads them to accept needlessly low performance from students. Certainly if they never check their assumptions, they are not going to change.

The central issue here is the importance of teacher attitude. IQ scores and other sources of information are neither bad nor good, per se. The use that the teacher makes of the information is what is crucial. Of vital importance is that he see information about a child as merely hypothesis—the best guess at the moment.

In conclusion, let us identify those desirable teacher attitudes and expectations that are inextricably linked with effective teaching:

1. The teacher believes that skill acquisition is the major (though not the only) goal of the program and that deliberate instruction is a major responsibility of the teacher.

2. The teacher genuinely and seriously expects all children to meet at least the minimal program objectives and is willing to spend extra time with the children who have difficulty.

3. The teacher understands that the crucial aspects of the teaching role are instruction, diagnosis, and remediation rather than the giving of directions and evaluations.

4. The teacher expects to talk to and with the children, not merely at them.

5. The teacher realizes that when his behavior is appropriate, his pupils will find skill acquisition inherently enjoyable and rewarding.

Teaching is a very complex activity, but teachers who enjoy children, who have mastered basic teaching techniques, and who are open to corrective feedback are well on their way toward becoming outstanding teachers.

For a
Disciplinarian's Manual

By DON L. EMBLEN

T hose critics of modern education who fall back, finally, on that happy phrase, "the good old days," might do well to study the suggestions of a London schoolmaster of 160 years ago, who published an elaborate improvement scheme based upon an inventive schedule of corporal and psychological punishments remarkably well designed to pinch the young where they are most tender. Not only were his punishments less severe, he said, than those commonly in practice at the dawn of the nineteenth century, but they would not interfere with the young scholars' going ahead with their work. Moreover, each of them had the very great virtue of making the miscreant the instrument of his own pain and discomfort. That his own description of these devices sounds today more like notes from the commonplace book of a Dachau sadist than the sober recommendations of a respected schoolman is beside the point. "Some persons *will* plead for the rod," the old schoolmaster said, "as the partisans of Robespierre did for the guillotine, with an unrelenting fury."

The recommendations are those of Joseph Lancaster (1778-1838),[1] whose book, *Improvements in Education*,[2] was abstracted in the "Useful Projects" section of the *Annual Register* of 1808

(London), pages 143-51, from which the following excerpts are taken. Typically, Lancaster presented his prize punishments (as a good housewife might her favorite recipes) in carefully arranged categories: Instruments of Punishment, Proclamation of Faults, Confinement After School Hours, and Other. It should be remembered, in the following descriptions, that Lancaster's corrective measures had all been tested and found effective in the schools under his command, and further, that these highly practical answers to the problem of discipline were applied to *all* of his subjects, from the youngest children beginning work on their ABC's to the oldest monitors of the sixth and seventh grade.

Instruments

The Log consisted of a wooden log, weighing from four to six pounds, with a cord attached to each end. Lancaster found this particularly effective in correcting the child who fidgets and squirms at his desk. The cord was slipped over the victim's head and the log was balanced on his shoulders. "The neck is not pinched or closely confined," Lancaster explained. "It is chiefly burthensome by the manner in which it encumbers the neck when the delinquent turns to the

PHI DELTA KAPPAN, Feb. 1969, pp. 339-340.

right or left. While it rests on his shoulders, the equilibrium is preserved; but, on the least motion one way or the other, it is lost, and the log operates as a dead weight upon the neck. Thus he is confined to sit in his proper position and go on with his work."

The Shackle was a piece of wood about a foot long (it could be as short as six inches for particularly recalcitrant cases), with a loop of cord at each end, making a shackle or hobble. The legs of the offender were tied together with one or more of these shackles. As Lancaster pointed out, "When shackled, [the offender] cannot walk but in a very slow, measured pace. . . ." [Presumably this would be particularly appropriate for the vicious child who cannot restrain his impulse to run or skip or leap.] "Thus accoutered he is ordered to walk around the schoolroom until he is glad to sue for liberty and promise his endeavour to behave more steadily in future." If the simple leg shackle didn't prove effective, Lancaster recommended these alternatives: adding a second or third shackle, or tying the left hand behind the back, or providing a wooden shackle from elbow to elbow. "Sometimes," Lancaster conceded, "the legs [must be] tied together."

The Caravan was a kind of gang-shackle or portable pillory, consisting of a long piece of wood, cut out so that it could be fastened around the necks of from four to six boys. "Thus confined, they parade the school, being obliged to pay very great attention to their footsteps for fear of running against any object that might cause the yoke to hurt their necks, or to keep from falling down." Lancaster added a useful refinement of this treatment—make the boys walk backwards.

The Basket was the most horrendous of Lancaster's instruments and as such was resorted to rarely and only after all else had failed. It was simple, drastic, and had a profound effect on the whole school. "Occasionally boys are put in a sack, or in a basket, suspended to the roof of the school, in sight of all the pupils, who frequently smile at the birds in the cage." Lancaster declared that this was the "most terrible punishment that could be inflicted on boys of sense and abilities," and was particularly dreaded by the monitors— so much so that often simply mentioning the device was sufficient.

Proclamation of Faults

The Parade was instituted when a boy was disobedient to his parents, profane in his language, had committed any offense against morality, or was remarkable for slovenliness. "It is usual for him to be dressed up with labels describing his offence, and a tin or paper crown on his head." The offender, preceded by two other boys proclaiming his faults to the world at large, was thus marched around the school. Lancaster also found the parade, or variations of it, useful as a teaching device, for example, in correcting a sing-song tone in oral reading. "Decorate the offender with matches, ballads, (dying speeches if needful) and send him around the school, with some boys before him crying 'Matches!,' etc., exactly imitating the dismal tones with which such things are hawked about the streets in London." Sometimes Lancaster would dispense with the marching part of this punishment and simply have the delinquent stand in front of the class, with various labels pinned to his front. He recommended such signs as "Idle Boy," or "Nasty," or "Suck-finger Baby."

The Bashaw Coat drew its name from the word "bashaw," which was, and still is in some parts of England and the U.S., a colloquial expression roughly equivalent to "big shot." This was a slightly more sophisticated version of the parade—the device of hanging up in a conspicuous place in the school a ridiculous-looking coat bearing the name of the offender in large letters and the legend, "Bashaw of Three Tails." It was important, Lancaster said, that three birch rods be suspended from the tail of the coat. He found this "excellent for the senior boys and will not need many repetitions."

159

Confinement After School Hours

After-school Detention was a favorite punishment in 1808, as in 1968. "It is, however, attended with one unpleasant circumstance," noted Lancaster. "In order to confine the bad boys in the schoolroom after school hours, it is often needful the master, or some proper substitute, should confine himself in school to keep them in order." But Lancaster was more than a match for this problem. "This inconvenience may be avoided by tying them to the desks, or putting them in logs, etc., in such a manner that they cannot loose themselves."

Lancaster did not publish his *Improvements* in any impulsive, offhand manner. They were the product of much practical experience and experimentation in how best to hurt or embarrass the young. He followed certain punitive principles which he set forth in his book as a foundation on which others could build to similar heights. Abstracted from his prolix eighteenth-century prose, these precepts might read like this:

1. Novelty and variation in the mode of punishment are essential. "Any single kind of punishment continued constantly in use becomes familiar and loses its effect."

2. Punishments should be designed "to give as much uneasiness to the delinquents as possible without disturbing the mind or temper of the master."

3. Punishments should be such that they can easily be repeated. "When he finds how easily his punishments are repeated . . . it is more than probable he will change for the better."

4. The most effective punishments are the self-administered types—the log, the shackle, etc.—in the use of which the boy himself is the chief instrument of pain or discomfort. He thereby soon learns that there will be "no respite or comfort for him but by behaving well."

5. Use punishment by exhibition (see Proclamation of Faults) for the most sensitive children.

6. Punishments are best when they do not interfere with the child's regular work. Lancaster found that the log, the shackle, the badge of disgrace, for example, did not interrupt the pupil's attention to business.

7. "Lively, active-tempered boys are the most frequent transgressors of good order, and the most difficult to reduce to reason; the best way to reform them is by making monitors of them. It diverts the activity of their minds from mischief by useful employment, which at the same time adds greatly to their improvement."

8. There is little the school can do to offset the bad example at home: "Many punishments fall to the lot of that child who, however well regulated at school, is spoiled at home."

9. Lancaster urged that teachers recommend no punishment unless they had actually employed it themselves and thus could speak from firsthand experience.

[1]Lancaster was a Quaker educationalist who took over a school in the Borough Road, Southwark, in 1801 and offered free education to children whose parents could not afford fees. Lack of funds to pay teachers caused him to devise his monitorial system. After *Improvements* was published, the system caught the public eye as a cheap way of providing a rudimentary education for the poor. By 1832, Lancaster's system accounted for most of the elementary education available to the English poor.
[2]*Improvements in Education as it respects the industrious classes of the community: containing a short account of its present state, hints toward its improvement, and a detail of some practical experiments conducive to that end.* Originally published in London in 1803, *Improvements* appeared in greatly expanded second (1803), third (1805), fourth (1806), and fifth (1808) editions.

THE REINFORCEMENT HIERARCHY[1]

STEVEN R. FORNESS

While it is clear that the technology of behavior modification has been demonstrated and its usefulness widely applied (Forness, 1970), it is equally clear that an analysis is overdue of certain issues that practitioners understandably seem to have neglected in their developing stages. One of these issues concerns the notion of "reinforcement overkill" (Forness & MacMillan, 1972; MacMillan & Forness, 1970), which refers to the use of more primitive levels of reinforcement than are actually necessary to initiate or maintain behavior, for example, the use of food or tokens to reinforce a child who perhaps would respond just as efficiently to systematic use of praise or other social reinforcers. The fact that reinforcement overkill occurs is due in part to the fact that the first behavioristic programs in educational settings that appeared in the literature were token economy programs (Axelrod 1971; Forness & MacMillan 1970; O'Leary & Drabman, 1971) that served as prototypes for subsequent efforts in the field. What appears to have been overlooked is the fact that these programs were initiated for children who actually may have *required* primitive levels of reinforcement, e.g., witness the Ranier School program (Birnbrauer & Lawler, 1964) for institutionalized trainable mentally retarded children. It is not surprising that teachers derived the idea that behavior modification was somehow

[1]This work was supported in part by U. S. Office of Education Grant OEG-0-72-3974(603) and NICHD Grant HD 04612.

PSYCHOLOGY IN THE SCHOOLS, April 1973, pp. 168-177.

synonymous with tokens and checkmarks and that these systems should be imitated in the classroom.

One cannot fault teachers or other professionals, nor can one blame the researchers in the field. A relevant illustration is Hewett's (1968) Santa Monica Project. Among the first to demonstrate experimentally the effectiveness of a token economy, it was designed primarily as a research project and only subsequently as an ongoing school program. The fact that children were on check marks in some classes for a whole year or a whole semester was part of the research design and was not meant to imply that, in practice, children should always be on checkmarks on such rigid sustained schedules. It is interesting that some (O'Leary & Drabman, 1971) have interpreted as a partial failure the fact that some of Hewett's classes continued to improve after they were taken off check marks.

What needs to be done at this point, and it is long overdue, is to reiterate the notion of movement along a reinforcement continuum toward eventual higher-order reinforcers that occur naturally in the classroom environment—reinforcers that are extant in the real world, so to speak. This is a particularly critical notion in view of the current trend toward the reintegration of atypical children into the regular classroom.

Crucial to such a practical problem is the concept of a reinforcement hierarchy. The concept is not novel, and several have suggested critical aspects of reinforcement hierarchy. Hewett (1968) has stressed the pairing of praise with check marks so as to render social reinforcement solely effective. Whelan and Haring (1966) have stressed the difference between the reinforcement necessary in the acquisition phase of behavior *vs.* that necessary to maintain the behavior once it is acquired. Zigler and his colleagues (1966) have stressed the differences in response to social approval of deprived and/or retarded children. Bijou and Baer (1961) have illustrated how responsiveness to social reinforcement is acquired through pairing with maternal nurturance. Finally, MacMillan and Forness (MacMillan, 1969, MacMillan & Forness, in press) have outlined the shape that such a hierarchy might take.

Before the hierarchy is outlined and some evidence for its form is presented it should be stressed that there is considerable difference between the *idea* of such a hierarchy and the *fact* of a hierarchy. The idea is suggested as a framework from which teachers might view more systematically the problem of getting a child ready to respond to the motivational system of the real world. The fact that such a hierarchy empirically exists has yet to be demonstrated.

In a form somewhat different from that originally presented by MacMillan (1969), the hierarchy is as follows:

Competence	(skill acquisition)
Being Correct	(feedback)
Social Approval	(praise)

Contingent Activity (Premack Principle)

Tokens or Check marks (exchanged for other reinforcers)

Tangibles (toys, trinkets)

Edibles (food, M & M's)

In this hierarchy the bottommost rewards are considered the more primitive (and more powerful), and the topmost are considered the more mature (and less powerful). The line in the middle separates what are considered to be those reinforcers that exist naturally in the world (the regular classroom) from those that exist in special settings (special classes, learning groups) or in special instances (behavioristic program used for a particular child who is having difficulty in the regular classroom). With some reservations, it might be used to distinguish exceptional children from normal children, *i.e.*, those who do not seem to respond to the motivational system of the real world (no value judgment implied) might be considered exceptional children.

There are some obvious difficulties with and exceptions to the hierarchy. To begin at the top, competence is not only difficult to define (herein defined as a sense of mastery over one's environment), but it connotes the joy of learning for learning's sake, of being compelled by the fun of solving a problem or the sheer satisfaction of acquiring a skill. In our present educational system, some may doubt that anyone ever gets to that point. Next, "being correct," that is, getting a problem right or solving a task correctly, usually is never completely separate from a sense of competence, nor is it completely disassociated from social approval; furthermore, it implies a sense of competition and may even be *equated* with it on this hierarchy. This is why competition is not included as a separate item. Social approval, the next reinforcer, is usually a very subjective item and depends on the age of the child, on who gives it, and ranges from a glance or slight smile all the way to effusive social praise. Furthermore, social approval in the real world is usually noncontingent and capricious, and the use of systematic social approval (contingent use of praise and ignoring) is relatively rare. Systematic social approval probably would fall below the line on this hierarchy as a more powerful type of reinforcer. There is also some question that social approval is actually a higher order of motivation than the next item, "contingent activity." That is to say, completing one task so you can do another that is more enjoyable (which also might turn out to be a learning task) may be a more mature level than simply doing something to gain approval, which implies that one has an external locus of control. There also is some question whether this item should be above or below the line; herein it is placed below because the Premack Principle (in which one uses high-frequency behaviors to reinforce low-frequency behaviors) implies a more systematic use of this technique. There is obviously less difficulty with the order of the lowest three reinforcers, but even these function at times as feedback on correctness of response and, of therapeutic necessity, always are paired with social approval. As will be seen, there is also research evidence that further modifies even their place on the hierarchy.

Evidence for the Hierarchical or Developmental Nature of Reinforcers

While there is no comprehensive body of literature that deals with all the reinforcers on the hierarchy, there is some that deals with various elements as these relate to children with psychological or emotional problems. Zigler and his colleagues (Stevenson & Cruse 1961; Stevenson & Fahel, 1961; Turnure, 1970; Zigler, 1966; Zigler & Butterfield, 1968) have done considerable work in this area, and without going into depth on their findings it is helpful to mention some of their major conclusions.[2] Zigler contends that some retarded children are more apt to come from socially deprived backgrounds (such as homes with minimal social interaction) and, as such, are more likely to respond to the social aspects of a task than to the task itself. That is, retarded children who have been deprived of meaningful adult social contact are more motivated to obtain that contact than normals and thus will respond more to the adult or the teacher than they will to the task at hand. In effect, to be right or correct is not as high on their reinforcement hierarchy as is social approval. While he desires the social approval of adults, it should be noted that at the same time the retarded child is apt to be leery of interacting with them, *i.e.*, to have a negative reaction tendency, because he probably has experienced failure and frustration in previous encounters with adults. Zigler further contends that retardates are more apt to look to others for cues.

It should be noted that the effects of social deprivation on retarded children and their responsiveness to social cues are nonetheless similar to those found in normal children after brief social isolation. For example, Gewirtz and Baer (1958a, 1958b) found that when a normal child was left alone in a room for a brief period (usually 20 minutes), the child was significantly more responsive to social reinforcement than when the task was begun immediately. The effects of social reinforcement were greatly attenuated, on the other hand, when a period of social satiation (talking with the experimenter for 20 minutes) preceded the task. Clinical impressions are that in some settings in which social satiation may exist for the retarded (for example, university mental retardation centers) check marks tend to be *de rigueur* in the classroom simply because social approval is so easy to come by and hence may lose much of its power as a reinforcer.

To consider research that contrasts various reinforcers on the hierarchy with each other, Ellis and Distefano (1959) found that an adult's encouragement added significantly to the performance of the retarded above and beyond that added by knowledge of results. Gordon, O'Connor and Tizand (1954), however, found that goal setting (analogous to being correct on the present hierarchy) was a better incentive than verbal encouragement for his retarded *S*s, which would be somewhat puzzling except that there was a possibility that the novelty of the task (leg persistance) may have accounted for the contradictory findings. Locke (1961) was able to demonstrate that social approval significantly increased the retarded child's performance on matching tasks; however, he found that this social approval was more effective after it had been paired in a prior training session with tokens. When he compared the two alone, he found that social praise alone was more effective than tokens on successive trials. McManis (1967) found that pairing praise with a competitive situation resulted in the best performance for retarded adolescents and that competition attenuated the effects of mild reproof given by the experimenter. He also found that praise given to a partner enhanced the performance of his *S*s even though they were not praised directly. In a study that compared social approval with edible rewards (M & M's), Tramontana (1972) found a slight trend for social approval to be less effective, and this trend became more pronounced with more severely retarded children. In one of the few studies of long-term programs reported, Baldwin (1966) also found that food was more powerful than tokens and

[2]For a practical review of this work, see MacMillan (1971).

further that tokens were more powerful than social reinforcement in a social skills development program in an institution. His findings, however, were subject to age differences—older Ss responded better to tokens than to food.

The developmental nature of the hierarchy should be stressed at this point in addition to other qualifiers. The prevailing assumption is that children become less reliant on social approval as they grow older. Stevenson and Cruse (1961) found that older retarded children were similar to younger MA-matched normals in their response to social rewards and attention, but that older normal children worked better when the adult was not present or even when the adult was mildly critical of their performance. Terrell (1958) and Terrell and Kennedy (1957) also found significant age differences with normal children under various incentive conditions that generally reflected the present hierarchy, although there were no differences between 4- to 5-year-olds and 8- to 9-year-olds in response to tokens as a reinforcer. Srivastava (1968) found no differences between the same age groups in response to social reinforcement vs. candy, but did find a tendency for the effectiveness of the reinforcement used to be related to the type of task at hand. Social reinforcement was more effective than candy on a motor task, and the reverse was true on a discrimination task.

The above findings must be interpreted further in the light of social class. Zigler and Kanzer (1962) indicated that lower socioeconomic status children performed more effectively when reinforced with the words "good" or "fine" than when reinforced with "right" or "correct," consistent with the findings of retarded and/or younger children. This finding has been challenged by McGrade (1966, 1968), who failed to replicate Zigler's results and further suggested that, methodologically, previous studies may well have been measuring practice effects rather than the effects of social reinforcement. However, she did find differences in the effect of "good-fine" vs. "right-correct" vs. a third category "great-swell" to indicate that the first of these functions as feedback, while the second and third function more like social approval. Unikel, Strain and Adams (1969) found no differences in 5- to 6-year-old lower-class children between social approval as a reinforcer and edible reinforcement and suggested that previous research was difficult to assess in this area because differing measures of social class had been employed. Terrell, Durkin and Wiesley (1959) found that lower-class children performed best with feedback only. Their findings suggested that middle-class children would rather do something, as they put it, "for the fun of it," while lower-class children do something "to get something."

Another aspect of incentives that bears on this discussion is the type of tangible or edible reinforcer used. For example, Stevenson and Knight (1961) found that retarded Ss worked longer than normals for visual reinforcement (animal pictures). Unfortunately, little research seems to have been done on this type of reinforcement. Cantor and Hottel (1955) studied the magnitude of incentive (4 peanuts vs. 1), but found no differences in retarded Ss. In a study of retardates drawn from the same population, Heber (1955) suggested that peanuts were not highly preferred incentives for these Ss. When Ss were asked to designate highly preferred rewards, there were differences as a result of magnitude of reinforcement. To the contrary, Wolfensberg (1960) found no differences as a function of magnitude, even with highly preferred tangible rewards, but the fact of institutional deprivation and the small groups used may have overshadowed his results. Ellis and Pryer (1958) found, interestingly, that yellow paper squares were more powerful reinforcers than edible rewards (jelly beans), but there was a suggestion that paper squares might have been associated previously in that setting with edible reinforcers.

The above research on the retarded and socioeconomically deprived, while difficult to resolve in many areas, nonetheless seems to indicate some support for the reinforcement hierarchy, at least as far as these groups are concerned.

The case with other atypical children is less clear, with far less research available. Often quoted is the work by Levin and Simmons (1962a, 1962b) on emotionally disturbed boys, which indicated that social approval had a debilitating effect on the performance of latency age boys with emotional or behavioral problems. In their first study, Ss responded on a marble dropping task until praised for their performance, at which time they ceased to perform. In the second, one group was reinforced with peanuts, while the other was reinforced with peanuts plus praise. Again, praise depressed the performance of the latter group. It should be noted that both studies involved very small Ns, with only 3 Ss in each group in the latter study. Little has been done with hyperactive or brain-injured children, but the evidence seems to indicate that they respond to a variety of token and social reinforcement ysstems (Hall & Broden, 1967; Patterson 1965), despite the prevailing assumption that their behavior is organically based and not a problem of motivation.

Ferster and DeMeyer (1962) analyzed the behavior of two autistic children under various reinforcement conditions in which, after Ss first had obtained coins from a dispenser, they selected a reinforcer by dropping coins in one of several vending devices that delivered reinforcement. The three most preferred rewards appeared to be candy, trinkets, and listening to a record player, though the trinket vending machine also delivered part of the child's lunch. Forness and Saltzman (1970) compared food, social praise, and physical contact (hugging) with two autistic children. One S responded best to praise, with hugging and food next and nearly equal in potency, while the other preferred food, hugging, and social praise in that order.

With little definitive evidence available on atypical children, and this subject to differing interpretations based on developmental and social class differences, the validity of the present hierarchy has yet to be established empirically. At this point it is merely an intuitive practical guideline, and both between and within categories of exceptional children *it needs to be applied on an individual basis.* One of the crucial aspects of the hierarchy that deserves further mention is the topmost incentive, because it appears to have implications for lower levels as well.

THE COMPETENCY MOTIVE

While emphasis in reinforcement theory traditionally has been on incentives necessary to engage a child in a task, little mention has been made on the nature of the task and, more importantly, on what the task means to the child. The notion of competency, the organism's ability to interact effectively with its environment, has been discussed by White (1959) in reference to psychosocial development. He suggests that children have a developing need to master their environment, to do things for themselves. The infant's first attempts to feed himself are an example.

166

Even though the attempts are far from successful, the mother needs to realize that the infant thereby is learning to fend for himself. During latency age, this phenomenon takes the form of a striving for achievement and success in school, which generally is interpreted as a sublimation of the Oedipal conflict. Psychodynamic interpretations aside, the notion of competency striving as motivation receives considerable support from other theorists.

As several have suggested, infants and young children are compelled to interact with situations or objects in their environment as these challenge their existing notions of the environment (Bruner, 1971; Festinger, 1963; Flavel, 1963; Hunt, 1961). These authors draw principally from the work of Piaget and suggest that when a child encounters a situation that is somewhat different from those that he has experienced previously, the child is motivated to discover the source of the discrepancy through observation or manipulation. If the discrepancy is too great, the child may become frustrated, bored or disinterested and not motivated to resolve it; if the situation is too similar to those that he has experienced already, he also may not be as compelled to engage in exploration. Most theorists suggest a novelty factor that is sufficient to challenge but not too great to discourage the child.

Others have illustrated that self-competency may be motivational only when basic needs have been met (Maslow, 1954). Harlow (1953) has shown, furthermore, that this need may affect performance beyond the effects of other lower-order reinforcers. He has demonstrated how monkeys rewarded with food for solving problems continued to attempt to solve problems even though their cheeks were full of food. Harlow suggests that his monkeys were inherently interested in the problems. Lastly, it long has been evident that behavior disorders can be caused by presenting problems that require for their solution capacity beyond that which the child possesses (Krasmagorski, 1930).

While placed at the top of the hierarchy, the competency motive obviously relates to lower levels in that the task for which the child is being reinforced, regardless of the reinforcer used, presents at least some form of competency incentive. The question is whether the task can be made sufficiently challenging in and of itself such that external reinforcements (edibles, tangibles, social praise) are unnecessary. Ferster (1966) has suggested that many reinforcers that are used are arbitrary or unnatural and are unrelated to the motivational system in the natural environment. By the use of these reinforcers we often may prevent the child from establishing, at critical periods of his development, responses necessary for eventual competence.

While it is no doubt necessary with some atypical children to use these reinforcers, it is possible that their use is testimony to the fact that we have failed to find the right competency "match" between child and task. That is, we have selected for the child a task that either is not sufficiently challenging or that is too much of a challenge for him at that particular stage. We thus have to resort to some other form of reinforcement to get him to attempt the task. As a related example, Cobb (in press) reported a study in which various behavioristic approaches were used with problem children in regular classrooms. One approach emphasized individual behavioral contingencies, another emphasized group contingencies, another combined individual contingencies with assistance to the teacher from a curriculum expert, and the last employed the curriculum expert alone. Cobb's findings indicated that the last approach (curriculum expert alone) gave the best results and that the curriculum consultant accounted for a great deal of the variance in the other approaches. Possibly the task materials presented to the children were more important than the consequences of completing the tasks.

It is clear that more systematic study needs to be done in this area, and it is altogether obvious that the fields of cognitive development and curriculum are light years away from being able to prescribe developmentally based tasks with any sense of precision such that these tasks become motivating in and of themselves. It does, however, illustrate how behaviorists must pay considerable attention to developments in these areas. A sound curriculum hierarchy may render the reinforcement hierarchy considerably less important.

Conclusion

While it is beyond the scope of this paper to describe the practical application of a reinforcement hierarchy, it should be noted that the hierarchy implies movement along a continuum from top to bottom, from primitive levels of reinforcement to more sophisticated levels. Unless it is immediately obvious that a child cannot function without the use of lower-order reinforcers, a rule of thumb should be that we approach him as though he responds to topmost reinforcers until such time as he demonstrates otherwise. He then should be moved downward, perhaps gradually, to that level required for acceptable functioning, but with the ever-present intention of moving him to higher levels as soon as he is ready. While reinforcement schedules have not been mentioned here, they are indispensable in moving from one level to the next, as is the notion of pairing lower-order reinforcement with higher reinforcers, *e.g.*, always giving social praise with feedback so that feedback eventually will become reinforcing in and of itself.

Any use of the reinforcement hierarchy should remain flexible and individualized. As indicated previously, there is individual variability both between and within groups of atypical children. There should be no excuse for having all children in the same class, no matter how small the class size, on the same level of the hierarchy. It also is important to note that what is reinforcing at any one level for the child may not be immediately apparent to the teacher and that the child's preference and/or performance should be the guide as to what is reinforcing. We are all notorious for thinking that we know what is "good" for children. The setting of the task may determine the type of reinforcement. For example, preschool children may require only social reinforcement if the task is done on a one-to-one basis, but require tangible reinforcement for the same task done in a group of children (Graham, Kass, & Forness, 1971).

As mentioned before, the hierarchy should be considered only tenuous in fact. Available research evidence suggests that many of the reinforcers are indeed "floaters," that is, they position at various levels on the hierarchy depending on myriad factors such as age, social class, preference and magnitude of incentive, to name but a few. Even after the evidence is reviewed, the validity of the reinforcement hierarchy, like so many other aspects of classroom management and motivation, appears to rely at present on a good deal of intuition. It should, however, serve as a practical framework for teachers as they approach the problem of preparing certain children for the motivational system of the regular classroom.

REFERENCES

AXELROD, S. Token reinforcement programs in special classes. *Exceptional Children*, 1971, *37*, 371-379.

BALDWIN, L. Development of social skills in retardates as a function of three types of reinforcement programs. Unpublished doctoral dissertation, University of Oregon, 1966.

BIJOU, S. W., & BAER, D. *Child development. (Vol. I)* New York: Appleton-Century-Crofts, 1961.

BIRNBRAUER, J., & LAWLER, J. Token reinforcement for learning. *Mental Retardation*, 1964, *2*, 275-279.

BRUNER, J. S. *The relevance of education.* New York: Norton, 1971.

CANTOR, G. N., & HOTTEL, J. Discrimination learning in mental defectives as a function of magnitude of food reward and intelligence level. *American Journal of Mental Deficiency*, 1955, *60*, 380-384.

COBB, J. A., & HOPS, H. Effects of academic survival skill training on low achieving first graders. *Journal of Educational Research*, in press.

ELLIS, N. R., & DISTEFANO, M. Effects of verbal urging and praise upon rotary pursuit performance in mental defectives. *American Journal of Mental Deficiency*, 1959, *64*, 486-490.

ELLIS, N. R., & PRYER, M. Primary versus secondary reinforcement in simple discrimination learning of mental defectives. *Psychological Reports*, 1958, *4*, 67-70.

FERSTER, C. B. Arbitrary and natural reinforcement. *Psychological Record*, 1967, *17*, 341-347.

FERSTER, C. B., & DE MEYER, M. A method for the experimental analysis of autistic children. *American Journal of Orthopsychiatry*, 1962, *32*, 89-98.

FESTINGER, L. A. *A theory of cognitive dissonance.* Evanston, Ill.: Row, Peterson, 1957.

FLAVELL, J. H. *The developmental psychology of Jean Piaget.* Princeton, N. J.: Van Nostrand, 1963.

FORNESS, S. Behavioristic approach to classroom management and motivation. *Psychology in the Schools*, 1970, *7*, 356-363.

FORNESS, S., & MACMILLAN, D. Origins of behavior modification with exceptional children. *Exceptional Children*, 1970, *37*, 93-100.

FORNESS, S., & MACMILLAN, D. Reinforcement overkill: implications for education of the retarded. *Journal of Special Education*, in press.

FORNESS, S., & SALTZMAN, S. Effectiveness of physical-social contact as reinforcement. Paper presented at the meeting of California Educational Research Association, San Francisco, February 1970.

GEWIRTZ, J., & BAER, D. Deprivation and satiation of social reinforcers as drive conditions. *Journal of Abnormal and Social Psychology*, 1958, *57*, 167-172. (a)

GEWIRTZ, J., & BAER, D. The effect of brief social deprivation on behaviors for a social reinforcer. *Journal of Abnormal and Social Psychology*, 1958, *56*, 49-56. (b)

GORDON, S., O'CONNOR, N., & TIZARD, J. Some effects of incentives on the performance of imbeciles. *British Journal of Psychology*, 1954, *45*, 277-287.

GRAHAM, V., KASS, E. W., & FORNESS, S. Development of a behavior baseline for educational intervention with preschool children. Paper presented at the meeting of California Educational Research Association, San Diego, November 1971.

HALL, R., & BRODEN, M. Behavior changes in brain injured children through social reinforcement. *Journal of Experimental Psychology*, 1967, *5*, 467-479.

HARLOW, H. Mice, monkeys, men and motives. *Psychological Review*, 1953, *60*, 23-32.

HEBER, R. Motor task performance of high grade mentally retarded males as a function of the magnitude of incentive. *American Journal of Mental Deficiency*, 1959, *63*, 667-671.

HEWETT, F. *The emotionally disturbed child in the classroom.* Boston: Allyn and Bacon, 1968.

HUNT, J. McV. *Intelligence and experience.* New York: Ronald Press, 1961.

KRASMAGORSKI, N. Conditioned reflex and childhood neurosis. *American Journal of Disturbed Children*, 1930, *30*, 753-768.

LEVIN, G. R., & SIMMONS, J. J. Response to praise by emotionally disturbed boys. *Psychological Reports*, 1962, *11*, 10. (a)

LEVIN, G. R., & SIMMONS, J. J. Response to food and praise by emotionally disturbed boys. *Psychological Reports*, 1962, *11*, 539-546. (b)

LOCKE, B. J. Verbal conditioning with retarded subjects: establishment or reinstatement of effective reinforcing consequences. *American Journal of Mental Deficiency*, 1969, *73*, 621-626.

MACMILLAN, D. Behavior modification: a teacher strategy to control behavior. Report of the proceedings of the forty-fourth meeting of the convention of American Instructors of the Deaf. Berkeley, June 1969.

MACMILLAN, D. The problem of motivation in the education of the mentally retarded. *Exceptional Children*, 1971, *37*, 579-586.

MACMILLAN, D., & FORNESS, S. Behavior modification: limitations and liabilities. *Exceptional Children*, 1970, *37*, 291-297.

MacMILLAN, D., & FORNESS, S. Behavior modification: savior or savant? *American Journal of Mental Deficiency*, in press.

MASLOW, A. *Motivation and personality*. New York: Harper & Row, 1954.

McGRADE, B. J. Effectiveness of verbal reinforcers in relation to age and social class. *Journal of Personality and Social Psychology*, 1966, *4*, 555-560.

McGRADE, B. J. Social class and reinforcer effects in discrimination learning. *Psychonomic Science*, 1968, *12*, 140.

McMANIS, D. L. Marble sorting persistence in mixed verbal incentive and performance-level pairings. *American Journal of Mental Deficiency*, 1967, *71*, 811-817.

O'LEARY, K. D., & DRABMAN, R. Token reinforcement programs in the classroom. *Psychological Bulletin*, 1971, *75*, 379-398.

PATTERSON, G. R. An application of conditioning techniques to the control of a hyperactive child. In L. Ullman and L. Krasner (Eds.), *Case studies in behavior modification*. New York: Holt, Rinehart & Winston, 1965, 370-375.

PREMACK, D. Toward empirical behavior laws: I. positive reinforcement. *Psychological Review*, 1959, *66*, 219-233.

SRIVASTAVA, R. K. The effectiveness of the type of reinforcement as a function of mental age. Unpublished doctoral dissertation, University of Kansas, 1968.

STEVENSON, H. W., & CRUSE, D. B. The effectiveness of social reinforcement with normal and feeble-minded children. *Journal of Personality*, 1961, *29*, 124-135.

STEVENSON, H. W., & FAHEL, L. S. The effect of social reinforcement on the performance of institutionalized and non-institutionalized normal and retarded children. *Journal of Personality*, 1961, *29*, 136-147.

STEVENSON, H. W., & KNIGHTS, R. M. The effect of visual reinforcement on the performance of normal and retarded children. *Perceptual and Motor Skills*, 1961, *13*, 119-126.

TERRELL, G. The role of incentive in discrimination learning in children. *Child Development*, 1958, *29*, 231-236.

TERRELL, G., DURKIN, G., & WIESLEY, M. Social class and the nature of the incentive in discrimination learning. *Journal of Abnormal and Social Psychology*, 1959, *59*, 270-272.

TERRELL, G., & KENNEDY, W. A. Discrimination learning and transposition in children as a function of the nature of the reward. *Journal of Experimental Psychology* 1957, *53*, 257-260.

TRAMONTANA, J. Social versus edible rewards as a function of intellectual level and socio-economic class. *American Journal of Mental Deficiency*, 1972, *77*, 33-38.

TURNURE, J. Distractibility in the mentally retarded: negative evidence for an orienting inadequacy. *Exceptional Children*, 1970, *37*, 181-186.

UNIKEL, I. P., STRAIN, G. S., & ADAMS, H. E. Learning of lower socio-economic status children as a function of social and tangible reward. *Developmental Psychology*, 1969, *1*, 553-555.

WHELAN, R., & HARING, N. Modification and maintenance of behavior through systematic application of consequences. *Exceptional Children*, 1966, *32*, 281-289.

WHITE, R. Motivation reconsidered: the concept of competence. *Psychological Review*, 1958, *66*, 297-333.

WOLFENSBERGER, W. Differential rewards as motivating factors in mental deficiency research. *American Journal of Mental Deficiency*, 1960, *64*, 902-906.

ZIGLER, E. Research on personality structure in the retardate. In N. Ellis (Ed.), *International review of research in mental retardation*. (Vol. I) New York: Academic Press, 1966.

ZIGLER, E., & BUTTERFIELD, E. Motivational aspects of changes in IQ test performance of culturally deprived nursery school children. *Child Development*, 1968, *39*, 1-14.

ZIGLER, E., & KANZER, P. The effectiveness of verbal reinforcers on the performance of middle and lower class children. *Journal of Personality*, 1962, *30*, 157-163.

THE USE OF BEHAVIOR MODIFICATION BY STUDENT TEACHERS—A CASE STUDY IN CONTINGENCY MANAGEMENT

William Ray Heitzmann

During the spring semester of 1971 I introduced the concept of contingency contracting* to a student teacher following my observation of a class which contained a disruptive student.

The student teacher, unknown to the student, counted the number of "unauthorized talkouts" for three consecutive days. These "talkouts" numbered thirteen (13), fourteen (14), and thirteen (13). At this point the student was approached by the student teacher and asked if he would like to sign a contract in which he would agree to limit his "unauthorized talkouts" to an average of two (2) per day or a total of six (6) for three days. The reward to be given by the student teacher was a picture of Howard Porter, Villanova basketball star. Teacher and student both signed the contract.

Unfortunately the student was unable to meet his requirements of the contract—"unauthorized talkouts" numbered seven (7), six (6), and zero (0). This was complicated by two weeks of team teaching and two "snow days" when he was not in his regular classroom.

The student teacher and I decided that because of the improvement shown, the student deserved another chance, with an improved reward—the picture of Howard Porter with a note written to the student signed by Porter. A new contract was signed by both parties.

The student completed his requirements for the contract—"unauthorized talkouts"—two (2), three (3), one (1). He received the reward.

This was a learning experience for all involved; in fact, the above experiment was presented to the student teaching seminar for discussion. Follow-up (post reward) data were collected—"unauthorized talkouts"—two (2), one (1), two (2). This behavior was the best of any period observed. In addition the student showed significant academic improvement.

* Contingency contracting is a form of behavior modification in which a contract is signed. It attempts to reward one party for performing a desired behavior or omitting undesirable behavior.

THE TEACHER EDUCATOR, Winter 1971-72, vol. 7, p. 36.

BEHAVIOR MODIFICATION: SOME DOUBTS AND DANGERS

Bryan L. Lindsey and James W. Cunningham

For some time "the modification of behavior" has been the textbook definition of learning, but "behavior modification" has been redefined to focus more on discipline than on intellectual growth. It seeks to mold human behavior by arranging the events in a learner's environment so that he responds in a desirable and predictable direction. These contingencies are managed by offering rewards for acceptable behavior and by withholding rewards for unacceptable behavior.

There are a number of inconsistencies in logic and some serious dangers involved in the use of behavior modification techniques in group and classroom situations. If behavior modification is used:

1. *It makes discipline a system of rewards,* which is no better than making it a system of punishments; good discipline is more than rewards and punishment; it is progress toward mutually established and worthwhile goals. A good disciplinarian is a leader who instigates and directs action toward these goals without great dependence on

rewards or punishments but with an awareness of what to teach and how to teach it.

2. *It prepares students for a nonexistent world;* to ignore unacceptable behavior is to socialize for an unexisting society. An important aspect of most behavior modification is to disregard, as much as possible, inappropriate behavior. Society and nature do not ignore such behavior.

3. *It undermines existing internal control.* Behavior modification is a system to modify behavior in a classroom. But if students showing internal control in a class are learning, why should they be externally rewarded? Might they not then stop being self-directed and begin working only for external rewards?

4. *It is unfair.* To refrain from externally rewarding the behavior of some students for fear of weakening their internal control is to be faced with the alternative of providing rewards only for those without internal control. It will seem unfair to the students who have been doing what is expected of them

PHI DELTA KAPPAN, May 1973, pp. 596-597.

172

without reward, while those having difficulty in doing what is expected of them are being rewarded. A point system or other reinforcement schedule shows a major weakness if allowance is made for individual differences, in that students already behaving in acceptable ways will remain unrewarded, while those exhibiting unacceptable behavior will be rewarded ("paid off") on occasions when they show modified behavior. But if no allowance is made for individual differences, students having a history of unacceptable behavior will receive fewer total rewards than those who can easily conform and obtain maximum rewards.

5. *It could instruct children to be mercenary.* A system of rewards or punishments or both requires the teacher to decide how much conformity or nonconformity is enough. Since the student is exposed to many teachers with divergent standards of behavior, he could easily become confused about what acceptable behavior is and conclude that it is whatever is profitable in a material sense.

6. *It limits the expression of student discontent.* Unacceptable classroom behavior is often an indication that content and methods used in teaching are inappropriate for the needs of students. To this extent, such behavior is healthy; it is evidence that change is in order. A system of rewards or punishments which causes students to accept instruction they should reject might make it seem less necessary to modify that instruction, and thus limit student input into the curriculum.

7. *It denies human reasoning.* Many parents and teachers treat with ridicule the practice of reasoning with children about their behavior and academic performance. But despite the obvious imperfections of man, history and contemporary times are evidence of his

overall good sense and practicality. A system of rewards which would "pay" for acceptable behavior and academic effort surrenders the appeal of the reasonableness of what the child is expected to do, substituting payoffs. The denial of reason, the opposite extreme from always reasoning with children, is no less ridiculous.

8. *It teaches action/reaction principles.* The complexity of human behavior is not adequately considered, since behavior modification uses action/reaction principles where there may be no logical action/reaction pattern for the learner, but only for the teacher (manipulator). Such techniques deal with behavior in the cognitive domain when behavior should be dealt with in all domains. For behavior to be internalized, it is best that it be understood by the individual whose behavior is being changed.

9. *It encourages students to "act" as if they are learning, in order to obtain rewards.* Once the range of acceptable behaviors is established by the teacher, the student will be able to affect responses within that range, causing the teacher to assume that desired behavior patterns are being established, when in fact the student is merely "playing the game."

10. *It emphasizes short-range rather than long-range effects.* It emphasizes to a fault the conditions under which learning is to take place rather than appropriately emphasizing what the outcome should be. This limitation results in fragmented educational experiences, and may result in long-term ill effects.

11. *It would make the student assume a passive role in his own education.* Behavior modification focuses the student's attention on behavioral responses that are acceptable by the teacher, thus limiting the choice of behaviors for the student. This could result in frustration of personal goals

toward creativity and self-actualization, weakening individual motives.

12. *It is a totalitarian concept in which the behavior shown by an individual is regarded as more important than the state of affairs in the individual's life leading to his behavior.* The use of behavior modification techniques is very often an attack upon symptoms of problems rather than an attack upon problems. Because it makes teachers the sole legitimizers of classroom behavior, it gives them an "out" from really confronting the problems met in teaching children.

QUALITY
RESEARCH–

A Goal for Every Teacher

BYRON G. MASSIALAS

FREDERICK R. SMITH

PERIODIC reviews generally reveal that the volume of research conducted in elementary and secondary schools by school personnel is steadily increasing. Although one could not safely claim that we have reached our research peak, one could probably advance the proposition that classroom teachers are beginning to exhibit some interest in pursuing inquiries in their respective fields of specialization. In the social studies, for example, examination of some of the specialized journals will justify the latter statement.[1] Additional evidence can be found in bibliographies and reviews of research.[2]

Research must have a qualitative as well as a quantitative dimension, however, and here much remains to be done. By quality research we mean research which is planned and carried out under conditions which are educationally and experimentally sound. The matter of quality is primarily

[1] For example, see the volumes of *Social Education* and *Social Studies* for the last five years.

[2] Clarence D. Samford, *Social Studies Bibliography: Curriculum and Methodology*, Southern Illinois University Press, Carbondale, Illinois, 1959. Also see Richard E. Gross and William V. Badger, "Social Studies," in the *Encyclopedia of Educational Research*, pp. 1296-1319, edited by Chester W. Harris, Third Edition, The Macmillan Co., New York, 1960.

PHI DELTA KAPPAN, March 1962, pp. 253-256.

a question of research design. It logically follows, then, that the reporting of the findings and conclusions of a study is really incomplete unless accompanied by an explicit and perhaps even elaborate discussion of the method and frame of reference which governed the study. Many times in journal reports we see findings and claims concerning a variety of pupil outcomes attributed to certain variables (content or teacher). These frequently fail to indicate the strategy of attack and technique of investigation utilized in arriving at such findings. It is practically impossible to assess the end product of research when there is no statement about the methodological approach used.

The classroom teacher is in a key position to study the effect of new materials, methodology, and similar innovations upon the learning process. Yet no matter how research-minded he may be, he is apt to miss an opportunity for worthwhile basic investigation if he is not aware of the research potential of the situation. Even when research opportunities are recognized, the classroom teacher or even an entire department may fail to take into account some of the basic considerations crucial to quality research.

Let us assume, for example, that we are faculty members of a social studies department eager to embark on a research project.[3] Here are some of the questions which we could ask ourselves. There is little doubt that the consideration of these questions will have significant influence upon the strength of our investigation.

1. *What is our research philosophy? For what purpose do we intend to conduct research?*

A number of alternative responses, not necessarily mutually exclusive, can be anticipated. A justification of research for purposes of problem solving might be to meet a specific and immediate problem confronting us. For example, in view of the fact that students are currently showing concern with fall-out and atomic radiation, or with the implications of our Berlin policy, how can we provide a new educational experience

[3] The social studies were selected for illustrative purposes only. The authors assume that these questions and the considerations which they imply are basic to research in most subject areas.

which would allow them to discuss these and related problems in a thoughtful manner? Could this problem be better met by creating a "current events club," or would it be more profitable to discuss such issues in regular classes?

On the other hand, a department might want to conduct research because of a long-range problem, i.e., since 90 per cent of our graduates continue their education in college, what kind of social studies curriculum should we be offering? Should we include anthropology and social psychology or should we concentrate on history? What would be the best way of selecting content from a vast body of socio-economic data? Should we try to introduce a seminar at the senior level for the purpose of familiarizing our mature students with social science research tools and techniques?

The attitude of the school administration and the community itself may set limitations or offer encouragement to classroom investigation and experimentation. Thus we might legitimately ask ourselves what the prevailing attitude is toward studies such as we contemplate. What is more important is a determination that we as a department will take a position as curriculum leaders in our subject field while simultaneously working toward the creation of an atmosphere which will be conducive to research and possible curricular innovation.

Professional growth can be offered as an additional incentive for research activity. Through participation in research the teacher may become interested in readings about his subject and new approaches to teaching and learning; he could find himself involved in curriculum meetings, lectures, conventions, and summer workshops. Furthermore, research can provide a climate whereby communication and exchange of ideas and teamwork are made possible not only for members within one faculty but also among several faculties. A spirit of scholarly competition and drive to excel might be the justification and the outcome of such inquiry.

Finally and most significantly, one could justify research on its own merit. That is, our research could contribute to the building of a systematic body of social studies theory. Here, for

177

example, a faculty could discuss and investigate basic philosophies appropriate to social studies instruction and research, conceptualization concerning logical operations employed in the act of teaching, or elements which could be operationally identifiable in the decision-making process in the classroom. The purpose of this approach is to accurately classify and systematize social studies knowledge. The ultimate ends are explanatory. Usually in pure research there are no immediate pay-off considerations, although many times there are measurable and tangible outcomes. We must remember that since Ptolemy it has taken many generations of scientists to build up, slowly and painstakingly, a satisfactory theory of our solar system; finally, one individual, Copernicus, published his thesis of a heliocentric universe in 1543.[4]

2. What are some fruitful areas of investigation in the social studies? Considering our limitations and resources, what can we do productively?

Here a number of considerations demand further discussion and analysis. For example, a team of teachers might desire to study the daily activities in the social studies classroom. Paradoxically enough, although many investigators have conducted research in the social studies, very few have dealt with actual happenings at the purely descriptive level. It seems only logical to assume that unless we can conclusively respond to the "what is" question we cannot intelligently proceed with questions of "why" and "how."

Teachers will also have to assess their strengths and weaknesses concerning the research process. Major weak spots are, generally, the following: (1) lack of background and formal preparation in the statistical and measurement procedures in education; (2) certain limitations in time and/or ability to pursue studies that go beyond the confines of the classroom, i.e., follow-up studies; (3) heavy teaching loads and extracurricular responsibilities. On the other hand, the classroom teacher also has a number of advantages appropriate to the conduct of quality research: (1) He has direct contact with the

[4] For an elaborate statement concerning the value of basic research, see Nicholas A. Fattu, "The Teacher and Educational Research," *High School Journal* 44:194-203, March, 1961.

pupil and a knowledge of his problems, his intellectual potential, his socio-emotional development, and the like. (2) He is able to record happenings in the classroom and to put them in proper perspective as they affect the teaching-learning process. (3) He can, with certain limits, manipulate the educational environment and observe the corresponding reactions of the pupils.

In addition, the faculty will have to consider some seemingly unimportant yet indispensable factors, such as availability of physical facilities and equipment, space for trained observers, and the like. This is not to imply that quality experimentation demands excessively expensive equipment of facilities. It is only realistic, however, to evaluate these factors in terms of their appropriateness to the over-all design of the study.

3. *What is the domain of inquiry? How do we delimit our problem?*

Acknowledging the fact that there is interrelatedness in nature, we realize that we need to reduce the problem to one which is manageable and operationally definable. For certain objectives, perhaps, global views are necessary and important. But for our purposes as classroom teachers we need to be selective; thus we attempt systematically to delimit our sphere of investigation.

A five-year research project conducted at the University of Illinois under the auspices of the United States Office of Education identified three domains of inquiry in the classroom: the linguistic, the expressive, and the performative. The first referred to the verbal intercourse that takes place in the classroom. The second referred to the behavior of children as expressed through certain signs, facial or others. The last referred to behavior centered on demonstration or performance of certain tasks associated with laboratory work. Although all these domains were identified, Smith chose to investigate only the linguistic in terms of logical operations involved in the act of teaching.[5]

[5] B. Othanel Smith, *A Study of the Logic of Teaching: The Logical Structure of Teaching and the Development of Critical Thinking.* A Report of the First Phase of a Five-Year Research Project, Bureau of Educational Research, College of Education, University of Illinois, 1959. (Dittoed.) Also see, by the same author, "How Can You Help the Student Teacher Become a Real Teacher?" *Teacher College Journal* 32:15-21, October, 1960.

Bloom[6] and his associates, in an effort to classify and systematize educational objectives, identified three main domains: the cognitive, the affective, and the manipulative. The first included those objectives normally associated with knowledge, intellectual abilities, and skills. The second referred to objectives associated with interests, values, attitudes, preferences, adjustment, etc. The last included aspects of motor skill development. After he had operationally distinguished among the foregoing domains, he proceeded to investigate the first.

4. *What philosophical and psychological rationale are we employing? What constructs do we want to use?*

What assumptions appear to be warranted in planning our research? What postulates and propositions are we taking for granted? Are we going to accept Smith's[7] proposition that the act of teaching is related to but distinct from the act of learning? Does teaching involve a set of operations which could be logically and empirically discernible? Is it possible to categorize linguistic discourse in the social studies classroom? Can we assume, as Bruner[8] has stated, that there is an inherent "structure" underlying each discipline and subject matter area? Are we going to accept one particular theory of learning as valid and reliable and thus try to evaluate student behavior in such a light? Will we accept a connectionist theory of learning or a field theory as being most appropriate for achieving the desired outcomes in our subject area?

5. *What is our unit of measurement? What strategies and techniques could we utilize?*

Typical of the questions we might ask are the following: Would an existing standardized test provide an adequate measuring instrument? Do we need to construct our own evaluative instruments? If we are to measure or assess verbal exchange, what kind of measurement device can we apply?

Can we rely on teacher or student daily logs or anecdotal records as part of our evaluative de-

[6] Benjamin S. Bloom, editor, *Taxonomy of Educational Objectives*, Longmans, Green and Co., New York, 1956.
[7] Smith, *op. cit.*
[8] Jerome S. Bruner, *The Process of Education*, Harvard University Press, Cambridge, 1960.

sign?[9] Would we need some additional objective evidence for purposes of validating our instruments? Can we use tapes and video-tapes to maintain a permanent record of our investigation in the classroom? Will it be desirable to hire trained observers to visit our classrooms and record activities using, perhaps, a time-sampling technique? Can we justify one approach or technique over another within the total project and its underlying rationale?

6. In what aspects of this research would we need help from a specialist?

A faculty ready to initiate a research project will have to determine what kind of professional, expert help it will need. For example, if we are utilizing standardized tests, or even tests constructed by individual researchers for specific purposes, we would need assistance in tabulating the scores and in determining whether the instruments are valid and reliable. We may need advice on the selection of statistical techniques which will enable us to determine whether outcomes are statistically significant, or whether our purported correlations are indeed positive. We may need to consider the possibility of consulting with a specialist in the content area to attest to the reliability of certain propositions and key concepts that we are using in our teaching.

7. How do we evaluate and confirm our procedures and findings?

Here we are mainly concerned with the validity of our product. We might be thinking in terms of replication and follow-up studies which will provide the necessary justification of our propositions. In this connection we might want to refine our procedures and investigate techniques as we proceed with our study. Ryans'[10] seven year project in teacher competence is an example of untiring devotion to obtain a logical and empirical confirmation of findings through an exhaustive attempt at the refinement of research tools and a continuous search for reconstruction of generalizations.

[9] For an analysis of promising new techniques in conducting research in the social studies see Byron G. Massialas, *Research Prospects in the Social Studies,* in the *Bulletin* of the School of Education, Indiana University, Vol. 38, No. 1, January, 1962.

[10] David G. Ryans, *Characteristics of Teachers,* Council on Education, Washington, D. C., 1960.

Summary

At the fingertips of the classroom teacher lie innumerable opportunities for research which may be the source of additional insight into many of the problems of understanding the teaching-learning process. While we must operate within the limits set by the nature of our teaching assignment, level of training in research techniques, and necessary content background, the teacher should and can become capable of conducting quality research. Among the principal points of justification for such endeavors, professional growth, problem solving, and systematic theory building are especially worthy of consideration. But whatever purpose the research is to serve, a statement of the underlying philosophy and rationale is indispensable. A systematic, thoughtful, and vigorous approach to the investigation is necessary if we are to expect a clear design and a valid strategy of attack. Only when tight and organized frames of reference are consciously employed will the field of education move toward quality research.

Humanizing
Teacher
Education

By Robert Blume

There is no single method of teaching which can be demonstrated to be superior for all teachers. Nor will knowledge about good teaching insure superior performance. These findings from research conducted over the past 10 years have thrown teacher education into a dilemma. If not knowledge and methods, what shall we have our prospective teachers learn in college?

A study published in 1961 by the National Education Association, in which all of the research available on good and poor teaching was reviewed, failed to find any method of teaching which was clearly superior to all others.

At about the same time, Combs and Soper conducted research with good and poor teachers to determine if the good ones knew better than the poor ones the characteristics of a good helping relationship.[1] They found no significant difference between the knowledge of the two categories of teachers.

What does distinguish between good and poor teachers? Certainly we all think we can tell the difference, but does research bear out our beliefs?

Twenty years ago a startling finding came out of a study of various styles of psychotherapy. At that time the psychoanalysts and the Rogerians were debating whether it was more effective for the therapist to be direct and forceful in dealing with his client, or whether the client should be encouraged to think out his own solutions to problems while the therapist assumes a client-centered role.

Fiedler found that expert therapists, no matter what school of thought they belonged to, tended to advocate the same kind of relationship with their clients. In fact, these experts were more alike in their beliefs about the therapeutic relationship than were the beginners and experts in the same school. This relationship has come to be called "the helping rela-

PHI DELTA KAPPAN, March 1971, pp. 411-415.

tionship."

Combs and Soper modified the questions Fiedler used with the therapists, in order to make them appropriate for educators, and administered the instrument to a group of expert classroom teachers. They found that these teachers agreed with the expert therapists about the relationship which was most desirable and productive for helpers and helpees.

As mentioned above, when they asked poor teachers the same questions, they found that they, too, knew the answers. They concluded that a good helping relationship is something most people know about, but not all are capable of practicing.

With these questions in mind — "What does make a difference in the ability of teachers to practice the good helping relationship?" and "What shall we have future teachers learn in college?" — let us turn to some of the recent criticism of the schools.

The new critics (as opposed to the three-R's proponents of an earlier day) tell us that our schools are ineffective and dehumanizing institutions. Evidence of ineffective education surrounds us, they say. School dropouts, increasing crime, drugs and alcohol, racism — the list could go on and on — all testify to the failure of the school to educate people in a way that gives them a feeling of dignity and an understanding of their world.

Some consider this indictment too harsh. They hold that the school can't be blamed for all of society's ills. Whether or not the school is responsible for causing our problems, it is the institution responsible for producing educated people, who will in turn make the wise decisions, both large

and small, that will gradually improve life. Unfortunately, we are not moving in this direction now; on the contrary, life is becoming more grim and joyless all the time, and therefore the school *is* vulnerable to the above charge.

Education must include more than the acquisition of a few more facts and a faster reading rate. It must be the instrument through which people release the tremendous creative potential that was born into all of us. Whatever methods and materials are needed to do the job — that is education.

But this isn't enough. We must also help our young to develop compassion, concern for others, faith in themselves, the ability to think critically, the ability to love, the ability to cooperate with others, the ability to maintain good health, and, above all, the ability to remain open to other people and new experiences. This is *humanistic* education.

In order to achieve this kind of school we must abandon the old patterns along with the old assumptions, and search together for a concept of education that will in Jourard's words "turn on and awaken more people to expanded perspectives of the world, new challenges, possible ways to experience the world and our own embodied being." We *can* create educational patterns that are much more exciting than anything we adults have experienced in our elementary or secondary schooling. The University of Florida has begun a program of elementary teacher education which is a radical departure from those of the past. This program has abolished courses and regularly scheduled classes, replacing them with individual study and small discussion groups. Each student becomes a member of a seminar led by the same faculty member for the two years he is enrolled in the program. Students have the opportunity to work with children every week, and almost every day, from the beginning of their teacher education to the end.

This program is based on principles which have emerged in educational literature over the past two decades, and more specifically on extensive research which Arthur Combs and his associates have conducted at the University of Florida. These principles are:

○ People do only what they would rather do (from Freud). That is, people behave according to choices they make from among alternatives they see available to them at the moment.

○ Learning has two aspects: 1) acquiring new information, and 2) discovering the *personal meaning* of that information. Information itself is useless. Only when individuals find the link between specific information and their own lives are they able to put it to use. This principle is not well understood by educators. Most of our efforts to improve education involve new ways to deliver information to people. Very few innovations involve helping learners to discover the personal meaning of that information.

○ It is more appropriate for people to learn a few concepts rather than many facts.

○ Learning is much more efficient if the learner first feels a need to know that which is to be learned. This principle has been known for a long time, but the response of educators to it has been to artificially "motivate" students with letter grades and other rewards. None of these schemes works as well as the genuine desire to learn, and in fact they frequently get in the way of that desire by substituting artificial for real motivation.

○ No one specific item of information, and no specific skill, is essential for effective teaching. Any one fact or skill that could be mentioned might be missing in a very effective teacher. Furthermore, it would be presumptuous for teacher educators in the 1970's, drawing on their experience in the 40's, 50's, and 60's, to declare certain teaching skills or knowledge essential for teachers in the 80's, and 90's, and beyond. We just don't know what the job of the teacher will be in 20 years, or even 10. Hopefully it will be quite different from what it is today.

○ People learn more easily and rapidly if they help make the important decisions about their learning.

○ People learn and grow more quickly if they aren't afraid to make mistakes. They can be creative only if they can risk making errors.

○ Objectivity is a valuable asset for a researcher, but it is not very useful for workers in the helping professions, such as teaching. What is needed instead is the opposite of objectivity — concern and caring. As Jack Frymier has said, we want students not only to know about cold, hard facts, but to have some "hot feelings about hard facts." We must produce teachers who have developed strong values about teaching.

○ Teachers teach the way they have been taught — not the way they have been taught to teach. If we want elementary and secondary teachers to be warm, friendly people who relate positively and openly with their students, then we must treat them that way in our college programs. We must respect our teacher education students if we expect them to respect their pupils.

O Pressure on students produces negative behaviors, such as cheating, avoidance, fearfulness, and psychosomatic illness. Students tend to become more closed in their interpersonal relationships when they are pressured.

O Our teachers would be more effective if they were self-actualizers. Teachers ideally should be more healthy than "normal" people. They should be creative, self-motivated, well-liked persons.

In his book, *The Professional Education of Teachers*, Arthur Combs reviews "third force psychology," the alternative to the Freudian and stimulus-response theories which have dominated our educational thought for the past half century. Three basic principles of perceptual psychology are significant for humanistic education:

1. All behavior of an individual is the direct result of his field of perceptions at the moment of his behaving.

2. The most important perceptions an individual has are those he has about himself. The self-concept is the most important single influence affecting an individual's behavior.

3. All individuals have a basic need for personal adequacy. We all behave in ways which will, according to our view of the situation, lead to our self enhancement. Once aware of this fundamental drive toward growth and improvement, we can see that it is unnecessary to reward a child to encourage him to learn. If he already wants to learn, we need only help him, by giving him the environment which makes it easy and the materials which are appropriate for the kind of learning toward which he is motivated. We need to become aware of his motivation and plan learning experiences which will fit into it. The role of the

teacher, then, is that of facilitator, encourager, helper, assister, colleague, and friend of his students.

Teaching is therefore a helping relationship rather than a command relationship. It is similar to counseling, psychotherapy, nursing, human relations work, social work, and many other helping professions.

A number of studies have been conducted at the University of Florida which have investigated the nature of the helping relationship. Combs and others have studied counselors, teachers, Episcopal priests, nurses, and college teachers to see if the more effective practitioners in these fields have different ways of perceiving than do the ineffective ones. The perceptual organizations of these professionals were examined in great detail in the following four categories:

Category 1: *The general perceptual organization.* Is he more interested in people or things? Does he look at people from the outside, or does he try to see the world as they see it? Does he look for the reasons people behave as they do in the here and now, or does he try to find historical reasons for behavior?

Category 2: *Perceptions of other people.* Does he see people generally as able to do things or unable? As friendly or unfriendly? As worthy or unworthy? As dependable or undependable?

Category 3: *Perceptions of self.* Does he see himself as with people or apart from them? As able or unable? As dependable or undependable? As worthy or unworthy? As wanted or unwanted?

Category 4: *Perceptions of the professional task.* Does he see his job as one of freeing people or controlling them? Does he see his role as one of revealing or concealing? As being involved or uninvolved? As encouraging process or achieving goals?

The results of these studies consistently indicated that the effective helpers saw people from the inside rather than the outside. They were more sensitive to the feelings of students. They were more concerned with people than things. They saw behavior as caused by the here-and-now perceptions, rather than by historical events. They saw others and themselves as able, worthy, and dependable; they saw their task as freeing rather than controlling, and as involved, revealing, and encouraging process.

As mentioned above, one significant finding of these studies was that objectivity had a *negative* correlation with effectiveness as a helper. For example, the teacher who observes two boys fighting and tries to "get to the bottom of the problem" by asking how it started, what led up to the first blow being struck, etc., is not helping as effectively as the teacher in a similar situation who says, "Mike, I can see you are very angry with David and you want to hurt him, but I can't let you do that. How do you feel, David? Are you mad too?" The latter teacher is not being so objective; he isn't trying to place the blame logically on one boy or the other. Instead he is trying to show the two boys that he recognizes the way they feel *at this moment,* and he wants them to know that he is a friend of each of them and will help them to express their feelings. Violence is usually an attempt to express strong feelings. The best helpers are those who help people to express these feelings without violence.

The implications of this research are important for the Florida New Elementary Program. For example, if good teachers are more sensitive to the feelings of students, we should provide more opportunities for teacher education students to enter into more personal, meaningful relationships with other students, faculty, and children. If effective teachers see others as able, well-intentioned, and dependable, they need a warm, friendly, cooperative atmosphere in which to interact with children and in-service teachers during their teacher education. If the effective teacher sees himself as able, likable, and dependable, he must be treated as a person of worth, dignity, and integrity from the very beginning of his professional program. Finally, if effective teachers see the teaching task as one of freeing and assisting, rather than controlling or coercing, we must provide teacher education which does not insist on particular methods, but which encourages students to seek their own best methods. These programs themselves should encompass a wide variety of approaches. The instructors will need to be concerned with the attitudes and perceptions of teachers, not merely with subject matter and methods.

Various members of the College of Education saw a challenge in this research and in the book Combs published in 1965. They decided to build a new program for the preparation of elementary teachers. This program consists of three parts: the seminar the substantive panel, and field experience.

The seminar is the heart of the program. It is here most of all that the student develops a close relationship with a faculty member, one who knows him well over the entire period of his professional program. He also becomes a member of a small group of students. Thirty students are assigned to each of the three seminar leaders. They range from beginners, who have just come into the program, to seniors, who have completed all but the final phases of their work. When a student graduates, a new one is taken in to replace him. The 30 students are divided into two groups of 15 for discussion purposes, and each small group meets for two hours per week. These meetings are for the purpose of discussing everything which comes to the minds of the students and their leader relative to education. More specifically, the purpose is the discovery of the personal meaning of the information and experiences which the students are encountering in the other aspects of the program.

The seminar leader serves as advisor to each of the 30 students in his group. He is responsible for helping them schedule outside course work and for keeping the records of their work within the program. He also conducts evaluation activities for his group in the form of weekly activity sheets and the midpoint and final review conferences.

The second aspect is the substantive panel. It includes faculty members who normally teach methods, foundations, and curriculum courses. Included are math, reading, language arts, social studies, science, art, social foundations, psychological foundations, curriculum, black studies, and testing and research. In each of these areas the faculty member distributes lists of competencies for students to complete and hand in, or to discuss in faculty-student conferences. The competencies range over the entire area of didactic learnings within each of the fields mentioned. Certain competencies are required, while others are optional. In the area of curriculum, for example, there are four required competencies, and each student must do three more from a list of seven optional ones. Even the required competencies may be done in two different ways, thus carrying through the idea of giving students wide latitude for choice making. Some of the competencies involve working with a small group of children and writing a critique. The students do these while they are involved in their field experience. Others include reading in the library and writing papers summarizing the literature, or reacting to it. Students are encouraged to design their own competencies as alternatives to some of the optional ones. They write out a contract form for this purpose. The faculty member signs the contract when he has approved the design, and again when the competency has been completed. Substantive panel members conduct some small-group sessions each week to help students develop the understanding needed to complete the competencies. Students are free to sign up for these meetings or not as they choose, but if they sign up they are expected to attend. These meetings are usually offered as a series of three or four. Some competencies consist of passing a test over material which has been presented in these small-group meetings.

Obviously, the student can't work in all substantive areas at once. He must choose which three or four he will work on each quarter, depending on his schedule of field experiences and outside classes. With this much freedom and responsibility, there is danger that students who have been spoon-fed all of their lives will goof off and get behind in their completion of the competencies. We feel this is a calculated risk worth taking, in order to gain the advantages of having students feel free to explore and probe in directions dictated by their growing interest in becoming teachers.

The field experience aspect of the program begins with level one, which consists of tutoring an individual child and observing classrooms in the Gainesville area. The student and his advisor decide when he has had enough observation experience — usually about 10 one-hour observations. The tutoring continues for an entire quarter. In level two, the student is designated "teacher assistant." He does whatever needs to be done — work with individual children or small groups, or even record keeping. Teacher assistants spend a minimum of six hours per week in the classroom. In level three, the student is designated "teacher associate." He now accepts more responsibility for planning and teaching certain groups of children within the class, or certain aspects of the curriculum for the whole class. As teacher associate he teaches two hours every day. Eventually he must do an intensive period of teaching, level four, which requires full time in the classroom for five weeks.

One of the unique aspects of this program is the flexibility of time requirements. The program is expected to take six quarters to complete, but a student who wants to push harder can complete it in as little as four quarters. The student who needs more time to finish, or to develop confidence or maturity, might take a longer period of time. This is as it should be, we feel. If we seriously believe in individual differences in learners, we must make

provision for people to go through our program at different rates.

The evaluation of each student's work within the program is handled by the seminar leader, the student himself, and the members of the substantive panel. The student completes competencies in each substantive area, and they are evaluated by the panel member. He rates them on a pass-fail basis and checks them off as the student completes his list for his area. He sends a list of the competencies completed to the seminar leader who keeps the student's records.

Approximately half-way through the program each student has a midpoint evaluation, during which he goes over his progress with the seminar leader and one member of the substantive panel. The number of competencies completed in each area, the number yet to be done, and the field experiences to date are all discussed, and a proposed timetable for completion of the program is written down in his folder. When the student has completed all of the requirements he sits for a final review in the same way, and it is determined if he is ready to teach. The seminar leader is aware of each student's progress each quarter, because he keeps all of the records, and he receives feedback from other faculty members who have observations about particular students.

One of the strongest features of the program is the participation of students in every phase of decision making. The students feel ownership in the program as a result of being on various faculty-student committees, such as a committee to write a handbook for new students, a committee to evaluate the competencies in the various substantive areas, or a committee to plan next term's schedule. Each seminar sends a representative to the bi-weekly staff meetings, not only to observe and report back, but to participate in the discussions as a full-fledged member of the group.

Within one year, two very significant, student-initiated changes were made in the program. The group petitioned the dean of the College of Education to place the entire program on a pass-fail basis rather than the letter-grading system then in use. Their logic was persuasive and the change was made.

In another case, a small group of students asked for some academic preparation for teaching in integrated schools. They were all having some teaching experience in schools that were predominantly black, and they recognized their own lack of background for teaching in those classrooms. This suggestion was followed by the creation of a faculty-student committee, which eventually planned a black-studies program and received some limited funding for its operation.

Whether students learn as much about teaching here as they would in a more standard program will have to be determined by the research which is under way at the present time, but several perceptions are generally shared by the staff members who work most closely with these future teachers. One perception is that the students leave our campus with a solid feeling of confidence about their ability to teach.

A fact which pleases the staff is that *many* of our students ask for an intensive teaching assignment in a school which has large numbers of disadvantaged children. It isn't clear just why this is happening, but it reflects the kind of attitudes we hope to see students developing.

One coed who was having her final review conference said, "It took me almost a year in this program before I felt like these ideas were mine – and then it was easy after that." That statement summarizes what this program is trying to do: not merely to have students *learn about* principles of humanistic education, but to have them feel that they are *their* ideas.

The specific elements of the Florida New Elementary Program are still evolving, and will continue to evolve. What is more important, we believe, are the ideas on which they are based. These principles are valid for humanistic education at any level. We hope to introduce them into elementary classrooms by preparing teachers in ways that are consistent with those principles, because teachers teach the way they were taught.

Notes on Teacher Education

By Richard H. Brown

T eaching is becoming an unnerving experience. Teachers are unsure of themselves and uncertain of their roles. Many are dreadfully disoriented. The more conservative take recourse in caricaturing the forces of change, defying the bricks coming through the window, growing steadily more unhappy. Others despair or take recourse in an abdication of responsibility, deluding themselves with the thought that they are heeding the popular message and contributing, somehow, to an education that by some mysterious means will be "better." All find themselves badly equipped by programs of teacher education in which substantive changes have been few and far between and which have been confined, with rare exceptions, to alterations in who teaches what to whom, in requirements narrowly defined, and in administrative procedures. For teachers at the collegiate level there are no programs at all.

Nowhere is it more true than in teacher education that even new ways of doing things are obsolete before they are effected. Nowhere is the need greater to go beyond tinkering, to look at the assumptions that are built into our thinking, and to heed a pro-

CHANGE, March/April, 1970, pp. 44-47.

cedural version of the idea that, after all, the medium *is* the message.

The comments that follow rest on certain convictions. Chief of these is that the problems of American education are a product of our efforts, unwitting for the most part, to perpetuate basically authoritarian institutions in an increasingly democratic society in which the clamor for freedom grows steadily more strident. Second is the conviction that learning proceeds essentially from an act of the individual learner, whether it takes place in the context of a classroom or outside; that it takes place at different rates and times for each individual and can be expressed only in terms of his own change as a human being; and that it results from some form of inquiry which begins where the individual learner is and grows out of his desire to know something, as well as his feeling that he is free to learn. A corollary to this conviction is that the chief aim of education is not the transmission of an abstract body of knowledge but the growth of individual learners as they confront new experiences, including knowledge, and in turn transform those experiences.

These hypotheses about learning, in one way or another, link together modern curriculum work and pressures for change in the government of institutions; movements for flexible scheduling, nongraded classes and achievement or competence as a measure of progress; the outcry for independent work and for "relevance." They are equally applicable to schools and to colleges and they are being asserted loudly, if not always clearly, both from within the ranks of the academy and from outside.

At times we hear the message too narrowly, as though it had to do only with methods, and at times we hear it too portentously, as though it sounded the doom of all formal education. It does in fact explode the classroom. It challenges all of us to re-think not only what we do but who we are. And yet it has within it the potential to make formal education an infinitely richer and personally more rewarding experience for all who are involved. It calls for teachers to be different kinds of human beings, for new attitudes more than for new skills, for new assumptions more than for new knowledge. It calls for teachers who are able to view themselves and their role differently from the way most view them at present, for teachers who see knowledge and learning differently, and for teachers who will see differently the relationship of schools and colleges to the outside world. It calls for teachers who are able to do a good deal more than take refuge in telling students something, and able at the same time to do a good deal more than merely providing "comfortable" classrooms.

We need teachers who are capable of being leaders in inquiry, who have an urgent sense of the processes and the possibilities of human growth, and a realistic sense of and respect for the mutuality of the teaching/learning process. Above all, we need teachers with a higher and clearer sense of purpose as teachers than many now have; a confident awareness of what they themselves have to offer in terms of maturity, experience, knowledge and skills; an awareness that students can avail themselves of what the teachers offer only if they— the students—sense and feel and understand what is available, and that they will do none of this unless they respect both the teacher and the situation in which they encounter him.

I f we are to get this kind of teacher with any regularity and in any significant number, we shall need to provide not new courses based on and inculcating the same old assumptions but new experiences designed specifically to challenge those assumptions, enabling teachers to be as a consequence both freer and more flexible people.

We need to free teachers from the assumption that prevails in so much of our education that knowledge exists independently of the knower, and that the disciplines constitute bodies of knowledge that can be "covered" rather than ways of inquiring into reality. To do this, we need to give them a good deal of working experience with the relationship between knowledge and process. In the discipline of history, to take an example, they will need enough experience to perceive, not only in their minds but in their very being, the sublime significance of the fact that all we have of the past is inert data to which we go with organizing questions that grow out of our own experience, and that enable us to see some things and not others. They will need to see, not only intellectually but as a fact of life, that because of this, history is always changing, always being rewritten, and thus, in the largest sense, every man is his own historian.

We come closest to giving students this kind of experience when we ask them to do creative scholarly research in a discipline. But seldom do we give such opportunities to teachers going into the schools, and even when we do, rarely do we connect it with their preparation for teaching. Nor is it enough by itself; the task, to be effective, must repeatedly go beyond the doing of the discipline to a consideration of the implications of the "doing" for human beings. The point is not alone to use the skills of the scholar as a way of training the mind, but to enable students to perceive that knowledge cannot be separated from the processes by which it was acquired or the uses to which it is put; that its character is instrumental and dynamic rather than abstract or static; and that it is something that each man constantly works on, however well or badly.

We need to afford teachers new kinds of experiences that challenge them to reflect analytically and intuitively on how they themselves learn, perceiving the relationship of learning to their total experience, to everything they do, and to everyone with whom they come into significant contact. To cite a simple example, how does one explain the phenomenon of returning to a book one has read and underlined five years before, and finding totally inexplicable why certain passages were underlined and not others? What has changed, obviously, is not the book, but the experience and questions one has brought to the book. Again, how does one explain the phenomenon of "learning from kids"—

the sudden new insight in the middle of an expository lecture, or in watching one's own three-year-old? Is the learning in such situations self-generated, or is it the result of a quizzical look on a face in the lecture hall, or the fact that the three-year-old's presence altered our experience? Who is the teacher and who the learner? Is the three-year-old less a teacher than the college professor lecturing on the Peloponnesian War, who was also altering our experience? Is it not true that the only significant consideration insofar as learning is concerned is what the learner was doing with the new data or experience in his own mind, and that this in turn was as much a function of the questions he brought to the experience as it was of the experience itself?

To an educational culture determined by word and deed to separate content from process, such phenomena are at worst trivial riddles fit only for methods courses, or at best philosophical questions beyond the ken of educators. But to a culture conscious of the relationship of content to process, they are significant. If we find ways to build consideration of them continually into the experience of teachers, we shall make the question of how people learn intensely human and personal rather than abstract, sensitize teachers to the mutuality of the learning process, and foster their consciousness of the ongoing nature of the teaching/learning relationship both in their own lives and beyond the walls of the classroom.

We need to challenge teachers in fundamental ways to come to grips with the purposes and goals of teaching in contexts in which they deal with and are challenged by students, and in which they have none of the traditional thought-evading armor of established requirements. Perhaps we shall do this best by allowing them extensive opportunity to plan and organize formal and continuing learning situations with students: in short, creative opportunities to design curricula, develop materials, and practice teach. But such programs must go beyond all of these as we now see them if they are to be effective. They must give the teacher both more responsibility and more experience in learning from students than the A to B relationship (with C watching) of most practice teaching. Prospective teachers must be removed from the procrustean bed of teaching six weeks in someone else's course, or the equally procrustean bed of teaching even one's own course in "history" or "English" or "chemistry." They must go beyond the task of consuming a given amount of time in a given curriculum in a given school.

It is important in these experiences that teachers be given both the responsibility and the freedom to plan and work out with students the "ideal" learning experience, without any of the props of the established order. (Postman and Weingartner in their challenging book, *Teaching as a Subversive Activity,* have described a version of this.) If they would teach history, they must be challenged continually as to *why* history, and *why* they do what they do with it, in a situation in which they are afforded no easy outs, either through established authority or through students rendered disinterested through having no responsibility. They must be challenged to match purpose to materials and to classroom methods—if they opt for a classroom—and to learn in the process to create learning situations mutually with their students.

Teachers need experiences that enable them more effectively to relate what they do in schools and colleges to what goes on outside those institutions, both in their own lives and in those of their students. The evidence is plain for all to see that the days of the self-enclosed school and college are gone. New curricula, whether "modern" in style or not, will partake more of the world around us than the old curricula they supersede. The once little-observed maxim that the best teachers will be those who best know the world outside the school grows more important than ever. Nor will it be enough merely to know that world in a static sense. For if we are to have open classrooms from which students are free to go to the evidence in their own lives and to which they bring that evidence, we shall need teachers who themselves have lives to which they go.

The only counter to the "relevance" argument is to make our schools and colleges relevant. We shall not be doing this responsibly if we merely jettison the academy, turning our institutions into forums for the discussion of current affairs or into political societies. If we would preserve the values of the academy we must find ways of asking in it the questions that are important to us and to our students in our own lives. If our teachers are to be effective leaders in inquiry they must be able to move easily and comfortably between their classrooms and the outside world, and to make the two one. They will not do this without significant experiences in the outside world, and without encouragement to view those experiences as part and parcel of their growth as teachers.

If it is true in any sense that the medium is the message, we shall have to provide all these experiences in ways that themselves broaden the perspectives of teachers and free them from the unquestioned assumptions of the past. We shall not prepare teachers adequately for an age that challenges caste and class by teaching them in a caste and class system. We shall not prepare them for an age that is beginning to question the ultimate logic of the course system and of the regularly scheduled class period by teaching them everywhere in courses and in class periods. And we shall not prepare them for an age that questions the logic of separating content and method in institutions and through experiences that themselves preserve that distinction.

Ultimately, the search for the experiences teachers need in the modern world is likely to lead us to new views of our own institutions, of their relationships to each other, and of their relationships to the outer world. It is likely to raise among us questions of purpose, values and style, and to bring us face to face with assumptions about the way we do things and the way we live that have been too long unexamined. It will not hurt us if it does.

197

CLASSROOM INCIDENT

I still cringe when I think back on the year Laura Grayson (not her real name) was assigned to me as a student teacher.

Although she was an outstanding student in the Mathematics Department of a nearby college, she had great difficulty in relating to people— young and old. She returned the smiles and greetings of the staff at our junior high with a curt nod and completely turned off my seventh grade math students with humorless lectures and grim admonitions.

I counseled Laura about how she might work more effectively with students, pointing out that youngsters— especially junior highs — welcome warmth and humor as well as facts and figures from their teachers. But my counseling fell on deaf ears. Laura said that a "cream puff" approach to teaching was just not possible for her and that she would have "to work out her own destiny."

Frustrated and somewhat angry, I turned to her college supervisor and the assistant principal for advice on how to help Laura with her difficulties. However, they both dismissed the problem saying in effect, "Laura has an excellent academic record. She'll improve with experience in the classroom."

But she didn't.

By the end of her student-teaching period, almost all of my seventh graders disliked her *and* math with equal intensity. When I prepared my final evaluation of Laura's student-teaching performance, I was at my wit's end. I didn't see how I could fail her, remembering the college supervisor's and the assistant principal's words. Yet, my heart sank when I thought about the youngsters who would be in her classes in future years.

In the end, I opted for a lukewarm appraisal, gently pointing up her weaknesses and praising her strength —mastery of subject matter.

What else could I or should I have done?

Consultants' Comments

To open Laura's "deaf ears," I would have gotten specific feedback from the students by means of a formal evaluation instrument. Many good evaluation instruments are available and should be used at least once during the student-teaching period.

The supervising teacher was correct to solicit the advice of the vice-principal and the college supervisor in working with Laura's problems, but he should have had more confidence in his own ability to evaluate. After all, Laura was working in his classroom with his students and with him on a daily basis.

I feel any would-be teacher who turns off others, especially students, should not end up in the classroom. In the written evaluation, I would have praised Laura's mastery of subject matter and made a strong statement recommending that she reassess her goals and pointing to her lack of success in student teaching as an indication that she would require careful supervision.

—Kelvin L. Schuchart, *economics teacher, Cedar Falls (Iowa) High School.*

Evaluating a preprofessional's teaching is a most difficult challenge. However, this is the realm in which the profession has the opportunity to make giant strides toward achieving self-governance. It is time to start seriously looking at who enters and remains in the teaching profession.

Laura is a good case in point. If she ranked low in the math teacher's opinion, giving a lukewarm appraisal was not the solution. Since Laura wished "to work out her own destiny," she needed to know her supervising teacher's professional opinion. As a student headed for the same job market, I would not want anyone with an untrue evaluation competing with me.

Mastery of subject matter is essential in quality teaching, but it is far from the only factor. If a teacher cannot relate the subject to the child and make that subject a functioning part of the child's life, then he is wasting his time and the child's.

The teacher was correct in believing he should not be allowed to "fail her" on his own, but he should have made sure that his evaluation was recorded right next to Laura's self-evaluation and the evaluations of her college supervisor and the principal.

Also, the teacher might have suggested that Laura conduct a class attitude survey and permit his students to indicate, anonymously of course, their reactions to her methods, personality, and so on. Too frequently, this valuable tool is overlooked. For Laura, findings of such a survey might have provided the necessary stimulus for change.

—Tom Creighton, *president, Student NEA.*

The teacher's response was not helpful to the growth of the student teacher or fair to her future students. However, in a similar situation, I would probably react the same way. The problem here has the same causes as other educational problems: societal pressure, which produces a lack of confidence in our perceptions; a limited ability to consider alternatives; and a lack of courage to stick to our decisions.

The teacher didn't just imagine that the children were turned off. The fact that the supervisors considered other qualities as paramount shouldn't have caused him to change his perceptions, especially since he was the only person to see the student teacher in a classroom situation.

The teacher's response was all too typical. He made the obvious choice. We can more closely approximate a rational choice, one we feel comfortable with, if we make a point of considering the opposite alternatives to our initial choices. Choosing becomes easier if we can determine the extremes.

We worry more about how others perceive us than about how we perceive our role and responsibility. If we accept our perceptions and consider alternatives we should feel confident with our decisions.

—Michael R. Cohen, *associate professor of education, Indiana University-Purdue University at Indianapolis.*